Managing Professional Communicati

COMMENTS AND CRITICAL APPR

"The PR industry is populated by some enormously talented, bright and creative people. However, most confine their talents to the work they do on behalf of their clients often neglecting the fact that they too are in business.

"Neil's book bridges this gap. With margins in PR still lagging behind similar disciplines, and the PR world often baffled as to why, this book should be the definitive reference for all PR people who want to match the success of their businesses to the quality of their client work.

"While acknowledging the peculiarities of the PR world, Neil's book is simple but hard nosed, a much-needed ingredient in a sector prone to undervaluing itself. The logic is unquestionable and the ground covered leaves no excuses for not grasping how PR businesses can be made better and, ultimately, more profitable."

Patrick Barrow
Director General, Public Relations Consultants Association

"Satisfied clients will normally agree transparent rates that enable your firm to operate with a healthy profit margin. This welcome transparency, largely brought about by the continuing rise of professional procurement functions within client companies, means it is crucial for any business manager to have a firm grasp on the key levers that drive profitability. Without this, no matter how able the professional is in their chosen field, their own business is unlikely to reach its full potential.

"Most managers know the theory – the gaps tend to appear when putting the theory into practice. Based on more than 30 years of practical experience, this is the business book your shareholders would pick for you."

Jonathan Harman
Senior Vice President, EMEA, Carlson Marketing

"Neil has an impressive understanding of the financial, people and legal aspects of a fee earning organisation, be it marketing or professional services. We seek his advice and wisdom on a range of operational and strategic issues on a regular basis and this advice is always sound, wise and of the highest quality."

Nick Helsby
Managing Director, Watson Helsby Limited

"Oh what a joy it would be to spend one's days simply thinking of how our companies can be more efficient both operationally and financially. Wouldn't that be nice? Reality is not like that. Many of the approaches and guidelines offered throughout this book are quick and easy to implement, deliver a profound impact on your PR business and allow you to continue being involved in the business of PR.

"Chameleon has worked with Neil over the last couple of years and has implemented many of his thoughts on running a successful PR business. I wholeheartedly agree that great PR people do not necessarily make sound business people; however you can learn. We have."

Helen Holland
Managing Director, Chameleon PR Limited

ABOUT THE AUTHOR

Neil Backwith was born in Hereford in 1952 and was educated at Bishop's Stortford College and University College London where he studied Psychology. At that time, psychology bridged the gap between the sciences and the arts and he was one of a minority of students who entered the degree course with a science background having studied maths, physics and chemistry for 'A' level. He was sponsored through his university course by the De La Rue Group on the condition that he joined them as a commercial management trainee both during the course and after graduation.

He trained during the university vacations at (De La Rue owned) Thomas Potterton Limited in Warwick, working his way through all the major departments and eventually joining them full time as a commercial planner in July 1973.

After Thomas Potterton was sold to Birmid Qualcast in 1974 he left to take up a junior marketing post at Guinness subsidiary GPG Holdings as sales development officer rising quickly to Marketing Manager by 1978.

In 1979 he left GPG to join the Hepworth Group as marketing manager where he was responsible for the market development of the first uPVC window system into the UK, called Astraseal.

By 1981 the frustrations, inertia and politics of working in large international organisations had taken its toll and Neil took the decision to leave the security of the corporate world and join a small privately owned market research agency to develop the UK's first database-marketing offering. The business took off but only a year later Neil was made redundant having established a highly profitable business division for a proprietor who brazenly announced that, with the business up and running, he no longer needed Neil's expertise.

Three weeks later in February 1982, he joined a small communications agency in Banbury called Countrywide Publicity Group to help establish an advertising agency. The group employed 20 people mostly in PR but with some in design and some producing corporate newsletters. The advertising business was embryonic to say the least!

By 1986, when Neil was appointed MD, the advertising agency had grown to 20 people and continued to expand until 1990 when, following a strategic decision to focus exclusively on the development of the even faster growing PR business, Neil became group strategic development director and the, then 50 strong, advertising agency was sold to the remaining directors.

A plan was developed to take Countrywide onto the international stage. Links were forged with US communications giant Omnicom and an affiliation with Omnicom's US PR group Porter Novelli was established. In 1992 Omnicom acquired Countrywide.

Neil took on the role of group MD for the UK business whilst Peter Hehir – the founder of the company – became international chairman and 'Porter Novelli' was adopted as the global brand. By 2000, Porter Novelli had grown to more than 100 offices across 50 countries and was one of the top three global PR brands.

Neil became UK CEO in 2000, CEO (EMEA) and a global board director in 2001.

Having always planned to 'retire' at 50, he resigned from Porter Novelli in November 2003, and left the firm after 22 years of service at Easter 2004.

Today he works as a management consultant, trainer and mentor to other professional service firms and their leaders. He holds a number of non-executive directorships, is a Fellow of the Royal Society for the Encouragement of Arts, Manufactures and Commerce and is a special advisor to the PRCA (the Public Relations Consultants Association).

In 2004, 2005 and 2006 Neil was a guest speaker on 'Commercial Issues in PR' at the PRCA annual conference in London and in 2005 was invited to speak at the EACA (European Association of Communications Agencies) congress in Brussels on the subject of fee-based remuneration systems.

Neil has been married to Lizzie for more than 30 years, has two grown-up children, two grandchildren and lives in the Cotswolds, one of the most picturesque regions of the UK.

For Lizzie, my long-suffering wife, who never failed to see the wood when all I could see was trees and who always encouraged me to do the 'right' thing regardless…

ACKNOWLEDGEMENTS

This book is the result of my '30 year apprenticeship', during which time I have had the privilege to work with some of the finest people in the marketing and communications sector from whom I learned so much – and to whom I am deeply indebted.

In particular I would like to take this opportunity to thank all my colleagues at Countrywide and more recently Porter Novelli, who provided the stimulation and 'collegiate' environment that encouraged fresh thinking. They are the unsung heroes of this book, the people (and they know who they are) that came up with ideas, helped to develop them and put them into practice.

I was fortunate indeed to work with colleagues and friends who shared a common vision and a passion for excellence in communication. No-one is an island and there is nothing more rewarding than working with a team of brilliant people in a culture that recognises and rewards both innovation and individuality.

I also want to recognise the contribution of both DAS and Omnicom without whose support and patience the creation of Porter Novelli as a global firm would never have been realised.

Finally, a few personal 'thank-yous': to both Peter Hehir and Geoff Lye for having the faith, in 1982, to recruit a young, jobless marketer with no 'agency' experience; to Jerry Brooks – financial wizard extraordinaire – who coached me in all matters of selling time and measurement (and the only man I have known who worked to a 36 hour, rather than a 24 hour, cycle); to Ian Cummings, calm personified, who got me out of numerous financial predicaments and who kindly ensured that my references to accounting in this book were accurate; to the late Andy Pittaway, deeply missed, whose wit was such relief in moments of utter madness; to Paul Miller who encouraged me to write it all down; to both Richard Houghton and Patrick Barrow (the Chairman and Director General of the PRCA respectively) and all the PRCA Board members who had the courage and faith to agree to publish this book having seen only the first chapter! And lastly, to all the friends, colleagues and advisors without whom none of this would have happened.

It was an amazing journey.

Neil Backwith
January 2007

Managing Professional Communications Agencies

How to double your profitability

by

Neil A Backwith

Public Relations Consultants Association

The Public Relations Consultants Association Limited
Willow House
Willow Place
London
SW1P 1JH

www.prca.org.uk

First published in Great Britain 2007

2 4 6 8 10 9 7 5 3 1

British Library Cataloguing in Publication Data
A catalogue record for this book is available from the British Library

978 0 9517397 1 6

Photography by Chris Metcalfe

Production Management by Amy Fairbairn, PRCA
Design and typesetting by Nicky Studdart
Printed in Great Britain by Piggott Black Bear Press Ltd, Cambridge

CONTENTS

FOREWORD

Had this book been written 20 years ago, it would have revolutionised the public relations industry. It still could.

Notable for poor financial management, public relations consultancies in the 1980s would have doubled their profits if they could have taken Neil Backwith's advice. With this extra money flowing into the business, the industry would have been more able to recruit better graduates, train them properly and so enhance the quality of the work they produced.

This virtuous circle would have attracted more clients, driven up fees, further improved profits, and seen communications advisors taking the place they say they seek but seldom achieve: the seat at the boardroom table.

It would have headed off some of the competition they have met from those, admittedly few, management consulting firms that were wising up to the fact that communications is THE central and fundamental role in management and deserves a lot better study, science and education than it has had so far.

It is 24 years since Neil joined the Countrywide Communications Group. We were at a crossroads, with big ideas, a passion for communicating but little management experience – typical perhaps of the sort of consultancy Neil refers to throughout this book. With our new management-trained CEO, Geoff Lye, already bringing unheard of disciplines to our board, such as three year plans, the disciplined curiosity Neil brought to every aspect of what we did soon brought dividends.

Through the early 1990s our PR company really took off, winning the UK Consultancy of the Year title an unprecedented three times and being a finalist in three other years. But we were stuck on profits of around 15% and struggling to understand how hard to pull which of the many business levers that would produce not only the award winning work we were known for, but the higher profitability the work deserved.

For some years I had been on the board of the PRCA, which embraced some 160 consultancies. When we called a meeting of all the organisations' managing directors and chairmen to discuss the financial management of our consultancies, only 30 turned up. But the result of that meeting and the subsequent creation of the industry's first Inter-Firm Comparison report, which showed how a range of companies' finances compared, slowly began to change the industry. It was the tool we needed to understand the dynamics of our business performance, though remarkably few consultancies were very interested, and the trade media also put this in the 'boring stuff for geeks' category.

This book delves into every facet of managing consultancy business. It is not based on academic theory, like so many management books. It is based on hard experience. We used to say at Countrywide Communications (later Porter Novelli) that we had tried just about everything and at least knew what didn't work! So please don't write to Neil saying what he advises can't be done – what he has written was learned in a real business after a great deal of trial and error and those of us who were there know that it does work.

The root of the problems in many creative consultancy businesses is the creative mind of the leader. This mind does not want to be sullied with dirty commerce. It wants to excite clients; change their worlds; deliver results. So often it does not understand that a well-run business, with a strong bottom line, has a far better chance of being able to sustain its creativity than one struggling along on a margin of 10% or less.

The creative mind is easily influenced by clients, well versed in the dark art of negotiation. "Your fees are too high" (rarely true and, if they are, why did they let you pitch and select you before saying so?) "Our budget is fixed" (how do you know what it takes to get the results you are looking for. You do KNOW what you are looking for, don't you?) The creative rolls over every time.

We used to tell our graduates never to believe half of what clients said about money, and impressed on them the fact that if they did over-service an account, they were giving away our money.

Incidentally, we turned that concept around in the 1990s by arguing "there is no such thing as over-servicing, only under-recovery". It's a line that has finally been taken up by others.

Recently I was glad to meet the brilliant head of a world-famous small consultancy (not in PR), who seemed rather glad that his business was not making much money. There was a genuine feeling that this somehow underlined his well-known ethical position. When I told him it would be easy to double his profits and suggested that some of the benefits to the company of doing so – more training, better research, more staff even – were surely not unethical, he was nearly convinced. "And if you still can't think how to use the extra profit, you could always give it away," I added. Now he was convinced.

To cut through any excuses for giving away consultancy time (which truly equals money) think of a shopping trip. You enter the supermarket with £50 in your pocket, put £75 worth of groceries in your trolley and head for the checkout. "My budget is £50. Sorry, but I am taking the lot," you announce.

As we say in New Zealand, "Yeah, right."

If there was just one lesson I would choose from the scores in this book, it is to value your work. If it is good, the client should pay for it. All of it.

If it is bad, good luck – you're going to need it even more than this book.

Peter Hehir

Wellington
New Zealand
2007

INTRODUCTION

Professional or Commercial?

I chose to open this book with a true story because it summarises beautifully what I consider to be the biggest issue for marketing and communications agencies and consultancies – the 'professionally driven' leader!

During the autumn of 2003, in my capacity as European CEO of a large international PR firm, I had been invited to speak at the 2004 PRCA (Public Relations Consultants Association) conference. At that time, I had already made the decision to leave my PR firm but no announcement had been made and it was possible that I would still be working out my notice period when the conference came around the following May.

As it turned out, my employers were happy for me to depart at Easter 2004, three weeks before the conference so I explained to the PRCA that, if they still wanted me to speak, I would have to do so as a recent 'ex-CEO'. "No problem," they said, "in fact what we'd really like you to do is run a break-out group on the subject of *alternative agency profitability models.*" There were to be four break-out groups and the 120 or so delegates would have the choice of which one they wanted to attend.

That suited me just fine because with only around a quarter of the delegates, I thought I could run the group without making a formal speech simply by asking a few well-chosen questions and getting them to think about and discuss the issues as they saw them. The session was scheduled for immediately after lunch and was due to run for 80 minutes.

On the day, I arrived at the central London venue complete with my five 'stimulus' questions during the mid-morning coffee break and joined the main sessions up until lunchtime. Delegates had chosen their break-out group preference at registration and the lists were posted in the conference lobby during lunch, so with about 20 minutes to go I went to check who was in my group and where to go.

This turned out to be a bit of a shock.

My group was to be 84 delegates in the main theatre. Clearly there was no way I could hold a discussion based on my five questions with that many people sat in rows facing a stage, podium and screen – and I had no presentation.

I could hardly dream up a major client crisis since many delegates already knew that I had left my job three weeks before. Thoughts of an anonymous threatening phone call to the hotel seemed attractive but a bit extreme and so there was little choice but to go for it.

So I made a decision.

Since (I thought at the time) I was unlikely to ever be in this position again I would use the opportunity to tell the great and the good of PR what I really thought about the way the industry was run. I'd arrived just in time that morning (fortunately) to hear the latest 'industry survey' statistics and they made pretty awful listening – average profitability 9%, over-servicing 38%, staff turnover 22% and so on – depressing most of all because it was no different from the surveys of the past ten years despite all the efforts of the PRCA.

I began by asking the audience how many of them would describe themselves as *professionals* – meaning that they had reached the top of their firm through practising their 'profession' – through the well-trodden 'client service' route. Almost all put their hands up.

Then I asked them how many of them were responsible for the 'running' of their firm (this was a slightly loaded question since the conference attracted almost exclusively MDs and directors) and not surprisingly all the same hands showed.

It was time for the opening salvo: "Well you're all in the wrong job," I said, "because those of us who have reached the top through our abilities to advise clients are generally lousy commercial managers and are to blame for the poor performance of the industry – the low margins, the huge over-servicing issue and the high staff turnover."

Silence.

"You see, 95% of MDs in our world are *professionally* driven; they believe that by providing excellent, professional service to clients, the profits will follow. History shows this to be *myth number 1*.

"However, the other 5% are what I call *commercially* driven; they **too** know that great client service is essential but that, on its own, it isn't enough to guarantee profitability; they know that a strong commercial grip, both internally and externally, is the only way to generate the profits that we need (and deserve) and which pay for the essential investment in growth and development of our businesses and our people."

I went on to explain why the marketing and communications sector generally suffers the problems that it does – because most of us grow up in the industry, learning on the job. There is little or no training other than in the *professional* skills that we need to advise clients and so we learn our *commercial* skills from our peers and perpetuate the falsehoods and pre-conceptions of the previous generation.

There seems to be some absolute 'truth' that over-servicing is a necessary part of delivering quality service; that winning new clients is *so* important that we should spend whatever it takes to win and that *profit* is what's left after you've deducted your costs from your income.

This is complete bunk.

This book aims to dispel the myths that have become accepted 'facts' within the marketing and communications sector and to show you how a few simple commercial skills can enable you to manage your firm to deliver the desired and deserved profitability, year in and year out. It isn't difficult – it just needs some basic understanding of the profit drivers and how to control them.

Don't expect to find the latest fads and marketing speak nonsense in here – you won't.

I won't give you checklists or 'clever' mnemonics, new theories or academic research; just plain common sense, structured in a way that will help you to get it.

It is my aim to give you a clear understanding of what *really* matters and, more importantly, *why?* Because once you understand that, you will be able to apply it in your business and the results will be spectacular.

As a by-product, your staff will be more satisfied, better paid **and** work fewer hours.

It may sound like a fantasy, but it isn't. I've done it and it works.

Managing the firm and its people

Part 1

MANAGING THE FIRM AND ITS PEOPLE

Chapter 1

PLANNING THE FUTURE OF YOUR BUSINESS
(Where are you heading?)

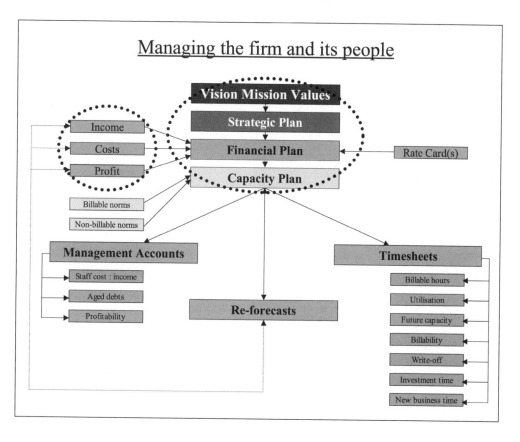

a. Taking the longer term view – strategic planning

It wasn't until I was in my 30s that I began to understand what was really meant by the (stupid) question – why do you get out of bed in the morning? Until then I had thought that it was just one of those management-speak, clever-clever, ego-driven questions asked by smart interviewers.

To me the answer had always been simple – because I've got a wife, two kids and a mortgage and I wasn't born into my rightful place in the wealthy aristocracy.

For most of us, of course, that's true.

But it wasn't the 'right' answer (and to be honest I wasn't brave enough to say it like that either). No, I was supposed to say something like: "Because I have an ambition to be the best in the industry, make a difference," or some other such nonsense.

The truth is that most of us work for someone else because *we need to earn an income* and once we've chosen a career (usually on the basis of very little information, no experience and a misguided belief that the person we met once in this career seemed like they were everything we aspired to being) we rarely change our path. But that's okay; I for one am far from sure that there is a perfect career out there for any of us. We make choices and then make the best of them. Most 'active career changes' are forced upon us if the truth be told. That's certainly been true for me and many of my contemporaries.

For owners and part-owners of private businesses, there is one relevant aspect to the question above and it explains why so many of us in this industry end up starting or running our own business. The answer is – to generate wealth!

The question might be better phrased as 'what are you doing this for?' or something like that; but the honest answer is always the same – to get rich, generate wealth, secure the future…

But for *shareholders* that raises a second question: how do you plan to achieve that, by generating as good an *income* for yourself as possible (and so build wealth year by year) *or* by aiming to build up an *asset,* which you could sell for a lump sum in the future?

Often the answer is "I haven't really thought about it, I just like the idea of working for myself".

So for shareholders the *question* is directly and personally relevant.

But the *answer* is relevant to everyone in the firm.

You see, if the owners of a firm want to maximise their *annual income*, then running the business for *profit* first is the 'right' strategy. Growth remains important but falls second to profit.

If, on the other hand, the owners want to build a saleable asset, then growth is crucial to build the business to a scale where the size (and at that point, profitability) can justify the sale price they are seeking.

It is the difference between these two objectives that affects every single employee in every firm.

A 'profit first' firm is likely to remain smaller, be more proprietorial and stay more dependent upon the owner, whereas a 'growth first' business is more likely to be expansive, take more risks and, perhaps, share the ownership more widely.

It is this choice that should determine the strategy that any firm follows.

Because the Vision, Mission, Values *and* Strategy of any business should reflect the *shareholders'* intentions and, once determined, they impact on each and every one of us employed.

And just to complete the picture, in wholly owned subsidiaries and public companies, the same is true: it is the shareholders (represented by the parent company in the case of subsidiaries) who determine the profit/growth objectives based on their desire for return on their investment in the firm.

Already I'm cross with myself because I haven't been able to get past chapter 1 without lapsing into gobbledegook management speak – Vision, Mission, Values and Strategy (and I really hate management speak); but I hope to redeem myself.

Most of us, whether in PR, advertising, marketing services or whatever, use business terms extremely loosely. Occasionally it's a deliberate bluff, sometimes a mistake but usually it stems from our irrational need to appear clever – and often it does just the opposite. Rarely do we take the time or trouble to find out exactly what the business terms really mean and how/where to use them. Most of us operate in our own worlds without ever seeing the whole picture of how business really functions. There *is* a logical structure to it and it *does* all make sense – but only once you've *really* understood what things mean, why and where they fit in the logical chain that is the business mechanism.

When you do, it's one of those rare 'eureka' moments when suddenly everything comes into focus. I went on for years thinking that so much of what we do in business seemed for the sake of it rather than for a real purpose. Sadly, that is all too often true because many of the people at the top of the business tree haven't 'got it' either and brief us to do things they have read about or been told are 'a useful exercise' without really knowing why. Think about all the firms that do staff surveys to see how their people are feeling about their employment; how many of them actually do anything with the information they've gathered?

That's why I thought it would be good to start off with a bit of clarity.

Let's look at the gobbledegook terms I used a few moments ago – Vision, Mission, Values and Strategy. I can't tell you how many times I have heard or read them used incorrectly or simply substituted (often randomly) one for another.

Does it really matter?

Well, yes, actually it does. Because used wrongly they confuse; used correctly they clarify, guide and make sense.

VISION:

As the word implies, a VISION is something that you *see*; a picture of the future as it relates to you. Normally a VISION is of a better world, something you might aspire to, something you want to create. It is a long-term aim and may never be fully realised, so don't restrict it to a time frame.

A VISION is a *passive* picture of the future, what you want your business to **BE**.

MISSION:

Again the clue is in the meaning of the word. Unlike the Vision, a MISSION is an *active* thing, something you go on. It describes the actions you need to take in order to *achieve* your VISION. It states what you are going to **DO**.

VALUES:

VALUES are things we hold dear, things that are important to us, that define how we conduct ourselves. Corporate (or management, as they are sometimes called) values define the *way* we do things, whether we are reliable or revolutionary, innovators or followers, put safety first or take risks, are ethical or fast and loose. Values MUST reflect what your business actually *is*. There is no point defining a set of values for your business that simply has no basis in the reality. Yet that is what so many business-es do. The values should define the **WAY** you do things.

In many ways, this is what makes the latest fad of referring to everything as a brand and assigning brand values to it such a nonsense. Brands don't generally do things and don't generally have values: they have *attributes*. It's just another example of how spe-cific terms get forever devalued and rendered next-to-useless by people who don't know what they are talking about and who try to impress through spouting jargon.

STRATEGY:

Here there *is* just the smallest amount of room for confusion because it could be argued that a MISSION is actually a STRATEGY and this would be true. However, a Mission is a very high level strategy indeed and on its own would be insufficiently detailed to define the precise jobs to be done. Think of it like this: if your VISION was to BE at the top of Everest in order to survey the world from its highest point, then your MISSION would be to get from where you are now onto the Everest summit.

By adding your VALUES to this you begin to define the way you are going to do it; for example, if one of your values was 'safety-first' you may decide that a solo climb without oxygen isn't for you.

Once you have the VISION, MISSION and VALUES defined, the STRATEGY is a more detailed appraisal of HOW you are going to achieve your VISION and conduct the MISSION. It is the plan that will guide you along the way; the map, if you like.

All of which leads us into the question of who should develop and who should 'own' the strategic plan for your business.

There is much truth in the sporting cliché that everyone should play to their strengths and it is true here. Some people are much more capable than others of seeing into the future and 'visioning' where the firm could be in years to come. Others are much more able to see what, precisely, might need to be done to get there. Few if any of us can do it all, so it makes sense to recognise that if you (or your MD, president or CEO) are a short term, detail sort of person then you probably aren't going to be best at the vision-ing process. On the other hand, the corporate visionary is unlikely to be great at detail-ing the plan.

So allocate the tasks appropriately and do check out the VISION with the sharehold-er(s) – after all, it is their company.

From then on, it should be the CEO's most *important* job to monitor progress against the strategic plan and to ensure that it is updated annually as circumstances and market forces change.

THE PLAN ITSELF

So what should go into your strategic plan?

Well, first things first.

Decide what period the plan is to cover; I've always found that three years is best, although some do five or even ten year plans. I've never been able to see three years ahead with any accuracy so any longer seems unnecessary. That said, there is a culture in Japan of much longer term strategies, 25 or even 50 year plans aren't unheard of, but within the marketing and communications sector, you probably can get away with three years.

Start with the Vision, Mission and Values and give them some serious thought. Don't make it a committee decision, though, or you'll end up with a weak compromise that will, frankly, be a total waste of time. I can't recall how many Vision/Mission mixes I've seen that say something about being the 'best in the field' or 'world class' or 'number one' or some such bland, meaningless nonsense. What does it mean? How will you know when you've got there? How will you measure that? And, most important of all, how on earth can you develop a plan to get you somewhere so ill defined?

Try to be really specific. Avoid ill-defined adjectives and generalisations like 'best' and try to answer the question – *how will I know when we're there?* It usually gives you exactly what you need to define the Vision and Mission precisely. Use words or phrases like *fastest, most respected, biggest, most recognised, most awarded, most profitable* or whatever you choose for your business. But be specific.

Then ensure that your Mission links directly to the Vision. So, for example, if your Vision is ultimately to be the *biggest* business in your sector, then specify in the Mission how big you're aiming to be, by when and where that will put you in your sector's league table (or, in other words, how you are going to measure progress).

Define the Values that have made your business what it is and how you want to use them to help you to achieve the Mission. Think about what your business is really good at and where it has clear weaknesses, look at the market and at your competitors and decide where you think you will best fit. Then – and only then – start to think about what you will need to do to achieve your Mission. If you have done a good job so far, the things that need to be achieved will begin to emerge quite easily.

I can't tell you exactly what should or shouldn't be in your strategic plan other than to say that it should provide you and your management team with a clear set of goals and interim objectives that, when achieved, will take you closer to being what you want to be. Be realistic about what can be achieved in the time period and be as precise as you can about what you are going to do and who is going to do it.

Typically the plans I have written over the years have varied quite considerably.

When my colleagues and I were trying to build the advertising agency, the focus of the plan always seemed to be about differentiation – something that the marketing and communications sector was, and still is, rather short of. We built a reputation as a media neutral, integrated communications agency many years before that became widespread. We operated on a fees-only basis with media commissions returned to the clients and in so doing, built a reputation for objective counsel, openness and honesty.

Perhaps most important of all, with a number of the most senior people being recruited from the 'client-side' (myself included), we understood the negative and cynical feelings that many clients held towards advertising agencies at that time – that they were expensive, ego-driven, commercially (and creatively) inconsistent, often inexperienced and unaware of the client-side pressures. Frequently, proposals from agencies would be highly creative but just not real-world practical.

We deliberately stood for the opposite; we minimised ego, opened our books to clients, charged fair prices and applied our own standards as ex-clients to deliver what would have delighted us. It worked brilliantly and generated consistent growth, healthy profitability and an excellent reputation.

That same philosophy worked within the PR sector just as well and led Countrywide Communications from its original foundations as a small, one-man firm in Banbury, Oxfordshire – not the centre of the PR universe – to its top three position in the world as Porter Novelli.

In addition, though, we always looked at the services that the firm offered and how to expand them; at the market sectors that the firm targeted and how to gain greater penetration and wider appeal; and at the quality of the staff and what could be done to help them grow, develop and perform better than anyone else.

Probably in itself that last point was the most important because the only significant assets we have in Marketing and Communications are the people who do the work. Keeping high morale and motivation is essential – as we all know – and nothing does it better than a declared (and carried through) strategy of investment in career development. It reduces staff turnover (which clients hate and erodes your profitability) and helps keep salary inflation under control too because, in my experience, many people value training and career growth just as much as they value their salary. Sure, they could probably earn a little more elsewhere – we all can – but is it really going to be as satisfying and lead to such rapid personal growth?

Finally (and I can say honestly that, even now, I am still surprised by the number of agencies who fail to do this), we always took our own advice – to communicate strongly and consistently about what it was that made us different and more attractive. We didn't always get it right and there were some notable failures along the way but we always had something to talk about and always made progress towards the vision.

Writing a strategic plan doesn't mean writing a tome, quite the opposite; make it clear, concise and to the point. Back up your assertions with data or evidence only where it is necessary for credibility. It isn't an exercise in completeness, it's a working document that will help you and your colleagues to work together, in a common direction towards the same goal. It's always worth remembering that the shorter and clearer it is, the more likely it is to be properly read and understood.

Done well, the plan will define for you one more thing: exactly what *roles* are needed in order to ensure that the plan is carried through. Those roles should be the ones that carry responsibility, authority and accountability to the MD – in other words they define what the directors' roles should be.

All too often in our service industry world, the title 'director' is meaningless; it is little more than a reward title for those who are good account team leaders. I've come across boards of 20 or more in businesses of only 50 to 100 people. This is a nonsense because there simply aren't that many areas of accountability; and no board of 20 ever 'runs' the company – that's done by a much smaller group of maybe two or three.

Having so many 'directors' does achieve one thing, though: it turns them into a group of mildly disgruntled senior employees who feel left out of the inner sanctum and who feel that they *should* be consulted on every aspect of the business, but *aren't*. It slows things down, creates huge debates and disagreements and produces unacceptable compromises. It really is very bad news and contributes to the failure of many good strategic plans because I've yet to meet a group of 20 intelligent and, dare I say, ego-driven individuals who can agree on much at all.

But that isn't the biggest cause of failure to achieve the goals of a strategic plan.

Most strategic plans fail because they are either simple wish lists without any clear direction on how to achieve them or because they don't link to a properly thought through long term goal (Vision). More plans end up in the cupboard only to be brought out when you want to impress your bank manager or shareholder(s) than those which are used monthly, weekly or even daily as a business guide.

All too often the inevitable conflict between the short-term realities and the long-term aims takes its toll – the tactical, day-to-day *needs* get in the way of the strategic *goals* or, as I prefer to refer to it, the *urgent* takes priority over the *important*.

Let's take a moment to consider exactly what this means and typically what happens.

We all work in a deadline driven business; we're interrupted constantly and are frequently switching from one task to the next. There's just too little time to do everything and so something has to give. Naturally the first things to give are the ones that don't have an immediate deadline – the longer-term tasks. They're the things that we all know we should do, we want to do, but somehow never get around to. We end up dealing with all the 'urgents' at the expense of the 'importants'. We do it in our personal lives too – forgetting birthdays or anniversaries, having to work late and missing story time with the children. It doesn't take a genius to see that a frequent failure to deal with the important things in our personal lives eventually takes its toll and so, too, does it in business.

At Countrywide, we once had a client who simply 'wasn't available' Thursday afternoons because it was his 'important' time; the time for thinking about the business; the time which was devoted to the big issues. He claimed it was the secret of his success and I think it was.

The most successful business people *always* create some time in their week for the 'importants' and you must too. Sadly, whilst they often get it right in their work, there aren't too many who get it right in their personal lives as well. Finding the optimum work/life balance is difficult, but, believe me, it is worth making the effort or else you could be one of those who looks back wistfully on their life with that glazed, 'if only' look; and you really don't want to be there.

But I digress. Let's get back to *planning* and bring the timescale back to the next 12 months because whether or not we achieve our three year strategic goals will be determined by the decisions and actions we take now.

So, in the light of all that's above, let's look at how we translate our strategic plan into the annual financial plan. The word 'translate' is pretty important here because all too often companies produce excellent strategic plans only to fall at the financial plan hurdle; they simply forget that the financial plan needs to reflect their strategic plan in every way. After all, it is simply a more detailed, costed version of the strategic plan for the year to come.

b. Taking the shorter term view – financial planning

I am going to start with an assumption – that the strategic plan has been written, approved and is ready to go. In itself that's fine but on its own it isn't enough.

In addition to the strategic plan (or the map as we referred to it earlier), we need the resources to be able to follow it and we need to measure our progress towards its achievement. Most commonly we measure our resource needs and progress in money; so think of the annual financial plan as the steps we need to take and the resources we're going to need in order to take them.

In simple terms, a financial plan is a forecast for the year ahead of what we believe is going to happen to our business measured in £s, €s, $s or whatever. It takes into account the overall aim of 'profit first' or 'growth first' and sits underneath (and is totally consistent with) the VISION, MISSION, VALUES and STRATEGY.

It sounds as if it should be a relatively simple process to put together a financial plan and it is, provided you follow a few basic rules:

–   Make sure it is a *realistic* prediction of what you think will happen; don't be seduced into making it an unachievable, 'in my dreams' wish list.
–   Do it early enough to be fully finalised and agreed by the board well before the start of the year.
–   Plan for the unexpected – it will happen!
–   Use history as a guide.
–   Be prepared to re-plan if circumstances dictate.
–   Remember it is a *prediction* not a guarantee.

Within the broad concept of financial planning, I am going to restrict this section to that which is relevant to you – those at, or heading for, the top in the marketing and communications services sector. Initially, let's concentrate on putting together the first draft of 'The financial plan'.

There are really only three areas to consider:

–   Planning the income.
–   Planning the costs.
–   Planning the profit.

Your accountant, CFO or finance director may disagree with the above and say that it is an over-simplification and to be honest they'd be right, because there are other considerations as well – cash flow, capital requirements, tax planning and more. However, for now we'll stick with the three above and come back to the others later.

You'll have noticed that I've chosen to use the term 'income' rather than turnover. By this I am referring to what most would understand as gross profit; that is the sum of all fees, mark-ups and commissions (where relevant). In a more conventional accounting sense, this is the total of all 'sales' less the 'direct cost of sales'. I have always found this to be the only really useful figure to use as my starting point as it is the true inflow from which the outflow of salaries and other overheads needs to be paid.

One could argue that turnover (or sales) ought to be the starting point, but in my experience the turnover of a professional service firm can vary widely depending on the nature of the business they do. In a conventional advertising agency – one buying media for clients – the turnover could be five or six times that of a PR consultancy employing the same number of staff. However the gross profit (or income) would be equivalent because one has to deduct the cost of the media purchases (the direct cost of sales) from the turnover. So for any realistic comparison of scale (and as we'll discuss later on, for any useful analysis of staff utilisation or efficiency of operation), the gross profit (or income) is the best measure.

This is not to say that turnover is irrelevant; it is not. We need to know the projected turnover if we are to have control of our cash flow and so an estimated turnover figure and monthly turnover forecast is necessary as well. However, for most fee-based businesses there is usually a relatively fixed relationship between income and turnover and a simple formula (based on historical data) is usually sufficient to 'calculate' expected turnover and so forecast the cash flow.

For the purposes of this section on financial planning I am going to ignore turnover and concentrate on the income stream as the starting point.

Before we start, we need to know what profit target we are aiming for. Usually this is defined as target *profitability* – the percentage of income that we want our profit to be – but it could equally well be an amount of money. Let's assume, for the moment at least, that we are aiming for 15% profitability. In other words our profit before tax is intended to be 15% of our income.

Planning income

Over the years, my colleagues and I came at this from a number of different directions and none of them was perfect. So what's suggested here is, I think, the best compromise I've been able to create and to be honest, it serves its purpose pretty well. It works on the basis of breaking down income streams into different types and forecasting each one, individually, on a best guess basis. History is a good guide here as a number of the required forecasts are going to be *educated* guesses based on what has happened before; and that's usually as accurate as you can get.

However, before getting into the actual income forecasting process there is one other thing to get clear and this is another of my lack of clarity beefs about us in this industry. I've already mentioned it earlier in this chapter but once again, it hits home here. This is what I said earlier:

> *Most of us, whether in PR, advertising, marketing services or whatever, use business terms extremely loosely. Occasionally it's a deliberate bluff, sometimes a mistake but usually it stems from our irrational need to appear clever – and all too often it does just the opposite. Rarely do we take the time or trouble to find out exactly what they mean and how/where to use them. Most of us operate in our own worlds without ever seeing the whole picture of how business really functions. There is a logical structure to it and it does all make sense – but only once you've really understood what things mean, why and where they fit in the logical chain that is the business mechanism.*

Here I want to apply my beef to the use of the words 'client' and 'account'. Think about them for a moment and ask yourself how *you* use them in your everyday work. Most people I talk to use the words interchangeably and can't offer a clear definition of them. However, there is a real difference and it is one that makes income planning a lot easier.

You should think of them like this:

CLIENT – an *organisation* for which we work.

ACCOUNT – the *specific area of client business* on which we are working.

So, for any given CLIENT there could be (and usually are) many ACCOUNTS.

These may be different brands, different divisions or different areas of service. For example, within any major organisation there may well be consumer marketing accounts, trade or business-to-business accounts, corporate accounts, city/financial accounts, internal communications and so on. We may not all have expertise in all these areas but often we do have capabilities that extend outside the account(s) we currently hold.

It is a widely held (and in my view accurate) belief that winning new accounts from *existing* clients is easier and less costly than winning new accounts from *new* clients.

So let's start our income planning with **Existing Accounts**.

These generally fall into two types:

— *contract accounts* for which there is an agreed annual fee or budget, generally broken down into monthly or quarterly instalments.
— *project accounts* where fees are paid on a job by job basis.

For *contract accounts* you (by which I mean the director/account director in charge) should be able to predict the coming year with reasonable certainty because the fee level is likely to be similar to the current year, allowing for any rate increases and known adjustments from the client end. So forecast the fee income on this basis, month by month for the year ahead.

Project accounts need a little more thought as you will need to take a view on what is likely to be coming your way; history overlaid with a little intelligence should do the trick well enough. Don't be tempted to only forecast what you *know about* today. It's tempting but very unhelpful as it will leave huge holes later in the year. Use your best judgement to guess what might come up later and put a reasonable estimate into the forecast.

Next, take a moment or two to consider how optimistically or pessimistically the forecasts have been done. In my experience everyone has a natural level of accuracy in their forecasting ability. Some will be pretty much spot on every time, others will always play it safe and under-forecast, whilst a few will treat the forecast as an opportunity to show you how go-getting they are by providing mildly to wildly optimistic estimates.

I'd put money on the fact that you'll get a greater number of pessimistic under-forecasts than any other sort so you'll need to add another line into the *existing accounts* section to allow for *growth/shrinkage of existing accounts*. Estimate this on the basis of *your judgement* of the forecasting approach that each of the team has taken. In my experience it is likely to net out to a small percentage of growth that you'll need to add (maybe 5% or so) but it does vary a lot depending on the mix of the forecasters.

A few years ago I was working in a team of directors where we all 'knew' that one of the account directors would always provide an absolutely accurate figure; if she said that her accounts would deliver £x or $y next year then that is exactly what they would do (barring totally unpredictable events). Another always gave figures that were at least 15% over-optimistic no matter how often we talked about 'sensible forecasting' and so we came to know that we would need to knock that 15% off before using those numbers for anything else. The rest were generally cautious (probably feeling that to over-deliver against a low forecast was preferable to under-delivering against a higher one). This is the norm and you will need to take all three types fully into account when estimating your *growth/shrinkage* line.

There is a clue in the previous paragraph as to the next forecast line to be written. The old adage that *'if it can happen, it will happen'* has never been truer than here. I can't recall a single year of my time running either the advertising agency or the PR firm when there wasn't at least one shock account loss or budget collapse that caught us by surprise. It could have been caused by almost anything from a personnel change at the client end to a merger announcement – or even (worst of all) poor performance that hadn't been admitted or dealt with properly. It happens even in the best firms so we need to protect against it as best we can. I am going to deal with Client/Account Satisfaction monitoring later on, so for now we'll only consider the financial planning implications.

To cover these unpredictable (but inevitable) events you should enter a line into your income forecast for *unexpected account losses.* It's another judgement call but one where, once again, history can be a good guide. Take a look at what has happened in previous years and then enter an amount that will cover you should the worst happen. Don't be too pessimistic by assuming, for example, that your top three accounts will all leave in month 1 but do put a fair estimate into the forecast, which could help offset an unexpected loss or two during the year. I have found through bitter experience that something between 5% and 10% of the *existing account* income seems about right.

If the worst does happen during the year, then you have already taken it into account and so you minimise the impact on the bottom line. If it doesn't, then you have additional income and profit that you weren't expecting and everyone likes that.

Before we move on to the next, obvious area of *new clients* there is one more area to consider – *new accounts from existing clients*. At this stage I hope it's becoming clear why I am such a stickler for accuracy in the use of terminology. It's easy to lump 'New biz' into a single line without any real thought and to end up not differentiating between *existing account growth, new accounts from existing clients* and *new accounts from new clients.* Yet we all know that winning these different income streams often requires quite different approaches. Given that around 50% of 'New biz' usually comes from existing clients – either through account growth or new accounts – it makes no sense to lump it all together.

The best way to forecast this line is, once again, by asking each of the account directors; the need to consider the opportunities for additional accounts from within their current clients. Recognising the different optimism/pessimism levels of each of them, take a view on what they give you, probe a bit and then, at the end, discount the total by a significant percentage to allow for the inevitable under-estimation of how long it takes to open up new accounts. In my experience a discount of around 50% works well. This way you can be reasonably confident that what you are forecasting is achievable rather than an ideal world scenario.

Finally, the bit that is most difficult of all – *new accounts from new clients*. Predicting business from new clients is a guessing game at best but once again experience and the judicious use of historical data can make it less unpredictable.

Let's start by looking at the likely extremes. First I need to assume that you are not a very small firm in its first few years of operation because if you are the following parameters don't apply. In some small firms 100% growth year-on-year is not uncommon. However, for the rest of us the growth rate is likely to be somewhat less.

I suspect it is pretty unlikely It is unlikely that you will go for a full year without winning *any* new clients; so at the lower end of the scale, a year when *new accounts from new clients* sum to less than 10% of your income would be unusual.

On the other hand, it is rare to find that *new accounts from new clients* amounts to more than 50% either, as that would mean a wholesale change in the nature of your business and would be incredibly hard to manage from a resourcing perspective, even should you be fortunate enough to win that much.

In reality, something between 10% and 50% would be normal; and, in my experience, for most 'established' businesses, it generally falls in the 20% to 30% bracket. So for your business you will need to make an educated guess based on what you have in the pipeline, what percentage you usually win and what stage you are at in the winning/losing cycle. By that I mean that every business seems to go through phases in its development where, at some points you seem to win almost everything you go for; at other times you seem to get onto a losing streak that knocks morale and confidence and seems hard to break. I wish I knew why this is but I don't. All I can conclude is that a run of wins builds confidence whilst a few consecutive 'very close seconds' knocks that confidence and it influences how clients react to you.

By now you have almost completed the income forecast part of your financial plan but remember that, so far, you have only been forecasting *fee income* and now you need to add the final two elements – *recharged account costs* and *recharged margin*.

Recharged account costs are the charges you (may or may not) make to your clients/accounts to cover the costs incurred in running their accounts on a day-to-day basis. These typically cover telephone calls, photocopying, postage, e-mail, subscriptions, copyright fees and so on. Some firms charge for these on an as-used basis, some don't charge at all and others use a flat-rate approach.

Personally I am a fan of the flat-rate approach as it covers all the costs and yet doesn't need all the systems and time taken to monitor everything. In my experience clients who are sent a breakdown of every photocopy and telephone call made on their behalf will only ever find it irritating and question why.

When we switched from 'as used' to a 'flat rate' there wasn't a single issue; not then or later. The norm seems to be about 8% of the fees and the sell is simple – "we waste too much of *your* time counting and invoicing all these different elements so we've decided not to do it any more and instead bill you an average flat rate based on a percentage of the fees. At x% [you decide for your business] it will actually cost you less than it used to because we no longer spend any time adding it all up."

Now on to the last line of the income forecast – the *recharged margin*. This is the mark-up you take on bought-in costs. For some firms it will be only a small element of their income but for others it can be very substantial. It needs to be forecast on an account-by-account basis by the account director. Whether you are forecasting a *contract fee* account or a *project account*, there is likely to be an agreed budget, which can be split into fees and costs (production costs, implementation costs etc.). It is the <u>margin</u> you intend to make on these costs that you need to forecast, not the total turnover.

The margin you earn will be determined by the mark-up percentage you use (typically 17.65%) and it is relatively easy to calculate. This needs to be added to each account income forecast as a subsidiary line. It must be kept separate from fee income because, as you will see later, the fee income alone is the element we need to convert into time to do our capacity planning (see chapter 2).

In talking to people about their level of recharged margin I often find that there seems to be little understanding of why we use the (odd) figure of 17.65%. Whilst not universal in its adoption, it is widespread and the generally recommended figure from the various industry bodies.

In fact, it has its origins in advertising. The advertising industry has, until quite recently, universally earned its income from media commission rather than client fees. Through the process of obtaining 'media recognition' (which means being 'recognised' by the media owners as financially sound and credit-worthy) agencies entitled themselves to commission on all media space sold to their clients at the (normally standard) rate of 15%. In other words, if a page in a journal or a slot on radio or TV was priced at, for the sake of argument, £1000, the client could buy it direct for that price or their agency would buy it for that price less 15% (their commission) and sell it to the client for the same £1,000. That way, the agency would earn £150 for themselves and pay the media £850. Frequently the £150 'commission' was used to fund the creative work needed to produce the advertisement or commercial, although production costs would be added on top.

However, if an agency was asked to do non-media work for a client – buying print, for example – they needed to ensure that they earned the equivalent of the media 'commission' and so simply applied the same formula in reverse. So if print costs were, for example, £850 they would want to charge the client £1,000, which requires a mark-up on the £850 cost of, yes you've guessed it, 17.65%. So adding a mark-up of 17.65% is exactly the same as earning a commission (or margin) of 15%.

Incidentally, the term 'agency' stems from the fact that they started out as the 'selling-agencies' for the media and added value by writing/designing the copy required to fill the space; and even though that's no longer the perception, the name has stuck and been applied even to non-media based consultancies – sales promotion, PR, direct marketing and so forth.

Again I digress, so let's get back to the financial plan.

In summary, we have an income forecast as the first element of our financial plan, which, once the account types have been summed together, looks a bit like this:

XYZ Company Limited
Income Forecast

	Jan	Feb	Mar	Apr	May	Jun	Jul	Aug	Sep	Oct	Nov	Dec	Total
Existing clients' accounts													
Contracted fees													
Project fees													
Growth/shrinkage													
Unexpected account losses													
Total of existing accounts													
New accounts from existing clients													
New accounts from new clients													
Total of new accounts													
Total Fee Income													
Recharged account costs													
Recharged margin													
Total Income													

By taking our desired amount of profit from the Total Income figure in the bottom, right-hand cell, we can calculate what we can *afford* to spend on 'costs'.

Sadly, this isn't what most of us do. Instead, we almost always **forecast** our costs, deduct them from our income and see what (if anything) we have left. Then most commonly, when it isn't enough we just add more income into the 'New biz' line until it is!

This is the most illogical way to go about it. First, it makes a complete mockery of the realistic approach to income planning that we've just been through and secondly, it doesn't really increase the likely profit at all. It just increases the number at the bottom of the plan, which means you won't achieve the profit you want or the plan – double failure.

There is only one right way; which is why, once we have been through the cost planning section below, we need to return to this issue and approach it rather differently.

Planning costs

In many ways planning the costs is a much easier exercise than planning the income stream as it has far fewer variables requiring 'guestimation'.
Let's start with the biggest cost of all – *people*.

In most professional service firms people costs represent well over half the total costs of the organisation – salaries, bonuses, incentive payments, freelancers' fees, National Insurance/social charges, pension contributions, health insurance and other benefits all sit under this heading. But the largest of these by far is salaries.

In Chapter 2, I am going to explain all about capacity planning, calculating exactly how many people you are going to need at each level in order to deliver all the services to clients that your income forecast dictates. However, and this is critical, I want to carry on here with the 'traditional' way of planning costs so that you can see where the problems arise and why it is unsatisfactory.

In the real world you are going to enter the coming year with the level of staffing that is already in place, *plus* any recruitment already in train and *less* any planned/unplanned departures. The salary levels are known and so it's relatively easy to list all staff and spread their known costs across the 12 months on an equal basis.

You'll need to include any planned salary increases and promotions and take a view on when they will come into effect. You'll also need to add in any additional staff that might be necessary to accommodate the growth that is reflected in your income stream across the year. Remember you always have a choice – you could recruit or, if the need seems to stem from a temporary, workload peak, you could hire freelance help to get you through.

Once you've listed all the salaries, together with additional staff and/or freelance costs, then move on to all the so-called 'on-costs' associated with employment – NI/social charges, pension (if you contribute), bonus allowances etc.

Once you've done all this you're ready to move on to the next block of costs – *the other overheads*.

Here the task is much simpler because these elements fall into one of three categories:

–   *Fixed costs* – those costs that stay constant regardless of the level of income you are enjoying. These include rent, rates, office service charges, heat/light, IT provision, equipment leases and so on. History will tell you what you should include and so I'm not going to give you a comprehensive list here as that isn't the point of this book; your FD or accountant can do that.

–   *Variable costs* – those costs that go up or down with your level of business. These include telephone charges, recruitment and/or termination costs, staff welfare, non-rechargeable expenses, interest charges and so on.

–   *Discretionary costs* – those costs over which you have complete discretion. Marketing, training, product development, new business research and so on.

This type of approach is the normal way of putting financial accounts together so your accountant or CFO/FD will have no problem sorting this for you. There are as many variations on this as there are accountants and to be honest, not all of them put every line in the same place but it really doesn't matter as long as you are consistent year on year. The need here is to ensure that you have allowed, properly, for all the costs you are likely to incur. It may be worth having a small contingency line somewhere, too, to absorb those unexpected costs that always seem to come and none of us can predict.

With that work done you should have a costs schedule that looks a bit like this:

XYZ Company Limited

Costs Schedule

	Jan	Feb	Mar	Apr	May	Jun	Jul	Aug	Sep	Oct	Nov	Dec	Total
Staff Costs													
Salaries (inc increases)													
Additional recruits													
Bonuses													
Pension/health ins													
NI/social charges													
Etc...													
Total staff costs													
Other overheads													
Fixed costs													
Rent													
Rates													
Heat/light													
Office services													
Etc...													
Total fixed costs													
Variable costs													
Telephone													
Recruitment/termination													
Welfare													
Expenses													
Bank interest													
Etc...													
Total variable costs													
Discretionary costs													
Marketing													
New business													
Product development													
Training													
Etc...													
Total discretionary costs													
Total costs													

Planning profit

The right way of planning profit isn't the obvious and simple route of subtracting your costs from your income to see what you have left.

If that really was all there was to it you would, in all likelihood, end up bankrupt pretty quickly because, most of the time, the calculation would lead to very little, if any, profit and, more likely, a thumping loss.

That isn't to say that you don't do the calculation. You do, but it doesn't stop there.

When I first approached financial planning this way, I calculated the profit exactly as I have described and found that, with the income and cost assumptions I had made, we would indeed make a loss. My solution? To look again at the income forecasts line by line and the costs, similarly, but with a rather more optimistic eye until I had added enough back in to cover the shortfall and deliver the desired profitability.

On the face of it, it worked and my boss was happy with the result. However, he shouldn't have been and nor should I because it was no longer a financial *plan* but a financial *hope*. It wasn't realistic and it bore little resemblance to what I had been given by the account directors or had learnt from history. It was at best a target but a very tough one and unlikely to be achieved.

Sure enough, we failed to get close.

A tough lesson to be sure but an invaluable one because, if I had been honest, I had known all along that, barring some extremely good luck, my plan wasn't sound. And planning for luck sounds like gambling and we all know that the only winners in that game are the bookies.

There had to be a better way – and there is.

Using the 'discretionary costs' balancer

First determine how much profit you are aiming to make – either as a simple number or as a margin on income. Let's assume, for the sake of argument, that you are aiming for a margin of 15%, which would generally be a pretty reasonable performance. Then do the calculation to see where your 'income minus costs' sum comes out and compare the two.

If you're ahead of the desired margin (unlikely, but possible), then look again at all your assumptions and double-check everything. If it's still true, then well done... probably. Before you give yourself a pat on the back, read the next chapter on capacity management and think about the number of heads you have included in your staff costs line and be sure that you really have allowed for enough capacity to do all the work.

If, as is more likely, your margin isn't even close to what you planned, you will need to look again at your discretionary costs line. Make the necessary adjustments to bring your margin into line with what you planned and there you are... maybe.

Once again it is probable that even if you take **all** the discretionary costs out – which is neither sensible nor realistic – you still won't be there. For this problem there is only one explanation: your staff costs are too high. It can *only* be this; because without any discretionary costs all your other costs are either 'fixed' or linked to the volume of business you are forecasting – 'variable'.

You have to ask yourself why your staff costs are out of kilter. It could be because your salaries are too high (but that's unlikely); maybe you're planning to give too much away in bonuses (but I'd be surprised). The truth is that almost certainly you are planning to have *too many people* in the business for the fee income you are forecasting.

One other possible explanation is that your day/hourly rates are too low but again that's not a very frequent occurrence and the chances are you know what the typical industry rates are and so can check easily.

No, the big issue here is the biggest issue in the industry – staff utilisation and capacity management. And that's what Chapter 2 is all about.

Chapter 2

CAPACITY MANAGEMENT AND UTILISATION

(How to make money along the way)

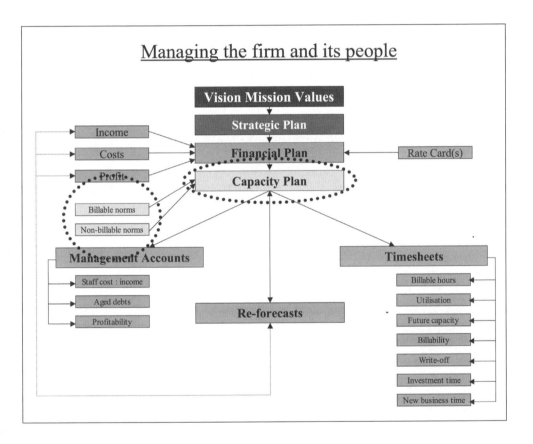

a. Why time really is money

I want to start off this important – probably most important – section by asking you a question.

How many hours a week do you work?

Across the professional marketing services sector the answer is invariably "a lot". Certainly it averages out to many more than the 37 or so hours that most of our employment contracts specify. But that's okay isn't it, because our employers make it clear that the nature of our 'profession' means we need to work according to the 'demands of the job'?

For years it has been normal to work long hours and for many of us it has become a habit; arrive early to avoid the traffic/phones/interruptions, leave late for the same reasons. But the big question I asked myself some years ago is "does it really have to be like this?"

Now, in Europe, with the EU Working Time Directive and ever more pressure (rightly in my view) to seek a sensible work/life balance, surely everything will change and we'll all find the perfect relationship between our jobs and our real lives outside, won't we?

As I sit writing this chapter, the latest information I have suggests that the average working week in our sector still seems to be about 44 hours and, in some cases, very much longer. And because we work in a 'professional' field we don't pay or get paid overtime.

So let's just spend a moment or two here to think about what this tells us.

Come with me on a little flight of fancy, to the land where no-one works any unpaid overtime, where we all start work at 9am take an hour for lunch and then head off home at 5.30pm or so. I did say it was a flight of fancy didn't I? A pleasant, though somewhat unrealistic thought, I must admit.

Nonetheless, stay with me here for a moment and let's calculate what that really means.

The first thing we can calculate (and it isn't too hard to do) is that we would each, on average, work seven hours a week less. That's almost a 16% reduction. If we assume that this seven hours is an average mix of activities roughly in proportion to the rest of the week then that would mean a 16% reduction in 'client time'; so either our firm would earn 16% less or we would need 16% more resource to do the same amount of work – to cover the extra work we currently do during our 'free overtime'.

Either we would have to accept a 16% reduction in our firm's income or we would need 16% more staff. If we accept the former then, given that the industry average profitability is running at about 11%, the average firm would be making *a loss of 5%*.

If, however, we chose to increase our headcount to make up for the shortfall, we could do a little better than that because staff costs only account for about 55% of the total overheads so a 16% increase in headcount would only add about 9% to our total costs. But we would need to find space for them and give them phones and computers and expenses and training and so in all we'd end up maybe adding about 12% to our overall costs. So the chances are we might just about break even.

Now what, you might well ask, has this got to do with anything?

The answer is deeply alarming.

Most of our firms, unless amongst the very best performers in the industry, *wouldn't make any profit at all if it wasn't for all the free overtime provided by the employees.* You could say, if you wanted to make a dramatic point, that it is only the overtime that makes any profit at all.

That's a really scary thought because it uncovers a most worrying question: what is it that the marketing and communications sector firms have so wrong that, without the free overtime and the goodwill of their staff, they can't make any profit?

And the answer?

Over-servicing.

That's what this chapter is **really** all about and even though we're going to have to take a little time to get there, we will address exactly why it happens, how to get rid of it and how to prevent it from arising in the first place.

b. Time as the currency

Forgive me if I start right from square one with a few real basics. First, another question: what is it that you are selling to your clients? Capability? Resource? Expertise? Outcomes?

The truth is that even with the very latest efforts by a few forward thinking agencies to sell 'value' through a 'what the job is worth' approach to pricing, most of us are really selling that precious commodity – time.

That's what our fees represent – the amount of time we have spent (or are going to spend, if you bill in advance) working on the client's behalf. No matter how we package it, our income stream depends largely on the amount of time we sell.

Think of it like this.

Imagine for a moment that you are running a bakery producing loaves of bread every day for shipping overnight to the supermarkets. If you produce 10,000 loaves a day but only sell 9,000 of them, you'll be throwing away 1,000 loaves a day. And with a wastage rate that high you will surely not be making any profit because your profit on the 9,000 will be going to pay for the cost of the 1,000 that are wasted.

So what do you do?

Well, either you scale back production to 9,000 loaves a day or you find a new customer for the extra 1,000. That way you minimise wastage and maximise profitability.

The same is true in our business. Simply substitute *hours* for *loaves* and the model works just the same. Except we do something the bakery would never do – we don't throw away the extra loaves – oh no - we *give* the extra loaves (hours) to the *existing* customers for free and in so doing give away the opportunity to sell them to anyone else. To make matters worse, we assume that if we ever stopped giving them the free loaves, we would lose the customers entirely and be left with an even bigger problem.

It's a killer isn't it?

What makes it more alarming still is that most of us don't even know with any accuracy how many loaves we're giving away or which customers are getting them. By which I mean that some agencies don't even keep timesheets (something I find beyond comprehension) and which, sticking with the analogy, means that they don't know how many loaves they're sending out to their customers or have any link between the number of loaves the customer is getting and the number they're paying for.

Transporting this back into our world is scary.

It means that, even though all of us monitor carefully how much income we are generating, we aren't properly logging how many hours we are providing in return. We only have half the equation.

So instead of sorting that out, we satisfy ourselves by checking that our total costs don't exceed our income and that, hopefully, there's a bit of a gap for profit.

Far from it!

That really is just plain foolhardy. Yet that's precisely what many firms do. It's completely mad.

Monitoring the number of hours available, sold and wasted (over-serviced) is critical if you want to be able to control profitability – and you wouldn't be reading this if that subject didn't interest you, now would you?

We need to understand how to manage timesheets and what they tell us. So that's what the next section is all about.

c. Timesheets

Time for a little aside.

A short while ago I was talking to a group of account directors from a variety of agencies about over-servicing. We talked about how widespread the issue was and what could be done about it and before long a debate about timesheets had emerged – whether the information was ever accurate, how different companies used them and so forth. After a while I noticed one of the account directors looking particularly pensive and so I asked him what was on his mind. "We don't keep timesheets at my agency," he said, "the MD doesn't believe in them."

Hmmm, I thought, this could be difficult and so probed a little to find out why that was. What I discovered was that the MD had been 'brought up' in an environment where timesheets were mandatory but no-one, it seems, had ever explained what they were for. He assumed, as many of us would, that timesheets were the agency equivalent of clocking in and out; the 'big brother' checking up on us to see that we did our jobs properly; the evidence with which to beat us up when we took too long over something.

Over the months and years that followed, the (now) MD concluded that the only way to avoid this problem was to complete the timesheet in such a way that it didn't raise any eyebrows, ever. In other words to fiddle the data so that it always added up to the desired number of hours and that the balance between activities always seemed about right. In other words, to lie. No wonder then that he didn't want a system like that in his business.

Let's look at an illustration of this phenomenon, here's a chart that shows what several hundred account handlers (at all levels) have told me is an average working week:

Typical week	
Billable client time	27 hrs
New biz	6 hrs
Investment time	2 hrs
Training	2 hrs
Internal management	4 hrs
Internal administration	3 hrs
TOTAL	**44 hrs**

On the face of it, the chart looks pretty reasonable. A balanced mix of activities with by far the majority of time spent on billable work for clients.

Now here's a chart that shows what you get when, instead of asking staff what they *think* they do, you analyse their timesheets:

Typical week		
Billable client time	~~27 hrs~~	21 hrs
New biz	~~6 hrs~~	5 hrs
Investment time	~~2 hrs~~	3 hrs
Training	2 hrs	2 hrs
Internal management	4 hrs	4 hrs
Internal administration	~~3 hrs~~	9 hrs
TOTAL	44 hrs	44 hrs

I have to make a confession here because for a long time I believed that the analysis above, showing 21 billable hours per person per week, was a good reflection of what was actually happening. But I was wrong.

For the above analysis to be true, in the firm I was looking at, **all** their recorded *billable* time would need to have been converted into *billed* time for it to balance with their fee income. That would have meant there was **no** *over-servicing*.

Would you believe that? No, nor did I so I needed to go 'mining'!

And what did I find?

Well it took a bit of digging but eventually I got to the answer; the firm I was analysing was a little bit like where the 'anti-timesheet MD' I mentioned earlier had 'trained' – the staff simply weren't telling the truth. If they felt they had taken too long to do a job for a client they simply put some of the time into *internal administration*. And that threw all the figures into a confused, unhelpful mess.

And this was the firm I was running!

It took a bit of sorting out, as you might imagine, but in the end we got it right and the figures suddenly made sense.

The truth, of course, lay somewhere between the two.

The staff were actually doing about 25 *billable* hours a week and about five hours of 'admin' but − and it is a very big but − only about 21 of the 25 billable hours were actually being *billed*. In other words, there was an average of about four hours per person per week of over-servicing − almost 20%.

In many ways our anti-timesheet MD was right not to want such a deceptive system in his business but his solution to dismiss timesheets altogether wasn't the right one.

What was wrong at his previous agency (and at mine) wasn't the timesheet system; it was the people who were administering it. Used properly, timesheets are an invaluable asset and helpful to everyone in the firm. But the way they're managed is critical to their success and so we'll cover how to do it properly a little further on.

Fortunately, most agencies do keep timesheets but, even amongst them, the data collected is often inaccurate or simply not put to good use. The truth is that *accurate* timesheet data is the *only* way to keep your business in control. Without that data you are running your business on guesswork, feel and hope. No wonder so many small agencies fail and so many more never achieve the founder's Vision.

Even that is only part of the story. To illustrate the rest, I need you to play a little game with me. It's called The Profitability Game.

d. The profitability game

Imagine for a moment that you are running a smallish firm providing professional services to a number of excellent clients. You've just finished another successful year's trading and have done okay with a very reasonable 13% margin.

Look at the key numbers below and work out how many *hours*, per week, per account handler, your firm was *paid* for.

<u>XYZ Company Limited – Full year results</u>
<u>10 people – all client facing</u>

Average hourly rate charged	£100
Total income	£1m
Staff costs	£520k
Other costs	£350k
Profit before tax	£130k
Profitability	13%

For those of you better with words than numbers I've done it for you over the page, but have a go yourself before looking over.

The calculation goes like this:

£1m (income) ÷ 10 (people) =
       £100k (income per person)

£100k (income per person) ÷ £100 (average hourly rate) =
       1000 (hours per person)

1000 (hours per person) ÷ 45* (working weeks per year) =

22.2
billed hours per person per week

---

* 45 = 52 − 4 (holiday) − 2 (public & given holidays) − 1 (sickness)

Now we already know that, on average, the team at XYZ will be working around 44 hours per week, so this tells us something extremely valuable and interesting: that the XYZ people are only doing paid work for clients for *half* their week; and with 13% margin (or profitability) they are amongst the better performing firms, above the average by at least a couple of percentage points.

So for 2.5 days a week they are earning money and for the other 2.5 days they aren't!

What on earth is going on? Why are they working so hard and yet only doing paid-for work for half their time? What are they doing for the rest of the time?

Before answering those questions, (and I'm sure you are way ahead of me already) I want to look at what would happen to XYZ's **profits** if they managed to increase their average 'billed' time from 22.2 hours to **25** hours per person per week.

The calculation goes like this:

25 (billed hours per person per week) x 10 (people) =
        250 (billed hours per week)

250 (billed hours per week) x 45 (weeks) =
        11,250 (billed hours per year)

11,250 (billed hours per year) x £100 (average hourly rate) =
        £1.125m (annual income)

£1.125m (annual income) − £520k (staff costs) − £350k
(other costs) =

£255k profit
22.7% profitability

So, simply by increasing its billed time *from 22.2 hours to 25* hours per person per week, XYZ has virtually *doubled* its profits.

A small shift from just 22.2 hours to 25 hours has a *dramatic* effect. Double the profit. And that is still from only 25 of the 44 hours per week that they are working.

These are what I call the **Three Magic Hours** – the three hours that *double* your profits.

Just to press the point home, let's look at what would happen if they were able to increase their billed time still further from 25 to 30 hours per person per week.

The calculation goes like this:

30 (billed hours per person per week) x 10 (people) =
300 (billed hours per week)

300 (billed hours per week) x 45 (weeks) =
13,500 (billed hours per year)

13,500 (billed hours per year) x £100 (average hourly rate) =
£1.350m (annual income)

£1.350m (annual income) – £520k (staff costs) – £350k (other costs) =

£480k profit
35.6% profitability

The same people, in the same company, working **30** billed hours per week (out of their normal 44 hours per week) would make nearly *half a million pounds profit* and still have 14 hours left each week for all the other things that need to be done.

Put another way, the same ten people could (should?) handle £1.35m of income (as opposed to the £1m they are handling now) – that's an extra £350k they don't currently have.

So they have a number of options facing them.

1.   They could put a freeze on any further recruitment until they've added the extra £350k of income, progressively improving their profitability as they add income.

2.   They could 'lose' two to three people and handle the existing £1m of income with seven or eight staff – cutting their staff costs by £100–£150k and doubling their profitability.

3.   They could combine 1 & 2 above by concentrating their existing work into seven or eight staff, freeing up two or three to focus on accelerating their growth. Then they'd get to their goal faster than in option 1 and without the pain (cost) of option 2.

For me, there's only one choice - option 3 every time.

Put like that, it doesn't seem all that unreasonable or unachievable does it? So what's stopping us? Why isn't it happening? What's going on here?

Understanding the answer starts by understanding the notion of billed and billable hours.

e. Billed and billable hours

During the previous section you'll have noticed that I introduced the term *billed hours* – the hours that you are paid for by your clients. Once again I have to get all pernickety about the accurate use of terminology because often, when we talk about time and fees, we use all sorts of confusing and inaccurate terms.

We talk about client time, invoiced time, fees invoiced, team hours, billable hours, billed time, retainers... the list is almost endless. So it's time for a few definitions.

Let's start with the definitions of time that we ought to put onto *timesheets*:

Billable time

> All time spent on client work – by account/job

New business

> All time spent on winning specific new accounts – by prospect

Investment time

> Planned non-billable time spent on growing/ securing existing accounts – by account

Training

> Time spent both on and off the job, giving and/or receiving training – not to be confused with account support work

Internal management

> Time spent managing people

Internal administration

> Non-billable time spent managing and adminis-
> tering the firm

On their own, the definitions above are helpful but still not really clear enough without some further explanation.

Take *billable time* for example: the definition is enough for us to distinguish between
'work for clients' and 'work for the firm' but what about some of the grey areas in
between? What about travel for instance? Is that billable time or not? If not where
should it go? What about re-writes or helping out a colleague?

In my list of definitions above I have assumed that travel time is billable but if you
decide, for your business, that it isn't, you'll need a timesheet category for it, otherwise
it will end up in *internal administration*. My logic for this is simple: if you are travelling
on the client's business and, as a result, unavailable to other clients/accounts then they
should pay for that time. However, if you are using that time to work on a different
client or account, then the time should be recorded to that other account – but still as
billable time.

That said, there aren't any absolutes here other than one: **you absolutely must be clear
and consistent within your own firm about what goes where.** You need clear policies; you need to communicate them to everyone (including every new starter); and
you need to manage the process consistently.

Given how important time is in our sector and how our use of time can affect profits
so dramatically, I am constantly shocked by the number of agencies where there is no
clear standard for recording time. We seem to assume that everyone joining the firm
will absorb the right way to do it without being shown and that everyone will end up
doing it the same way through some sort of mass osmosis.

Take it from me *that will never happen.*

Instead all you'll get is a timesheet system full of inconsistencies and data that is, at best,
misleading and, at worst, useless.

So put it all together, in writing, into a reference document that every member of staff
has and make sure they understand it and work to it.

And whilst we are on the subject it's worth taking some space here to look at exactly what *is* meant by each of the definitions we've just established:

Billable time

All time spent on client work – by account/job

This should account for every minute that is spent doing something that, if you didn't have the account, you wouldn't be doing. The only exceptions are for time that should be classified *properly* elsewhere on the timesheet – investment time, for instance.

New business

All time spent on winning specific new accounts – by prospect

I have a firm conviction that the amount of time spent to win a new account should be commensurate with what that account is 'worth' [I cover this later in the book]. So in this timesheet category you should only record the time spent against *specific* new business projects – from credentials meetings onwards to the pitch. Don't include general marketing in here.

Investment time

Planned *non-billable* time spent on growing/ securing existing accounts – by account

There is little doubt that clients want to see pro-activity from their agencies and nothing is more proactive than having unprompted ideas. It's all part of the service. However, there are occasions when either a client or an account has obvious growth potential or, sadly, when it may be under threat. In either case it makes sense to provide a little extra service. This isn't over-servicing in the tra-

ditional sense but investment − planned investment. Each account director needs to have some
flexibility to allocate some time to this, but in a
planned, controlled way.

Training

> Time spent both on and off the job, giving
> and/or receiving training − not to be confused
> with account support work

This one is fairly self-explanatory; time spent
showing somebody how to do something is training; time spent working with them on an account
may have the same effect but should be classed as
billable.

Internal management

> Time spent managing people

You should include here all general people management, such as appraisals and salary reviews, welfare issues, recruitment and all disciplinary matters.

Internal administration

> Non-billable time spent managing and adminis-
> tering the firm

This should include board and management meetings, general marketing, staff meetings and all other
internal monitoring.

With all of this clear, there can be no excuses for inaccurate timesheet information.

f. Setting the billable norms

As we've seen so far, understanding the timesheet categories is crucial if we are to get accurate data. But accuracy alone isn't enough; we need to give our staff a clear picture of what is expected from them – how much time they should expect to spend on each category in a *normal* week; the *norm*.

I've chosen here to work with hours and weeks – recording time in *hours* (and fractions of hours) onto a *weekly* timesheet – because it is a manageable combination. If you work with days per month, you have to deal with the issue of how long a day is. A monthly timesheet has the big drawback that staff will not start worrying about their mix of activities until the third or fourth week by which time it's too late. That isn't to say that a 'days per month' approach is no good, it's just not as good as it could be.

So how do we set the norms?

First we need to apply some common sense. It is inevitable that the people at the top of the organisation will need to allocate more time to non-billable management and administration than those at the lower levels; they will also be the ones leading the new business projects, so we will need to plan for less billable time from the senior staff than the junior.

The critical question to answer before we embark on setting the individual norms is 'how many billable hours per person per week are we aiming to *average* across the business as a whole?'

We've seen from the profitability game that the level of profit we earn is related directly to two variables: the number of hours we sell (the *billed* hours) and the rate we charge per hour; we've also seen that small differences can have a dramatic effect.

For the purposes of this section on 'Setting the norms' I am going to assume that you already have rates worked out for your people and that they are fixed. Later on we will look at how the rates should be determined but if we do that here we'll end up going round in circles asking what comes first, the rate we charge or the number of hours we sell? Let's start with the most important question of all – what level of profitability are we trying to achieve? And that takes us right back to the financial planning objective in Chapter 1.

In fact, this point ought to be a small 'eureka' moment because, if you've been following the logic so far, you ought to now see how the first few pieces of the agency management jigsaw fit together – strategic planning, financial planning, profit planning and billed hours – but there's still a long way to go.

Earlier on we worked out that *profit* isn't just what's left after you've taken your *projected costs* away from your *forecast income*, it's what you decide you want it to be. And that determines how much you can afford to spend on the *staff costs* and other *overheads*. Later we're going to look at *key ratios* and see what the relationships between all these numbers ought to be, but for now we'll stick to working out how we can set the *norms*.

Let's assume you've done your financial planning and determined your desired profitability to be 20% (time to be a little more ambitious than the 15% we used earlier). That will have led you to a budget figure of what you can afford to spend on costs. By deducting your *fixed* and *variable costs* and a reasonable allowance for *discretionary costs,* you'll be left with how much you can afford to spend on staff. **Keep that figure to hand**.

We also know, from the profitability game, that if XYZ Company averaged 30 *billed* hours per person per week, it ought to be highly profitable and that at 22 hours or so it would be struggling to get anywhere close to our 20% profitability goal. So we are probably looking to set an average somewhere in between, say around 27. It will vary according to your hourly rates; the lower your rates the more *billed hours* you will need to do and vice versa.

At about this point, you're probably starting to get a bit confused between *billable* and *billed* hours. The number of hours you *work* on client business is the *billable* total whereas the number of hours you are *paid for* is the *billed* total. Any difference (and there usually is) is *over-servicing,* and we'll look at how to minimise that later.

With nothing more than common sense as a guide and a view as to how your rates compare to the general marketplace, you need to decide how many *billable* hours per week you would expect the staff at each level in your business to do.

Typically you will end up with something like this, which I have put together for an average small/medium agency:

Level	How Many?	Billable Hours
Managing director/chairman	(2)	20
Directors	(4)	24
Associate/account directors	(4)	26
Account managers	(4)	28
Account executives	(6)	30
Team support	(4)	30
Intern/trainees	(2)	30
TOTAL	**(26)**	

Then you can calculate two things: the weighted average of billable hours per week and the income potential. Taking the weighted average first, the calculation is done like this:

Level	Billable Hours
2 x MD/chairman x 20 hrs pw	= 40
4 x directors x 24 hrs pw	= 96
4 x associates/ADs x 26 hrs pw	= 104
4 x account managers x 28 hrs pw	= 112
6 x account executives x 30 hrs pw	= 180
4 x team support x 30 hrs pw	= 120
2 x interns/trainees x 30 hrs pw	= 60
TOTAL	**= 712**

So, the *weighted average* of billable hours per person per week
= 712 hrs ÷ 26 people =

27.4

The calculation of income *potential* is pretty similar: you take the number of billable hours at each level and multiply it by the hourly rate you charge for that level as follows (I have taken rates that seem to be reasonably representative of a typical medium-sized agency):

2 x 20 hrs	=	40	x	£230 ph	=	£9,200
4 x 24 hrs	=	96	x	£160 ph	=	£15,360
4 x 26 hrs	=	104	x	£125 ph	=	£13,000
4 x 28 hrs	=	112	x	£90 ph	=	£10,080
6 x 30 hrs	=	180	x	£60 ph	=	£10,800
4 x 30 hrs	=	120	x	£45 ph	=	£5,400
2 x 30 hrs	=	60	x	£45 ph	=	£2,700
Total					=	£66,540

So, £66,540 x 45 weeks per year =

£3.0m income potential

On this basis, this 26-person agency ought to be able to earn £3.0m income per year, an average of almost £115k per billable head.

If you do this calculation of income potential for your firm, it may well turn out to be a shock as it probably won't compare with the outcome of your financial planning. In all likelihood your plan will show rather less income, which reinforces the point that *either* you aren't achieving the average 27+ billable hours per person per week (in simple terms, you have too many people for the income you are forecasting) *or*, if you are achieving the *norms*, then *over-servicing* accounts for the difference. As I said earlier, we're going to look at minimising over-servicing a little later, so park that issue for the moment.

Looking at your business like this also highlights why many agencies don't approach capacity planning in this way – because there is no right answer and everything seems to be connected to everything else: if you increase rates you can reduce the norms for billable hours; if you reduce the norms your rates need to increase; change the number of staff at each level and it all changes again and, of course, over-servicing plays a big part, too.

There is no perfect answer to this conundrum; it is simply an iterative process that requires you to break into it somewhere and then complete several 'cycles' before settling on a 'good' outcome. The most logical place to break into the process is by setting your rates at an appropriate market level and then working from there. (More on that later.)

For now, we'll stick with the assumption that you have rates in place. Next we'll look at how to work out how many people you should have.

g. Capacity planning

With a little application of logic you could conclude, from your financial plan, how many staff at each level you can afford. Which would be fine except for one thing: it takes no account of the nature of the accounts you have and what staffing mix is required for each of those accounts. So that's where you need to go next.

Each of the account directors has already contributed to the *financial plan* by forecasting the income expected from each account and now they have to turn that into a capacity requirement by working out how many hours per week (at each staffing level) the account should consume.

They do this by using a combination of judgement and calculation; judgement of the right team mix and calculation to ensure that 'hours' x 'hourly rate' for each of the team adds up to no more than the agreed fee level. In theory, at least, this should be exactly the reverse of the calculation you did when working out what the fee level should be in the first place (so you should have that information on file), although in my experience many 'calculations' of fees are little more that 'guestimates' and that is totally unacceptable.

Remember though to limit the amount of client work that any individual has allocated to them to around the norm for their level. It's a bit of a black art requiring a fair few iterations to get it right but it can be done fairly accurately and you'll end up with a capacity plan – a spreadsheet showing how many people you need at each level to do the work that you are forecasting to do.

One of the lessons learnt doing this a few times is that having fixed account teams handling a group of accounts is much less efficient than taking a resource pool approach. The pool approach will always give you more flexibility and less spare capacity. The logic for this is simple: if you have, say, four account groups each operating like a mini business, then most of the time *each* group will have a bit of spare capacity – say the equivalent of half a person extra. In total, that's the equivalent of two people unused.

If, on the other hand, you operate flexibly, with the resource being allocated across teams to where it is needed most, you can reduce the spare capacity to maybe half a person *in total*.

The difference in profitability terms can be quite substantial.

You now have a capacity plan and a staff costs budget, which ought, if you have done it properly, to marry up pretty well.

The final stage is to decide how you are going to bring your capacity plan and the reality of your actual staffing level into line — and this is a decision only you can make. The choices were covered earlier, as were the pros and cons, but in the end it comes down to your *values,* your level of commercial drive and the impact on the morale of the firm. For me, the choice was always to try to avoid redundancies unless the plan and reality were simply too far apart. The good news is that once you've achieved the desired balance between income and capacity, it isn't hard to keep it there.

h. Setting the non-billable norms

Having set the *billable* norms for each level of staff, you will need to give them guidance on how the rest of their working work should look. In my firm we always approached it like this: first we deducted the *billable norm* for each level from the contracted hours in the working week (usually 37 or so) and then we split the remaining hours between the other categories on the basis of judgement. The directors then looked at all the categories and we used judgement to decide on a few simple policies:

Billable time

As per the *norm* per level calculated above.

New business

Heavier for the more senior staff, lighter for the more junior. Generally around 10% of time overall, so with a 3.7 hours per week average maybe you should consider five to six hours per week for directors and two to three hours per week for execs.

Investment time

You will need to apply a strict limit on this as it can run out of control and become a hiding place for over-servicing. Setting it at <7.5% of total time seemed about right but, once again, set it higher for more senior staff, lower for more junior. Maybe three to four hours per week at the higher end.

Training

This one is the other way round. Training, or 'internal investment' if you like, is needed more at the lower level. Generally, allowing around one hour per week for the seniors and two to three hours per week for the juniors seems sensible.

Internal management

At the junior end this should be zero. At the senior end it will depend on how many staff they are managing; three to four hours per week ought to be enough.

Internal administration

Everyone will need to do some administration, even if it's just filling in their timesheets and expenses. At the more senior end it can be significant at three to four hours per week but at the lower end it ought not to be more than one hour.

So overall, the *norms* will look like this:

Hrs | Level	MD+	Dir	AD	AM	AE	PA/Sec	Trainee
Billable	20	24	26	28	30	30	30
New biz	4	4	3	2	1	2	2
Investment	3	4	3	2	1	1	0
Training	1	1	1	2	3	2	3
Int. mgmt.	5	2	2	2	1	1	1
Int. admin.	4	2	2	1	1	1	1
Total	37	37	37	37	37	37	37

In practice, there is little likelihood that anyone will work strictly to the contracted 37 hours per week but any additional time they do work provides you with flexibility and allows for the variation in workloads that inevitably arise with the natural peak and trough nature of the business.

i. Killing the 'admin' burden

The last section on non-billable *norms* still leaves a few loose ends, which I intend to tie up here. Setting the *norms* for each level is a great exercise and one that will help to get your firm closer to its desired profitability. But the theory and the practice can be a long way apart.

When I first worked out the way to do all this time management/capacity planning stuff, it wasn't long until I set about the timesheet analysis that I described in section c above.

At that time I believed that simply having a timesheet system and ensuring everyone completed it on time was sufficient to ensure that we would have all the data we needed to address the capacity/utilisation issue.

How wrong can you be?

So now I have to make my second confession.

You see, up until then we had been operating in the same way we always had (and many still do), judging the need for extra resource on the basis of two observations – staff feedback about how busy they were and my own/the directors' views on how pressurised it felt (generally judged by what time people came in and went home and how busy it seemed to be in-between).

I can tell you now that observation and judgement may work within a small firm but in a bigger one it's no good at all. To bring a little logic to the issue we decided that an analysis of the timesheets would provide much more objective data.

Having analysed all the timesheets we discovered (to my horror) that, on average, every staff member was only spending about 21 hours per week on billable work and nine hours a week on internal administration; so we set about finding out what 'admin' it was that was occupying so much of their time. I was sure that if we could find out what was using so much unproductive time we could streamline the processes to free up no end of billable time and, in so doing, relieve the pressure to recruit more staff at a time when we were still nowhere near the profitability we should have been delivering.

So we set about it.

We asked everyone about the problem, looked at all the systems we had in place and reviewed all the policies. If it could be dumped, it was dumped. If it could be slimmed, it was slimmed. If it had to stay, it was turned inside out until the slickest way of doing it was found.

We dropped the ISO 9000 quality standard that had taken a year to achieve (and required a filing cabinet of extra record keeping) because we discovered that, for a month before the ISO audit, almost everyone was involved in a massive updating of all the ISO files, writing pre-dated letters and reports and goodness knows what, just to ensure we passed. We dropped the Investor in People standard recognising that what really mattered was what we *did,* not having the badge. It was a thorough clean-out of the system.

We had to wait a full three months for the timesheet analysis. Then, finally, there was the analysis…

…and *not one single thing* was different; *nothing* had changed at all.

How on earth could that be? What had we missed? This had to have had an effect. But no, the facts were there to see. Internal administration: nine hours per person per week.

And then it dawned.

'Internal administration' was just a dumping ground for 'time that couldn't be classified anywhere else' – the bin in the corner into which everything that didn't fit anywhere else was thrown.

Internal administration time was never going to change by slimming down the systems because it wasn't internal administration; it was something else altogether. It was simply the balancing figure to make the timesheet add up to the desired number at the end of the week; it was all those odd quarter hours when we were talking about football or last night's TV; it was the rewrite that couldn't legitimately be billed to the client; it was the longer lunch hour or the popping out to the bank; in fact, it was almost anything other than admin.

I have to confess I felt like a complete idiot in hindsight, but at least an idiot who had finally worked it out.

The solution from that point on was simple. Ignore the admin time altogether and focus only on the billable time.

And so it turned out.

For every hour of extra billable work that was given, an hour disappeared off the admin line. We gave everyone a simple set of definitions to clarify what should go where on the timesheet and put one new policy in place – it stated simply that, provided everyone told the whole truth on their timesheet, there would never be any inquisition and no-one would ever be taken to task over what they put down. Instead it would be quietly dealt with quietly through their manager and they would be helped to re-balance their work appropriately.

It was a big change, but it worked. It showed, for the first time, exactly where the time was going.

Before long we could see exactly where the spare capacity was and who was really over-worked. Recruitment could be planned ahead and put in place when and where it was needed – but *only* when and where it was needed; and profitability soared from 12% to 22% in a year.

j. Murdering over-servicing

If I had one wish it would be that we in the marketing/communications services sector never again use the term 'over-servicing'. I would wipe it from our vocabulary, expunge it from every report and fine anyone overheard using the term.

I hate it for one simple reason: it is the *term itself* that is preventing us, in part at least, from eliminating it from our business.

If we were manufacturers we would call it 'scrap' or 'waste' and it would be the central aim of the production director to minimise it and, ideally, get rid of it altogether. It is a voracious profit eater and the symbol of a business out of control.

But we call it 'over-*servicing*'.

There's almost a touch of pride hidden in the term, almost an inference of better quality; it seems as if, subconsciously, we have a need to '*over*-service' to make us feel that we are giving the client 'proper' value for money. In fact, I've even heard that stated by senior people in the industry who ought to know better.

In 2006, the annual PRCA survey uncovered an average level of over-servicing of around 25% and that's only what the participants were prepared to admit to. In my experience that's a significant understatement. But even at that level it's dire.

The arguments I hear time and time again always go the same way, something like this:

> "We know we over-service our clients but we can't seem to do anything about it. They're used to the level of service we provide and if we reduced it they'd notice and we'd probably lose the account."

Well I'm sorry but I just don't buy that – at all!

Let me try to explain why I feel so strongly about this. But to start off, we need to look at what 'over-servicing' really is.

First we need to recognise and understand that over-servicing is not just one thing. It is a combination of a number of different elements of time utilisation, where the only commonality is that we don't get paid for it by the client. Let's look at each one in turn:

–   Time we (deliberately or otherwise) misrecord on our timesheets; whether it is deliberate deception or error the effect is the same – the time is lost and never offset against the fees paid. We'll call this 'lost time'.

— Time we deliberately give away by discounting our standard rates. In other words, by discounting our rates for a specific client or failing to achieve our annual rate increases we are, in effect, giving them more time than they are really paying for. We'll call the first of these 'planned write-off' and the second 'legacy write-off'.

— The hours spent working for a client, where we take longer to do the job than we estimated and don't feel we can properly charge for all of it. Let's call this 'underestimation'.

— Sometimes, though we choose simply to give extra time to a client as a demonstration of our commitment or to help us to open up a new opportunity; and there's nothing wrong with this as long as it's controlled and not allowed to run rife through the business. We'll call this 'investment time'.

— Finally, there are those inevitable, human moments when we just get something wrong and have to do it again – and that takes extra time we haven't planned for, so we'll call this 'unplanned write-off'.

So you can see already that the concept of over-servicing is more complex and variable than the commonly held understanding.

However, this section is called 'Murdering over-servicing' so we need to look at what we can do to get rid of the single biggest issue that depresses our firms' profits.

I have long believed that the reason why most agencies have been so remarkably unsuccessful in eliminating over-servicing so far is that they simply don't understand what it really is; because if they did and were able to identify the individual components that make up the total, they would be well on the way to developing solutions. Sure, it takes a particular type of analytical approach, but this shouldn't be beyond the capabilities of most agency MDs – and yet it remains the biggest unresolved problem, year after year after year.

I've even heard highly respected and successful agency heads saying that over-servicing is a fact of life within this business and will always be so, we just have to learn how to live with it and stop getting hung up about it.

What's even worse is that some think it's a **good** thing because it keeps clients happy and makes them think they are getting good value. If that's true there's little hope for those agencies because they are on the downward spiral of commoditisation where price is everything, the lower the better, and the quality of what we do is of no consequence at all. Maybe we should all give up now and let the procurement officers take over. We can sell our services 'by the yard' and may the cheapest person win.

What an utter load of rubbish.

So let's deal with it now, once and for all. And here's how.

First let's recognise that not every element that makes up the total is the same; in fact, some **are** actually desirable. So we need to take each element of over-servicing one at a time and look at the strategy required to control and/or minimise it.

1.   Lost time

The key here is the culture and style of management of the people in the firm. Getting accurate timesheet information is **critical** as I have explained earlier. To do this there are two golden rules:

> **No-one** ever gets told off for what they, correctly, enter on to their timesheet.

> **Everyone** does timesheets from the very top to the very bottom.

But to make this work you need to ensure you have a number of things in place.

You need accurate definitions of each type of time and everyone needs to understand what they are and how to apply them.

You must establish clear policies that determine how certain grey areas of time utilisation should be handled – for example, is travel time billable time or not?

Timesheets <u>must</u> be submitted to the supervisor for approval and the supervisor <u>must</u> check them and discuss any areas of possible contention with the individual – providing friendly and helpful advice on any changes that might be required to comply with the policies.

Regular failure to comply with timesheet policies needs to be dealt with in the same, professional way as any other performance issue. Remember it is not *what* they have put on their timesheet that is at fault but their failure, repeatedly, to follow the policies.

Staff must understand that, even if they have taken too long to do something, the decision on whether or not this will be written off is not theirs to make. So they must record it as *billable time* even if, eventually, some of it may not be *billed*.

With all this in place and good supervisory practice, '*lost time*' can be reduced to zero; but even if you never quite get there, **any** reduction is worth having as it adds to your bottom line either directly or through better utilisation and capacity management, which we'll discuss in detail later.

2.   Planned write-off

There will be occasions when you decide that the standard hourly rates you charge are going to count against you in winning a particular account or project – and that winning it is particularly important. So important, in fact, that you are prepared to discount your rates to do so.

I am generally dead set against discounting in this way as it is almost impossible to recover from and remains as a legacy for as long as the account remains with you. The truth is that to have an effect, the level of discount you need to give is usually most, if not all, of your profit margin (10-15% maybe). I much prefer to offer extra 'free' time – investment time – instead. Clients usually see it in the same way but it keeps your billed hours at the standard rate which has two substantial advantages over 'discounting': first that all future increases are applied to the standard not discounted rate and therefore keep pace with inflation at least and second that the time you choose to give free can be altered (for which you should read 'reduced') in subsequent years.

If you do choose to offer discounted rates (and you position it that way to your client) you should look at it slightly differently internally; you should calculate the number of hours you are being paid at the discounted rate and compare that to the number of hours that the total fee would buy at your standard rates. The difference, *in hours*, is your *planned write-off*.

By so doing, you will be able to deduct the planned write-off hours from the recorded billable time to check that you are not over-servicing after the deduction has been made and that you are keeping the planned write-off to the agreed level.

Any hours of over-servicing that go beyond the agreed planned write-off level need to be investigated separately to see which category of over-servicing they fall into and then dealt with accordingly.

3.   Legacy write-off

There is a simple truth here, that within the marketing/communications agency world we are neither very skilled nor motivated enough to ensure that we increase our rates each year even though our costs inevitably seem to rise.

In fact the most common issue related to this seems to stem from the fact that whilst we might increase our standard rates or rate card, we often fail to secure (or even ask for) such an increase from our existing, contracted clients. The result of this failure is that the longer we hold off asking, the further behind 'standard' they fall. Yet, very often, we have a clause in our terms and conditions that allows for an annual, inflationary increase.

In parallel, we always respond to the pressure to review *salaries* every year (sometimes more frequently than that) and usually by more than the rate of inflation.

Put together, we are eroding our profitability on existing accounts year after year.

I have often discussed this issue with agency heads and frequently they tell me that their solution to this is to try to cut back on the amount of time allocated to the account to counterbalance the effect. Sadly, that rarely works and instead results in a gradual reduction of service levels and per-formance which, in turn, leads to client dissatisfaction and eventual loss of the account, which is then rationalised as 'being for the best because it was unprofitable anyway'.

How sad is that?

Yet it is completely avoidable.

We may think that asking clients for an increased hourly rate will be a big issue for them but, in my experience, clients expect a modest increase year on year. Provided that your increases are broadly in line with salary inflation, I've rarely found it an issue.

Where it has been a problem, it is usually because the client has 'forgotten' to allow for it in his/her budget request for the following year and so is embarrassed that the money won't be there. If this turns out to be the case (rather than a convenient excuse – and only you can judge that), you should counter by negotiating a 'sharper focus to the programme' requiring a small reduction in the client's time allocation that corresponds to the percentage increase in hourly rates. It doesn't increase the income stream but it does free up some time that can be sold elsewhere, once again improving utilisation.

The bigger issue for many, though, is the legacy write-off that dates back many years. This isn't easy to resolve – at least, not quickly. It requires a little-by-little approach, negotiating a slightly higher than standard increase each year (or the equivalent time reduction) over a number of years.

You may never get every client back to today's standard rates, but you can make a sizeable difference and every improvement leads to a pro-rata improvement in profitability. Every hour of time that is taken out of the legacy write-off pot is an hour that can be sold at a higher rate. What's more, it has the added bonus of delaying the need for the next recruitment by freeing up existing staff time.

Sadly, though, any discount you are left with after all these negotiations needs to be treated exactly as with *planned write-off* above.

There is one other issue that contributes to the legacy write-off problem and, like so many others in this section, it all comes down to your negotiation skills and general toughness. The issue is the failure of many agencies to negotiate an increase to the hourly rate for an account team member when they are promoted. In my view, if the individual is ready for promotion (and hence capable of a bigger, more responsible job), they have to be worth the higher rate that their new position commands.

But it isn't as simple as that: for some reason I haven't ever really been able to accept, we seem to believe that fast promotion of individuals is essential in our business if we are to retain them. Of course I understand their ambition and the opportunities that exist for good people right across the market sector, but I have also found that with proper management, rewards and training, staff are much more likely to stay with you if you can map out a *career* for them, in advance, and then work with them to an agreed set of goals and timescale. That way they reach a position when you both know that they are 'ready for promotion' and will be promoted when the next opportunity arises for someone at the higher level.

It is the absence of this last element in the chain which leads to the frequently encountered problem of an agency structure getting out of shape, with too many senior people and not enough junior; and that can only ever lead to staff dissatisfaction as they realise that their 'promotion' was nothing more than a change of title, hence the slightly ridiculous multitude of senior titles – account director, associate director, director, board director, head of, practice leader – and the over-large boards that are so prevalent in marketing/communications agencies.

4.   Underestimation

If it were possible to analyse what really goes on inside many agencies with big over-servicing problems, I'd bet that this would be the biggest culprit – by far.

Many years ago, my then boss Peter Hehir told me about one of the party pieces he used whenever he was in the company of a group of PR people. Sometimes it was a group of staff from one of the offices and other times it was a much broader cross section of the industry. Regardless of the audience, the outcome was always the same.

What he did was to ask the group he was addressing to work out for him the cost of a pretty standard client project, the organisation of a press conference at a hotel venue.

He would give them all the details needed – number of invitees, contents of the press pack, presentation materials, speakers, refreshments and so on. It left a little to be 'guestimated' but this was something every member of the audience would have done 'for real' many times before.

Unashamedly I have stolen this from him and used it myself many times since with exactly the results Peter told me about.

The estimates varied, of course, but not by 10% or 15%. Not even by 25% or 50% but by a factor of 10.

So if the lowest estimate was £2,000 the highest was probably £20,000.

And that is the fundamental problem here.

We simply aren't anywhere near good enough at estimating (error number 1) and most of us don't seem to know the difference between an estimate and a quotation (error number 2).

Every plumber, electrician, carpenter, painter and decorator in the land knows the difference but we in marketing and communications aren't so sure.

An estimate is a guide price, likely to be about right, but subject to variation according to the realities of doing the job. Within our business that's likely to mean accurate to +/- 15% or so.

A quotation is a fixed price, given in advance and which will be the final price regardless of the issues encountered along the way.

What I find time and time again is that agencies calculate an estimate and then provide it to the client as a quotation.

Unfortunately, underestimating (and then, worse, providing it as a quotation) has a serious downside – built-in over-servicing or, as I prefer to call it, unplanned write-off.

As luck would have it, the solution to this one isn't too hard and doesn't take long to implement.

First, make sure everyone knows the difference between an estimate and a quotation. Unless specifically asked for an absolute fixed price, always provide an estimate – and call it just that.

Work out who are best at estimating within your business and get them to check every estimate before it is sent to the client; and finally get everyone who pulls costs together to get someone else to check through it with them just in case they've forgotten something.

Then add 15% for the things you've still forgotten or underestimated.

That way you don't get a reputation for always coming in at the high end but more often come mid-way or even under. The 'trust and honesty points' to be gained for coming in 'under' are incalculable, so don't be tempted to invoice the estimated amount if the reality is less.

If you simply *have* to provide a quotation then use exactly the same system as above but add a further percentage for unknowns (I'd use 7.5%) so that most times you'll come out a little ahead and only occasionally will you be out of pocket. Do this properly and you could even end up with a small write-up instead of the more usual write-off.

5.   Investment time

I have to confess here that I love this concept. It works so well and in so many ways.

Earlier I defined investment time like this:

> *Planned non-billable time spent on growing/securing existing accounts – by account. There is little doubt that clients want to see pro-activity from their agencies and nothing is more proactive than having unprompted ideas. It's all part of the service. However, there are occasions when either a client or an account has obvious growth potential or, sadly, when it may be under threat. In either case it makes sense to provide a little 'extra' service. This isn't over-servicing in the traditional sense but investment – planned investment. Each account director needs to have some flexibility to allocate some time to this, but in a planned, controlled way.*

A few pages ago I mentioned the agency heads who think that over-servicing is unavoidable and maybe even a good thing. Well it would be easy just to write them off as misguided, perhaps even stupid to think that way… except I don't.

You see, I think what they are really saying is that with some clients it can be a good strategy to add a little extra time on to the servicing, to deliver a little extra and to occasionally surprise and delight them with a bit of unprompted pro-activity; and I agree.

Except I don't call it over-servicing; I call it investment time.

Earlier on I introduced the concept of splitting the working week into different types of time and having 'norms' for everyone. One of those categories was investment time and I suggested that a norm of 7.5% of the working week might be appropriate. This equated to three to four hours per week for each staff member at the more senior end of the scale.

This is time that you are not *expecting* to be paid for and which will not adversely affect your planned profitability as you have *budgeted for it to be given away* already.

There are three occasions when I would choose to use it:

As a negotiated alternative to discounted hourly rates offering, instead, to provide a fixed number of 'free hours' over and above the contracted time – for, say, the first six months or year.
To develop unprompted ideas for a client where you know that there is growth opportunity either within an existing account or through winning an additional account.
To prop up an ailing account where there is the risk of loss.

The real secret here is to only allow investment time to be allocated by the team leaders and to use it wisely.

By having a budget for investment time you can monitor it and measure the value it's providing in each of the three areas above. You must be vigilant, though, and keep it under control or else it will simply replace internal administration as the bin into which every bit of waste time gets thrown.

Used wisely it will help develop your high potential accounts and clients, avoid possible losses and enable you to maintain your standard rates and rate increases. It's a powerful concept.

6. Unplanned write-off

No matter how good you are at managing your accounts, there will always be mistakes and problems along the way – it's only human after all. However, that doesn't mean they will always turn into unplanned write-off.

Frequently I find that the largest sources of unplanned write-off are the moving goalposts or changes of plan by the client. This falls into one of two typical patterns:

1. The brief that was always rather loose and never properly defined in the first place, where the client's expectations and yours were never married up and where the work being done is open to quite wide interpretation.

2. The brief that was properly defined early on but has subsequently been changed.

In the former case you only have yourself to blame. It's a bit like the underestimation issue mentioned earlier. If you fail to properly define the work to be done, you will never be able to provide a reasonably accurate cost.

The solution here is simple to say but needs a fair bit of work internally if you are to get the behaviour change that is required. Train, train and train again in the ability to plan and estimate a programme. Then monitor, review and train again.

The only way to deal with the loose brief is to tighten it and to ensure that the client's expectations are realistic and agree with yours. Then price it accordingly.

In the second scenario above, the answer is really in the question. If the brief changes, in all likelihood so does the workload and the cost. Have the courage to go back to the client and explain the implications of the changes and what impact that will have on the costs. Give them the chance to either agree to the changed costs or amend the programme so that it can still be done for the original budget. It isn't difficult, it's just something that has to be done but which most times, most of us would rather not do – and so don't. It's laziness.

Think of it like this: imagine you have taken your car in for a service and been told that it will cost £150. Then during the day you telephone them to ask if, while they are doing the service, they would replace the two rear tyres, fit a cycle rack and clean the car inside and out. You wouldn't expect them to do all of that for the price of the service alone. In fact, if you went to collect the car and they only charged you the quoted £150, you'd be amazed.

Yet that's what we do all the time. Because we really don't like talking about money, or asking for higher fees for fear that we'll upset the client.

I know it's a competitive market out there but if we don't train ourselves out of this raging insecurity complex we will never break through the profitability barrier and earn the profits we deserve.

That said, there will still be occasions when we do have to take a hit, take it on the chin and accept that we have screwed up. We all get things wrong and when we do we have to face the consequences.

Sometimes those consequences will lead to unplanned write-off.

I know I called this section 'Murdering over-servicing' and maybe that was an exaggeration; perhaps we'll have to settle for attempted murder – but at least make the attempt. You may never eliminate it entirely but you can get very, very close.

I said earlier on that in my working life, we had introduced systems and behaviours like those above and doubled profitability and eliminated over-servicing. That was true, but it was only true *in aggregate*, across all clients.

There were always small pockets of unplanned write-off but they were offset by occasional *write-ups* through efficiency in delivering against fixed-price *quotations*.

Nothing is ever going to be perfect or absolutely consistent, but with will and determination you **can** minimise write-off and all those savings go straight to the bottom line.

If you succeed in cutting over-servicing from 25% to 15%, for example, you will either have an extra 10% profitability, 10% extra free capacity or a combination of the two. Any which way you look at it, that has to be a great improvement.

You can go further still by being strong and prepared to negotiate with clients when necessary, especially in the case of a substantial programme or project. To take this further step you will need to keep a record of the *cumulative actual time* taken per week/month versus the *estimated time*. Then by drawing a graph of the two lines and sharing this with the client on a regular basis, you begin to 'condition' the client into an understanding of the issue.

The graph below shows how this might look, in a bad case of *write-off*, after six months of a 12-month programme:

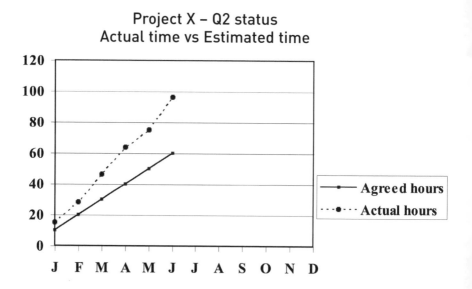

Clearly the time taken (the billable time) is running way ahead of the estimated (billed) time. Of course you will reassure the client that you are doing (and will continue to do) everything you can to pull the lines back together but in reality they are likely to end up with some gap, which you estimate to be xxx.

Then, using your best negotiating skills, you ask for the client's help to deal with the gap, either through finding some extra budget or, more likely, by agreeing with you those programme elements that are least important and could be dropped to help cut back on time.

You won't always succeed (and you'll need to be sensitive to when you are about to push too hard) but on the occasions when you do, you will either be paid for some/all of the write-off or have some/all of it removed from the equation. Either way, it is another significant contribution to the bottom line.

In my experience many clients will 'help' **once** but quickly point out that it is your responsibility to improve your estimating and not to expect their help again, which is fair enough isn't it?

Finally, remember this graph; you'll be seeing it again in the next section when we come to the question of 'annual budgets versus monthly fees'.

Chapter 3

DIFFERENT PAYMENT SYSTEMS
(What's profitable and what's not)

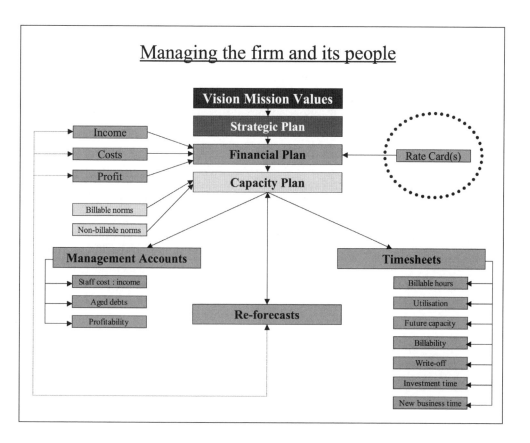

It seems to me that the more agencies I come into contact with, the greater the number of different payment systems I discover. By payment systems, I mean the way in which the agency or consultancy is remunerated for the work it does.

Certainly it is true that during recent years the balance between 'rolling contract' (or retained) business and 'projects' has shifted substantially with more and more clients opting for a project-based relationship and this is becoming quite an issue for many agencies as project business brings with it even more insecurity of tenure.

Add that uncertainty to the already insecure nature of the agency psyche and you have a recipe for declining margins and a price war, which is exactly what the bigger *clients* are aiming for through their adoption of procurement processes.

It is far from being the comfortable, long-term relationship business that it was.

Which brings me to another of my terminology gripes – retainers.

When I started out in this business back in the 1970s the use of the term retainer was quite widespread, although even then its meaning had been corrupted. Originally, the term retainer meant a fee paid to a provider of services simply to be available on demand for the client. Sometimes it would cover the provision of some basic advice, but it was always understood that a significant call on the services would attract additional fees. The retainer simply provided the security for the client that the service would be forthcoming upon request.

Interestingly, the term retainer goes way back to the noblemen of the Middle Ages who would often support a selected number of the lower classes financially and, in return, expect them to do their bidding when requested – often in areas outside the law.

Over the centuries the concept developed without very much change until it was applied to the family and household 'advisors' – the solicitors and accountants in particular. The 'old retainer' became almost a term of endearment for the (usually elderly) family advisor, who through years of faithful service became a friendly face in difficult times.

It was a short step from there to the application of the term to the fee paid rather than to the advisor personally. And there was little doubt that sometimes the fee would be paid for long periods without call on the service whilst at other times the service demands would far outstrip the payment. It was all a question of balance and the 'retained' would have little hesitation in rendering additional charges for the services when they stepped outside the general advice arena.

During my early career the term started to decline in use as agencies became more commercial and began to talk more about fees and contracts. It seemed to be replaced mostly by the term 'monthly fee'. And that was, without doubt, a beneficial change for those of us on the provision side of the equation.

For the first time, we were beginning to break away from the psychology that, by being paid a retainer we were at the client's beck and call to fulfil their requirements regardless of how often or how frequently the demands were made. Instead we were beginning to establish an elementary understanding that our monthly fee related to an estimated amount of time that our clients' demands were supposed to match.

Unfortunately, many agencies still hung on to the view that a monthly fee was a fixed 'contracted' amount whilst the workload was (at least in practice) variable – albeit usually upwards.

In the past few years the term retainer has re-entered the vocabulary and now seems as widespread as ever it was. It doesn't mean quite what it used to; it has taken on the mantle of the 'contracted fee' but the psychology remains largely unaltered with many agencies feeling they have to fulfil all their client's demands within the 'retainer' level agreed.

The procurement officers who are taking an ever-larger role in the sourcing of marketing and communications services are doing a great job in helping to bring it back into use. After all, it helps them to position themselves as the noblemen and the agencies as the servants. It's a manifestation of the superior/inferior positioning, the buyer/seller relationship and a clear statement of who calls the shots.

So here I make a plea.

Please, please, please stop using the term retainer. Ban it from your vocabulary and kill the psychology once and for all. Talk about monthly fees if you must or, preferably, contracted or project fees.

Now, let's get back to the different payment systems that are employed today and look at the pros and cons of each. But first we need to fill in one gap that links us back to the previous chapters – working out what we should be charging for our time.

a. Setting your rate card

One of the questions I am asked most frequently during training and mentoring sessions is 'How should I go about setting the charge-out rates for my team?'

It isn't an easy question to answer because there are many ways to come at it – 'cost plus', 'market averages', the 'three times' rule and many others.

Of course, there is no definitive answer. The logic for the process I'm about to propose though is pretty good and does give a rational and fair result. Before reading this section you would do well to remind yourself of 'The profitability game', 'Billed and billable hours' and 'Setting the billable norms' from Chapter 2 sections d, e and f.

You will recall that all the way through the sections referred to above we needed to make an assumption about the average charge-out rate and it was deliberately excluded from the calculation of the weekly norms for each level of staff.

That was because there is a clear relationship between the number of hours sold and the rate per hour achieved. The number of hours x rate = fee income.

The fee income determines how much you can afford to spend on staff, and the cost/number of staff determines how much you ought to charge. And that depends on the number of hours from each staff member that you expect to sell – the norm.

It's a circular argument with each element influencing the others.

Somehow you have to break in to the circle with one *fixed* element that can form the basis of all the others.

Most commonly, this is the number of hours that you expect to sell – the *norm*. That seems very reasonable because the one thing that *is* fixed is the number of hours per week (168) and the number of those you can reasonably expect (contract) someone to work (maybe 37 or so). Within that total you have to plan to do everything – new business, training, investment and so on. So you can see that setting the norms is at least a logical break-in point and one that can be set by consulting the *values* of your firm.

Interestingly, I did a little research into how other professional service firms, in accountancy, law and the like, set their norms and rates – accountants, law firms and the like.

It seems they take a pretty hard view. Certainly in the USA the approach is a very tough one indeed, with a typical year broken down into 2,000 hours and typical util-isation for a junior staff member set at 90%, or 1,800 billed hours. Which means that, over a 48-week year (only two weeks holiday and two weeks for public holidays and sickness), they expect an average 42-hour week with 37.5 of those billed to clients.

At the senior end of the scale, they are more generous with an expected 75% utilisa-tion, which equates to only 31.25 hours billed each week. Although with a bit more holiday allowance at the senior levels this is probably closer to 32–33 billed hours. This accounts for the exceptionally long hours these professions work in the USA.

The same sort of figures also seem to be true in the bigger international consulting firms and law firms in Europe, although the Working Time Directive must be having some effect. Assuming that it is, the firms in Europe must be under pressure to increase their rates or accept a lowering of profitability and, if a comparison of rates is to be believed, Europe is already more expensive per hour than the USA.

Fortunately, in the marketing and communications world we may expect to work long hours but we don't work as long as our colleagues in the law or accounting. Our salaries (particularly at the senior levels) are generally quite a bit lower too and that means that our rates and/or norms can be a bit less as well.

So let's get back to the rate setting processes that are most relevant to us. There are a number of approaches and it makes sense to look at all of them before settling on the approach that's best for you.

1. The 'cost plus' model

This is basically a number-crunching process for which I make no apol-ogy other than to say that it needs to be overlaid with a modicum of com-mon sense.

It is based on a simple concept that, by taking the salary of an individual and adding on an appropriate proportion of the overhead costs and an allowance for profit, we can reach a figure that represents the amount of income that the individual must generate for our desired profitability to be achieved. And that can then be divided by the number of weeks in the working year and the number of billable hours expected per week (the norm) to arrive at the rate per hour.

And the theory is fine. However, it would lead us to individual rates for every member of staff and the need for adjustment of the rates every time any overhead cost went up. That's why you need to overlay it with some common sense.

What I suggest is that you only work through the calculations once for *each level of staff* using the average salary for that level and an apportionment of overheads pro rata to the total salary bill for that level.

Let's go back and look, once again, at our theoretical agency with ten staff, who are all fee earners (the model we used in 'The profitability game' in Chapter 2d).

Here are the basic numbers:

XYZ Company Limited – Full year results

10 people – all client facing

Average hourly rate charged	£100
Total income	£1m
Staff costs	£520k
Other costs	£350k
Profit before tax	£130k
Profitability	13%

Here, for the purposes of these calculations, are the staff salaries that I am going to use:

XYZ Company Limited – Staff salaries	
Managing director	£100k
Director #1	£ 70k
Director #2	£ 60k
Associate director	£ 50k
Account manager #1	£ 37k
Account manager #2	£ 35k
Account manager #3	£ 33k
Account executive #1	£ 25k
Account executive #2	£ 20k
Account executive #3	£ 20k
Total Salaries	£450k
On-costs	£ 80k
Total Staff Costs	£530k

Assuming that the company was aiming for the 13% profitability margin they achieved, the calculation of hourly rates per level would be done like this.

First we need to calculate the apportionment of overheads/profit per £1 of salary, according to this formula (for a different profit % simply adjust the profit amount below to the figure you are targeting):

(Salary 'on-costs' + other costs + profit) ÷ total salaries

eg (£80k + £350k + £130k) ÷ £450k = £1.24 per £1 of salary.

Next we calculate the average salary per level:

XYZ Company Limited – Average salary per level

Managing director (1)   £100k

Directors (2) (£70k+£60k) ÷ 2   = £ 65k

Associate director (1)   £ 50k

Account mgrs. (3) (£37k+£35k+£33k) ÷ 3 = £ 35k

Account execs. (3) (£25k+£20k+£20k) ÷ 3 = £21.7k

Now we add the appropriate apportionment of overheads to each average salary to produce the total amount of income we need from each person at each level:

XYZ Company Limited – average total income per person per level

Managing director	£100k + £124k	=	£224k
Directors	£ 65k + £80.6k	=	£145.6k
Associate director	£ 50k + £62k	=	£112k
Account managers	£ 35k + £43.4k	=	£ 78.4k
Account executives	£21.7k + £26.9k	=	£ 48.6k

Now we have worked out the amount of fee income each individual needs to earn in a year to deliver the target of 13% profitability.

So to calculate the hourly rate per level we need to divide the total fee earned in a year by the number of working weeks in the year and then divide that by the *norm* number of *billable hours* that we expect from each level per week.

Level	Billable Hours
Managing director/chairman	20
Directors	24
Associate/account directors	26
Account managers	28
Account executives	30
Team support	30
Intern/trainees	30

If we apply these norms and use a 45-week year, we arrive at the following:

XYZ Company Limited – average total income per person per level

Managing director	£224k ÷ 45 ÷ 20 =	£249
Directors	£145.6k ÷ 45 ÷ 24 =	£135
Associate director	£112k ÷ 45 ÷ 26 =	£ 96
Account managers	£78.4k ÷ 45 ÷ 28 =	£ 62
Account executives	£48.8k ÷ 45 ÷ 30 =	£ 36

At this point you will notice that the spread of rates seems a little extreme. This is because not only does the calculated 'cost plus' rate allow for the difference in salaries, it also takes into account the different norms for billable time.

2.   The 'cost plus' *plus* model

Here, I thought it might be interesting to compare what we have calculated with the rates I used earlier when looking at setting the norms; these were rates based on the reality of the marketplace for a typical small/medium-sized agency:

Calculated rates vs Market rates		
	Calculated rate	Market rate
Managing director	£249	£230
Directors	£135	£160
Associate director	£ 96	£125
Account managers	£ 62	£ 90
Account executives	£ 36	£ 60

What is clear is that at the very top of the scale the calculated rates exceed the market whereas lower down, they fall short and get progressively more out of step. This is because in our calculation of rates we have assumed that everyone achieves their billable norm every week and that there is no write-off; in other words, a perfect scenario where every billable hour is billed and paid for.

And that is, of course, fantasy.

In reality, there will always be some write-off especially at the lower staff levels and we need to allow for that in our calculation of rates if we are to achieve the desired profitability.

Another reality is that the 13% margin that we targeted for our hypothetical firm, XYZ Company, is low. It may be what many firms actually achieve, but they were probably aiming (hoping) for more.

So it makes sense to add to the calculated rates an amount that allows for both the write-off we will have to carry and the increase in margin to, say, a better 20%.

We'll deal with the allowance for write-off in a moment but first let's look at the increased profitability target alone.

If XYZ Company had aimed for 20%, it would have had to increase its apportionment of overhead/profit per £ of salary from £1.24 to £1.40 and the calculations would have had a different result:

XYZ Company Limited – Average total income per person per level

Managing director	£100k + £140k	=	£240k
Directors	£65k + £91k	=	£156k
Associate director	£50k + £70k	=	£120k
Account managers	£35k + £49k	=	£ 84k
Account executives	£21.7k + £30.4k	=	£ 52k

XYZ Company Limited – hourly rate per level

Managing director	£240k ÷ 45 ÷ 20	=	£267
Directors	£156k ÷ 45 ÷ 24	=	£144
Associate director	£120k ÷ 45 ÷ 26	=	£103
Account managers	£84k ÷ 45 ÷ 28	=	£ 67
Account executives	£2k ÷ 45 ÷ 30	=	£ 39

Calculated rates vs Market rates

	Calculated rate	Market rate
Managing director	£267	£230
Directors	£144	£160
Associate director	£103	£125
Account managers	£ 67	£ 90
Account executives	£ 39	£ 60

Better, but still no cigar!

So now, let's allow for an element of write-off at each level.

The table below makes assumptions based on common sense rather than further calculation because write-off is not a precise factor but one that varies with the vagaries of people. It is always likely to be higher at the lower staff levels where lack of experience can wreak havoc with the time allowed for a job. In the calculation below, write-off averages to a little over 10%, which in my experience is rather better than most firms achieve.

Calculated rates allowing for write-off			
	Write-off %	Calculated rate	Market rate
Managing director	0	£267	£230
Directors	5%	£152	£160
Associate director	7.5%	£111	£125
Account managers	15%	£ 79	£ 90
Account executives	20%	£ 49	£ 60

Finally, in order to compensate for the fact that the MD's rate is too high and needs to be adjusted downwards to £230 to be in line with the market, the other rates will need to be revised upwards a little.

I am not going to go through the mathematics of that adjustment here; suffice to say that it takes all the calculated rates yet closer to the market rates and provides us with the best calculation we can get.

All of which suggests that the market seems to get it about right and, once again, suggests that the profitability issues faced by the marketing and communications service sector are not caused by low hourly rates, but are caused by failure to work sufficient billable hours, compounded by over-high levels of write-off.

And just to round things off neatly, that describes perfectly what was happening to XYZ Company in the profitability game earlier on.

At their earned 13% profitability, they averaged only 22.2 billed hours per person per week against the norm average of 27.4. Their high level of write-off (19% overall) reduced their margin dramatically.

3.   The 'three times' rule

For many years, across the whole marketing and communications services sector (and beyond into other professional services too) there has been a rule of thumb, which seemed to be the accumulated wisdom of the years. It's called the three times rule.

It works this way: that any client-facing staff member needs to earn fees equivalent to three times their salary in order for the firm to make a 15% margin.

Let's see if it works on the above example:

XYZ Company Limited – Three Times Rule			
	Avg. salary	3 x rule	Calc. rate ph
Managing director (1)	£100k	£333	£267
Directors (2)	£ 65k	£181	£152
Associate director (1)	£ 50k	£128	£111
Account managers (3)	£ 35k	£ 83	£ 79
Account executives (3)	£21.7k	£ 48	£ 49

On the face of it, it seems to work quite well at the lower levels but produces slightly higher rates at the top end.

That is because, having been around since time immemorial, it allows for much higher volumes of write-off within its figures.

It isn't the way I would come at it, because simply allowing for high levels of write-off by pushing hourly rates higher, creates the risk of becoming uncompetitive through being uncontrolled and inefficient – which is exactly what does happen and why controlling write-off is so important.

There is a limit to how much wastage you can build into your prices whilst still remaining competitive. It ought to be obvious that the more effective you are at minimising write-off, the more flexibility you have to choose between higher profitability and lower prices.

That said, the three times rule is a reasonable check to make sure that your rates are about right.

b. Standard and contractual rates

Hindsight is most certainly a wonderful thing and never more so than when trying to understand the evolutionary path that a business sector has followed.

Much earlier on, in my introduction to this Chapter, I explained how the term retainer had evolved and come to represent something rather different from that which was originally intended. And I pleaded with you to ban it from your vocabulary. This section is all about how I suggest you replace it.

From my most recent discussions with people from many different types of agencies and consultancies, it seems that clients generally fall into one of three different categories:

1.   Project clients

Those clients who buy your services on a one-off basis, paying fees that relate to the workload of the project(s) they have contracted from you. There may or may not be a contract of overall appointment and you may or may not be their sole agency/consultancy.

2.   Contracted clients

Those clients who pay a 'contracted' fee that continues for the duration of the contract, typically a monthly flat-rate fee spread across 12 months. This might be on a rolling contract (one which continues until either you or they give notice to terminate) or on a fixed-term contract (an agreement for a fixed period of time, which terminates on an agreed, preset date).

3.   Combination clients

Those clients who pay a (usually small) contracted fee for basic services on either a rolling or fixed-term contract but who buy further projects from you for which they pay additional project fees related to the additional workload.

Over the past few years there has been a marked change in the balance between these categories.

Not many years ago it was most common to find rolling contracts between clients and their agencies. The contract would continue in place until one or other of the parties decided to terminate by issuing the specified period of notice – most commonly three months – and there were usually provisions in the contract for an annual review of the fee levels/hourly rates and the workload.

Not surprisingly, there has always been pressure from the client side to minimise the period of notice in the contract and in many cases during recent years many rolling contracts have been agreed with just one month's notice required.

It was only a matter of time before the 'one month notice contract' evolved into its next guise, the fixed-term contract, usually for 12 months. And the latest evolution into project only clients followed fast on the heels of the fixed-term contract.

That is not to say that these different client/agency relationships didn't exist before, it's just that the balance of use has switched, considerably, away from the long-term rolling contract as sole agency handling all the client/account's needs, to a non-contractual, competitive, project-only relationship where the only security stems from the 'delivery' on the last project and where, as we all know, subjective assessment is the most common form of 'evaluation'.

So we can see that security, predictability and recognition of the benefits that arise from long-term relationships are all declining in favour of commoditisation, lower prices and the stick that is competition.

There is a clear pattern emerging: the professional services we provide to our clients are becoming less valued with every passing year as commoditisation is forced upon us by the pressures of procurement and cost-controls.

It is probably natural evolution and unlikely to be reversed quickly (although in my opinion everything is cyclical and a new generation of clients will soon rediscover the benefits of long-term relationships and begin to reverse the trend) and so we need to respond to the changing market environment with appropriate changes to our traditional fees.

Yet I see little sign of that happening. Instead we seem to be absorbing the changes, accepting the reductions in security and predictability and taking the hit to our bottom lines.

There is a better way and the solution lies in the way we position our fees and contract types to our clients.

There is, without doubt, a hierarchy of contract types:

1. Rolling, all-inclusive contracts with reasonable notice periods. Here I would suggest that, to qualify in this category, a contract should be for a minimum period of 12 months with a three-month notice period on top (ie 12 + 3 months rather than 9 + 3 months).

2. Rolling contracts as above but not all-inclusive and on to which projects may (or may not) be added.

3. Fixed-term contracts either with or without added projects. Here I would suggest a minimum of 12 months after which the contract is either renewed for a further 12 months or lost.

4. Project-only contracts for which there is no contracted fee, only work-load-based fees related to individual projects.

As we move down the hierarchy of contract types, it is clear that the level of security and predictability of the income stream declines markedly. It is this decline that provides the key for how we should respond to the pressure to move away from our comfort zone of rolling contracts.

Starting from the bottom, I suggest we introduce a new rate card that reflects the higher risk levels. It should list the hourly rates for all our staffing levels for *project-based* clients/accounts. It should carry a premium over our 'calculated' rates to allow for the fact that we will either have to accept periods of staff under-utilisation whilst we wait for projects to be signed off or carry lower staffing levels and top up with more expensive freelance support when needed. Either way, without higher rates, our profitability will suffer.

In my experience, a premium of around 15% seems about right. But don't think of it (or position it) as a **premium** rate; think of it as your **standard** rate.
Apply these rates to new clients who insist on working either with fixed-term contracts or on a project-only basis – after all, a fixed term contract is only a longer project; it still has no security beyond the end date.

For rolling contracts you can then offer discounted **contract** rates – special rates that provide an incentive to give you greater security. There aren't many clients (particularly procurement-based clients) who can resist a discount. For the full, all-encompassing rolling contract with a proper minimum period and a decent notice period, you will probably need to give the full 15% off, but for those in-between you can choose to offer/negotiate less.

The real beauty of this approach is that you can decide how far to go, but regardless of where you end up, you will be better off than before.

In practice you will probably only use the two rate cards – standard and contract – and rarely negotiate anything in-between. I found that the lure of a 15% saving frequently overcame the pressure for minimum commitment – and that was very welcome.

c. Day rates versus hourly rates

Often when asking firms about their charges the answer I get is 'so much per day'. In fact, when I started out in the communications sector that's exactly what I did.

But hidden behind that seemingly innocuous statement is an undeniable truth: that almost all day rates are in fact hourly rates in disguise.

You only have to probe a little beneath the surface of the 'day rate' to find that it refers to some sort of 'standard' day, maybe seven or eight hours. Never does it mean 'a calendar day', of 24 hours, because we rarely work that long in one go. Generally it means a 'working' day.

Now don't get me wrong, I have nothing against the day rate per se. It's just that, to work for you, you need to be precise about what it means (to how many hours it relates); and that sort of makes it redundant because you might as well quote an hourly rate in the first place.

All too often firms that quote a day rate *aren't* precise about what it means and different people from the same firm use a different conversion factor when converting their recorded hours into fees. It isn't uncommon to find people from the same firm using seven, seven-and-a-half and eight hours to represent a day – sometimes even choosing to call a long nine or ten hour session (on a single project), 'one day'.

The difference in income (or *write-off* if you're on a fixed fee) can be substantial. Simply using eight hours rather than seven represents almost 15% difference. With average profitability running at less than that, the impact on the bottom line can be dramatic – either way.

Scary isn't it?

The problem that this highlights is the common misconception that, unless you are 'working on the clock', the number of hours or days taken to do the job doesn't really affect profitability because the fee will be the same regardless. This is only partly true: the *fee* will be the same, but it isn't the whole story.

It's the same argument used to justify over-servicing and it misses the point entirely that the time you spend 'unpaid' is time that could be used for other, fee-paying work *if you have it; and if you haven't got extra work* then you have too much spare capacity because you can do *all* your 'paid-for' work and *still* be able to over-service your projects. Too much spare capacity means too much staff cost coming off your income and eating your profits.

Either way, you are losing profit by giving away the only commodity you have to sell – your time.

Think of it like this: every hour from every member of staff is a potential fee. If you don't earn income during any specific hour, that hour has been wasted and you can **never** get it back. It's gone forever.

Later on in this Chapter, in section e, I will explain one way that this fixed-fee problem can be overcome. For now, though, let's conclude that monitoring and estimating time *by the hour* is probably the best compromise and that hourly rates provide the most flexible way to offset your time against the fee paid with minimum loss. You just need to ensure that, if you still prefer to quote day rates, you agree, internally, how many hours make up a day and ensure that all your staff apply the same rule.

d. The problem with 'blended' rates

It is quite possible that you don't understand what I mean by 'blended' rates because across different businesses there are many different terms used to describe the same concept – team rates; averaged rates; single rates; flat rates; agency rates. I've heard all of them at one time or another.

They all mean a rate that is applied to a group of different people and charged irrespective of who is doing the work. So, for example, a team may comprise the MD, an associate director, an account manager and a couple of account executives and yet every recorded hour, irrespective of whose name is recorded against it, is charged at the agreed blended rate.

In theory, the rate is calculated as a weighted average of the team members' individual rates, the weighting being the proportion of their time included in the total amount of time allocated to that account.

For example:

Blended rate calculation				
	Indiv. Rate	Est. Wt %	Act. Wt %	Act. Rate
Managing director	£230	5 }	8 }	
Associate director	£125	15 }	22 }	
Account manager	£90	25 }	18 }	£93.30
Account executive #1	£60	30 }	30 }	
Account executive #2	£60	25 }	22 }	

On the face of it, the blended rate approach makes a lot of sense because it keeps everything very simple from an administration perspective but it does have one big flaw: the estimated weightings are never exactly right and so the balance of time spent by individual team members is always different from that which you expected.

Whilst that can work in your favour as well as against, most times, it seems to work against you. What's more, relatively small changes can have a big impact and generate large amounts of *write-off*.

Imagine that you've agreed a blended rate of £85 per hour – rounded down from the above calculation – but in reality the time split is slightly different as in the calculation below:

Blended rate calculation			
	Indiv. Rate	Weighting % of total	Blended rate
Managing director	£230	5 }	
Associate director	£125	15 }	
Account manager	£90	25 }	£85.75
Account executive #1	£60	30 }	
Account executive #2	£60	25 }	

As you can see, the actual time split is not very different from the original estimate – a bit higher in some areas and a bit lower in others.

But, ignoring the pence, the difference between what you should have been charging (£93 ph) and the estimated rate (£85 ph) is £8 ph. It may not seem like a big deal, but when you consider that it is the equivalent of a discount of almost 9% off your rates it puts it into perspective. For many agencies that could represent **all** their profit margin.

So you see that blended rates can have a big disadvantage.

A simple solution is to agree upfront with the client that the 'agreed blended rate' will need to be reconciled on a regular basis against the *actual* team mix that is needed in practice to manage the account. Ideally, that will need to apply retrospectively.

e. The 'annual budget' approach

Many of the problems that we have already looked at could be solved through one change in overall remuneration structure – the annual budget approach.

This is probably the one change that many firms could make, relatively easily and with a dramatically beneficial effect.

It works on the basis that most clients are concerned more by keeping within their **total budget** than keeping each individual element to its own limit. In PR, for example, most clients have a single PR budget and don't separate out (or in many cases even understand the difference between) fees and costs. They are concerned only to deliver the agreed programme or project for the agreed budget. Of course this does vary considerably depending on the communications discipline(s) in which you operate. Clearly in some fields – direct marketing, for instance – the cost budget may be substantially higher than the fee budget, whereas in PR the opposite is usually true; but the principles remain largely the same.

What I find surprising is that many agencies don't concern themselves with the overall budget at all; they remain focused on the fee element alone. This reduces their flexibility to operate.

There are almost as many ways to look at budgets, costs and fees as there are firms out there but, when all is said and done, it comes back to one simple statement: that the client has a limit to what they are prepared to spend.

Let's look at a hypothetical example where an account has a budget for activity of £100k. You may or may not know this to be the case because you may not have asked what the total budget is; you may simply have estimated fees to be £5,000 per month plus costs. Or you may have gone one stage further and estimated fees at £5,000 per month plus a cost budget of £40,000. Either way it doesn't really matter.

What you have done is to limit yourself to a fee total of £60,000, plus maybe some mark-up on some of the costs.

We all know that you will probably over-service and end up putting in rather more than £60k's worth of time.

In the worst case scenario, your client expects the £5,000 per month to be delivered (in time equivalent) *every* month regardless of any previous over-servicing and this is quite common amongst those firms where the monthly fee is referred to as a retainer.

The client expects you to do the work within the monthly fee agreed and each month starts afresh. (There have been occasions when even though the client wasn't so rigid, the team leader from the agency operated this way because they thought it ethical!)

To be crude, if you have agreed (or even chosen) to operate this way, you're pretty much stuck with it. There is no flexibility other than to control the time spent each month and be tough on refusing the extras that the client requests from time to time. It's very hard to do and even harder to do consistently.

Instead you should, as a minimum, endeavour to negotiate that your *annual* fee will be £60,000 and that there may be variations in time input month to month but you will do your utmost to bring the account in for the agreed overall amount.

Ideally you should negotiate that the *total budget* is £100k and that you will manage *the fees and costs* to ensure that you don't over-spend. That way, in theory at least, you have a certain amount of flexibility between fees and costs and can use any under-spend on costs to cover any over-spend on fees.

This is how it works in practice. First, you agree that keeping under the budget limit is the primary, financial imperative and that you will do everything you can to deliver the programme for the budgeted amount. Then you agree to invoice fees to the client at the flat rate of £5,000 per month plus costs as incurred.

So far so good.

You estimate the costs as you go with a clear view to try to spend less than the budgeted £40,000 – say £30,000. Then, every month you share with the client where you stand on the 'Actual vs estimated time' chart. The best way to do this is graphically as per the example below:

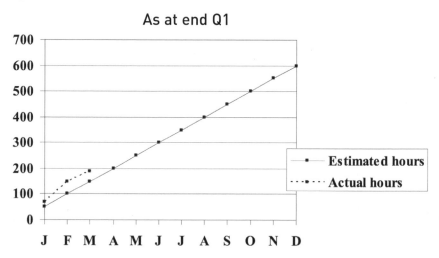

You explain to the client, in an easy going way, that the time the project is taking is running a little ahead of estimate but that you will keep working on getting it back into line. Then each month (or quarter) you update the client with the latest information and begin to introduce the concept of savings that might be made in the cost budget to offset the extra time required to do the job properly.

Then, when you get closer to the end of the programme and you're sharing the latest 'Actual vs estimated time' chart with the client (see below), you confirm that you will bring the programme in on budget overall but that the mix between fee and costs will be a little different from that originally estimated. However, the extra *time* needed has been funded by cost savings that you've achieved elsewhere, so it all balances nicely – provided that the client is happy to let you switch some invoicing from costs to fees.

As at mid Q4

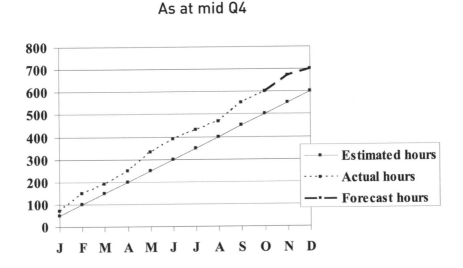

Handled professionally and sensitively, most clients will agree to the switch with a mild admonishment to improve your estimation of time for next year.

Now you may feel that this approach is unethical but I would disagree. It simply reflects that estimating the time and costs for any programme in advance is not and never can be absolutely precise; it needs a certain amount of flexibility. In an ideal world you would simply work to the overall budget anyway and not have to bother with this 'strategy'.

And that's what you should work towards – the annual budget not the monthly fee.

f. Account costs – flat rate or a la carte?

Yet again I find myself about to launch into an argument for a particular way of dealing with an issue in the marketing and communications services sector where there is no clear or universal understanding of a term. So what do I mean by 'account costs'?

There are many different terms used for the same thing and even more ways of dealing with them – account costs, house costs, disbursements, expenses, account overheads and more.

Every account, no matter how small or in which discipline, incurs administration costs. Typically these include telephone calls, photocopying, faxes, postage, local couriers and so on. Many of these costs are easy to identify whilst some are less obvious, yet equally important.

Some agencies choose to absorb these costs into their hourly rates; others charge them on to their clients 'as incurred'; and others charge a flat rate. But even here there is no standard system as some charge a fixed amount per invoiced day or hour whilst others charge a percentage of fee and, guess what – this percentage varies considerably too. What's more, the list of items included isn't consistent either. Frankly it's a mess.

Don't take this the wrong way; I am not trying to make all firms indistinguishable from each other, but I am trying to bring some sort of standardisation to the sector so that there is a sustainable and arguable logic to the way we charge for our services. Without such logic we are open to pressure for the lowest common denominator to become the norm and every negotiation will become more difficult and, ultimately, less profitable.

So what approach should you take?

As with most things in business there is no absolutely right answer. Much depends on the values of your firm and the pricing strategy you choose to adopt. However, one common myth is easy to dispel: the belief that clients want to see a long list of every telephone call, photocopy, fax and postage stamp that you have used on their account every month.

Generally, they don't.

Having said that, if you decide to send them a two-page invoice listing dozens of small cost items adding up to (probably) less than 10% of their 'one-line' fee invoice, then you shouldn't be surprised when they challenge one or two of the lines.

We seem to take this to mean that they're interested to see this information – and that's the first mistake. It's just that it is inevitable that faced with such a detailed list of items they will wonder what it was all for; and so they'll ask; and having asked then they may or may not like your answer and suddenly you're into a minor dispute over money and adding to the perception that agencies are expensive and/or over-charge.

Okay, maybe this is something of an over-generalisation and an exaggeration too, but it does suggest a certain, unnecessary inevitability: that if you provide an excess of information you'll get an equal excess of queries and issues in return.

Quite frankly, most clients would be much happier not to receive the listing in the first place and so not feel they have to study and approve it.

There is an even more compelling logic, though, which requires that we understand more about the elements that make up account costs.

Here's a list that I have pulled together, which is probably not representative of your specific firm or totally comprehensive, but it covers most areas of so-called administrative cost:

– Telephone calls
– Mobile telephone calls
– Text messages
– Faxes
– Photocopying/in-house printing
– Postage
– E-mail
– Stationery
– In-house client refreshments (food and drink)
– Copyright licence fees
– Other specific licence fees
– Specialist memberships
– Newspaper and magazine subscriptions
– Local couriers
– Local travel
– CDs, DVDs and memory sticks
– Other digital media
– Client intranets
– …

The logic I referred to above is this: that the time taken to keep track of each of these elements and to record the usage rates by account is vast. In my experience many agencies don't even record the time taken to do it as *billable* because it's probably done by someone who isn't considered as client-facing, an administrator or finance clerk.

So you have a real case of *lost time*.

At this point I want to tell you another true story. About ten years ago the firm I was working for billed clients for 'house costs' (that's what we called them) on an 'as incurred' basis. So we kept a record of everything that was used on every account – every photocopy, every telephone call (including how long it took), every envelope and postage stamp and so on and on and on... We then divided all the 'shared' costs pro rata to the account size. Then we constructed a detailed invoice every month for every account.

There was always at least one client (and often many more) who wanted more explanation of what was on the list and why. Often they didn't ask straight away, not until the invoice was overdue and they were prompted for payment. Then it took more time, usually the account director's time, to go back and sort out exactly what each queried item referred to and to explain it – yet more time that was recorded as internal administration.

So there we were, spending a vast amount of time recording information, calculating pro-rata amounts and preparing detailed invoices only to find that the effect was to slow down payment, waste more senior time answering queries, probably writing off cost elements that we couldn't adequately explain and damaging the client relationship into the bargain. What's more we were calling them *'house* costs', just to add to the client's perception that maybe he/she shouldn't be paying *our 'house* costs' anyway since they sounded like the costs of running *our* business. Clever!

So we did some analysis to work out what the typical (average) house costs were as a percentage of the fees. It took a little while to do but wasn't difficult and the result was fascinating. Allowing for the time taken to keep all the records and produce the invoice every month, it worked out at about 11% with a variation, account-to-account of only about +/- 1.5% – so somewhere between 9.5% and 12.5%.

Then we decided to introduce a flat-rate system across all accounts using a rate of 9.2% (the choice of 9.2% wasn't entirely scientific I admit but it represented a rate lower than the lowest calculated amount and so could be justified as a saving to every client through the elimination of the time taken to keep all the records).

Then we drafted a letter to all clients explaining that from now on they would see a single line on the bottom of their fee invoices called *'Account Costs'* and the amount would be calculated at 9.2% of their fee. This was to replace the long list of costs they had previously received and by doing it this way we would be delivering them better value by ensuring that *all* the time they were paying for was being used to deliver *their programme*, not to count photocopies and time telephone calls.

The letter was attached to their next fee invoice and from more than 100 clients only one complained and wanted to see a justification for the 9.2%. Even he eventually conceded. The rest accepted the logic (and I suspect breathed a sigh of relief that they wouldn't need to look through boring 'house cost' invoices ever again).

The moral of the tale is clear: don't assume that more detail equals greater transparency equals better practice – it often doesn't. Simple can frequently be more effective, more efficient and more profitable.

g. Payment by results

Another of the changes being brought about, at least in part, by the involvement of procurement is the ever-increasing pressure for payment to be based on results achieved.

It isn't a new idea but within the marketing and communications sector there aren't too many examples of it working well. Certainly there are some well-publicised success stories that have been written about in the trade press and there is quite a large body of evidence, particularly from the USA, that suggests that payment by results leads to improved results through better creativity and quality.

I have to confess that I remain pretty sceptical even having heard presentations with detailed statistics showing this to be the case. You see, statistics, or more precisely the interpretation of statistical data, is another one of those areas that gets me a little riled.

All too often presentations of research show the data and then leap to conclusions that are rubbish. You hear interpreted data being espoused in the news every day where anyone with any statistical knowledge would cringe. Collecting data is one thing; using it to *prove cause and effect* is quite another.

I guess it's my psychology background (where degree level statistics is essential), but I was taught never to leap to conclusions or assume anything unless you can repeatedly produce consistent data that can be used to theorise a link between two events which then can be shown to have statistical significance within certain, specified limits of confidence.

I don't want to get all technical here, so I won't. Suffice it to say that I read more and more 'surveys' purporting to show one thing or another when, singularly, they don't.

Let me give you an example.

Only a few years ago I was unfortunate enough to sit through a lecture by a management guru who was presenting the results of a major piece of research he had done. It purported to show that there was a link between satisfied staff and satisfied clients. He theorised that high motivation and morale amongst agency staff leads to high performance for clients and that in turn leads to high profitability; a variation on the theme that if you do good work the profits will follow.

Well as you will have gathered, I wasn't enamoured even at that stage. He went on to explain the major study, involving many leading agencies, which concluded that there was a statistically significant link between high profit agencies and high levels of staff motivation and morale.

Gosh.

But that wasn't the end of it. He then concluded that it was the high motivation and morale that led to the high profits – for which I could see not one scrap of evidence. Why could it not have been the other way round? Why could it not have been that highly profitable agencies (who will probably be highly confident and successful) generated a high morale and motivation through that success?

I don't claim to know the answer, nor I suspect did he because when I challenged him on that point he would only respond that it was he who had done the study and I would just have to take his word for it.

What all this has to do with payment by results is this: unless you can be confident that the 'results' to be measured will stem *solely and totally* from the work you are doing, then you might as well simply agree to a contract that says 'we'll pay you what we decide your work is worth – and our word will be final'.

So am I a fan of payment by results? Surprisingly, yes I am!

But only in those few circumstances where the generation of the effort and the measurement of the outcome can be seen, nay, *proven* to be causally linked. And that doesn't occur very often.

Even then, I would always restrict the incentive/penalty element of the payment by results system to that which I could afford to lose – the profit element and not a penny, cent or shekel more.

I would seek to establish a base level payment for the work that recovers all my costs – say 85% of the standard fees. Then I would only accept a results-based formula for the balance if there was at least an equal bonus element on top for over-performance.

For me the equation would be this:

Payment for the work, irrespective of outcome	*85%*
Sliding scale up to realistic expected outcome	*add up to 15%*
Sliding scale payment for exceeding expectations	*a further 15%*

Simply put, payment by results depends on being able to isolate results that stem from your work alone and then being able to measure those results sufficiently well (and fairly) to leave little room for doubt about the performance of your firm.

If you are confident you can do that, payment by results may work well for you. If not, my advice is to steer clear.

Hidden in that statement is one huge 'if'.

It is the question of measurement (and evaluation). It has taxed some of the best brains in the sector for decades and, whilst there are lots of proprietary schemes and 'specialists' around, I have yet to see a simple, universal methodology that really works. The truth is that it probably doesn't exist.

Measurement and evaluation of results depends on setting measurable objectives in the first place – objectives that can be solely and totally achieved by your work. All too often that means setting objectives that are not business *outcomes* (eg sales improvements, market share growth, share price enhancement and so on) but are interim business *outputs* (eg leads generated, enquiries received, listings achieved, analyst meetings…).

In itself this isn't a problem provided there is sufficient evidence to show these *outputs* do lead to the business *outcomes* that really matter; and that is pretty rare.

All too often there is an element of self-delusion here – if enough people tell you something is true, then it must be even if all your intelligence tells you otherwise; the leads are generated but do the sales really follow or are there other factors that get in the way – pricing, for instance? Or the media coverage target is exceeded and the messages are positive, but has it had an effect on the share price? Would the price have been lower without the work? Who knows?

I don't want to appear too negative here but we are talking about payment by *results* and, frankly, such systems are often little more than guesswork or a pretence at being scientific when, more practically, 'working together in partnership' could produce much better motivation and leave a far greater space for the input of common sense and intelligence.

All of which leads very nicely into value-based pricing, which we will look at next.

h. Value-based pricing

Running through all the previous sections in this chapter is one underlying assumption: that the fundamental constant across all we do is the selling of time – by the hour, day, month or whatever.

Now I have to confess that what I'm about to discuss is not very widespread in our sector of professional services but it isn't unheard of either. In some sectors, particularly when related to mergers and acquisitions, it is quite common. I'm talking about the concept of charging for work on the basis of what it's *worth* rather than how long it takes to do – market pricing if you like.

The difficulty it presents is fairly obvious: how can you decide what a programme, campaign or project is worth?

Fortunately, most of the time most of us don't need to answer the question because it doesn't arise; but what if it did? How often might we be able to put a financial value on our work or rather the outcome of our work?

The answer for some agencies is fairly often – or so they tell me. I'm referring here to agencies that price by the job type. Some PR agencies (more often Media Relations agencies) charge by output, in other words, a fixed price for drafting, issuing and 'selling-in' a press release to a fixed number of media. Other agencies have developed a standard pricing structure for all of their services.

But this isn't really what I mean by value-based pricing. What I have described above is just price 'standardisation' and the original calculations of 'how much to charge' were still based on time content.

What's more, this type of pricing just adds to the perception that what many of us do can be commoditised, packaged and sold for a standard price. It misses the point about professional counsel, advice and experience and dumbs down our profession to the lowest common denominator.

Real value-based pricing is much rarer and asks the question "if we were to succeed in this task, what would it be worth to you, the client?" Then it requires that a price is negotiated, which has nothing to do with how long it will take and everything to do with the expertise that you bring.

It's relatively easy to see how this might work in a crisis situation: the client has a major problem, which, if handled badly, could result in a major financial loss. If handled well, maybe the situation could be turned around and the loss averted. So a success fee related to the size of the potential loss could perhaps be negotiated.

The same principles can hold true in speculative business development situations. Imagine a situation where a client has the opportunity to win a major new contract for work but needs to put together a complex and detailed proposal, which includes how they will handle marketing and communications should they win. They ask for your help in putting together the proposal. It will take a lot of experience and expertise to get it right and they *need* your input.

Clearly there may be opportunities for you, too, if your client is successful, so you have a number of options as to how you provide the input needed:

1.   You simply do it on a time-based, fee equation and get paid at your agreed rates for the time you spend supporting their proposal.

2.   You agree to do the initial proposal work for nothing on the basis that, if successful, you 'win' the future work (on terms to be agreed now).

3.   You agree an 'at-cost' (85%) fee for the speculative work and a success fee (of rather more than 15%) if and when the proposal is won. The success fee might be, say, double your discount, around 30%.

4.   You agree to be paid on value. You agree a fee of somewhere between zero and 'at-cost' if the proposal *fails* but a percentage *of 'worth'* if it is successful. The percentage is negotiable and will depend on the profit opportunity that the proposal represents to the client – but could be many times more than any of the other formulae above.

Which route you choose really depends on how much of a risk you are prepared (or can afford) to take. When faced with this situation in the past I have always tried to assess the likelihood of the client being successful and made my judgements appropriately. But that is really difficult and often you can have little idea of the outcome, so I have tended towards the safer routes of 1 or 3.

I'd like to be able to say that I always went for the value-based approach but I didn't, although I regretted it on a number of occasions when, in hindsight, it became clear that a value basis would have been far more lucrative.

But I did learn one lesson – never to go for option 2.

Far be it for me to say that clients don't always stick to agreements made in advance – but they don't! People can change, circumstances alter and the best of intentions can quickly be reversed when large sums of money are at stake. Sure you may have a contract but the chances are there will be some loophole (or potential for one) that will lead you into either the threat of, or actual, legal action.

Taking clients to court is expensive, time-consuming, lengthy and damaging to everyone; what's more it rarely ends up with satisfaction for either party as no-one can be forced to fulfil a contract however watertight it is. All you can hope for is compensation for loss – and you'll probably have to risk more than the potential compensation in legal fees along the way.

Call me old-fashioned, but I believe that being *properly* paid for time is fine and trying to make a killing through a value-based approach doesn't sit comfortably with me.

That said, you may disagree and I, for one, would never say that you're wrong to do so; it's simply a case of 'each to their own'.

Chapter 4

THE KEY RATIOS

(What they are, what they tell you and how to measure them)

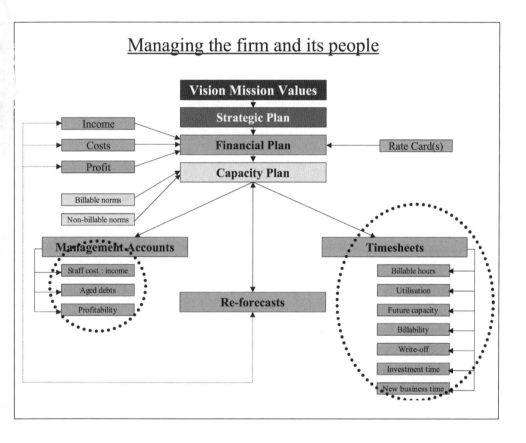

So far we have looked at planning the future of the firm, determining the level of profitability we are aiming for, establishing how many people we really need and how much we should be charging for our services. Now it's time to start looking at how we should monitor our *actual* performance and manage the business day to day.

The ideal way would be to have a single measure that tells us exactly how well or badly we are performing at a glance. Believe it or not, we do – it's called profit.

As a measure of performance it's pretty good because, when all is said and done, it's the one thing that really, really matters.

But as a way of monitoring the business day to day it's no good at all, as it only tells us the *outcome* of our efforts; it doesn't give any sense whatsoever as to *why* the outcome is what it is.

So, on its own, profit isn't a good enough measure of our business performance; we need a few more metrics to be able to identify exactly what issues we have and what needs to be done to put them right.

This is where key ratios come in.

Key ratios are a wonderful set of measures that can be presented as numbers (or better still as graphics). They tell us, at a glance, how we're performing (and what the trend is) in all the areas that affect profitability; but more than that, if set up thoughtfully, they can define the key management tasks and the scale of the problems to be resolved.

Below I am going to set out all the main ratios you should *consider* when putting together your monthly management reporting. You may not need *every* one for your business, but you will definitely need most if you are to see the whole picture.

Let's start with those that relate to time.

a. Billable hours ratio

This looks at the *actual* recorded billable hours and compares it to the *norm*.

Earlier on, when we were looking at XYZ Company we established a weighted average *norm* for billed hours, which, in the example, worked out at 27.4 hours per person per week (see Chapter 2f). By taking the information off timesheets, it is easy to calculate the total number of billable hours recorded for the week and divide it by the number of billable staff (remember to account for freelancers here by choosing to either include them or exclude them on **both sides** of the ratio – the *norm* and the actual). This will give you the *actual* billable hours for comparison with the *norm*.

No single week is likely to be representative on its own but averaged across a month you should arrive at a valuable figure that will tell you, at a glance, how busy your staff have been on client work that month.

You can calculate the comparison for an individual, a staff level, an account team or the firm as a whole. You may decide to do all of these or just some – that's up to you – but the figure for the firm as a whole was my first port of call.

By tracking these comparisons, month by month, you will begin to get a feel for the overall 'busy-ness' of the staff and, more specifically, where the pressure points are and where there is spare capacity.

Don't forget though, that you are only looking at *billable* time here and so you can only draw conclusions about workload. Without other ratios you still know nothing about *billed time* or *write-off*.

Finally, by calculating the percentage that *actual billable time* represents of the average *norm*, you get a picture of the workload of the firm as a whole, month by month. Ideally you are looking for it to be a consistent 100% (although it will always show some variation).

Here's an example of how it might look for XYZ Company:

XYZ Company	January	February	March	April	May	June	Total
Number of billable staff	10	10	10	10	10	10	10
Number of weeks	5	4	4	5	4	4	26
Recorded *billable* hours	1200	950	1040	1295	970	1020	6475
Ave. billable hrs. pp pw	24	23.8	26	25.9	24.3	25.5	24.9
Billable hours ratio %	87.6	86.9	94.9	94.5	88.7	93.1	90.9

Often, converting the data into a simple graph can provide a much more easily digested layout which gives an 'at a glance' message. This is certainly true in the data above – see below – and I would always prefer to see simple graphs rather than rows and columns of numbers.

Billable Hours Ratio

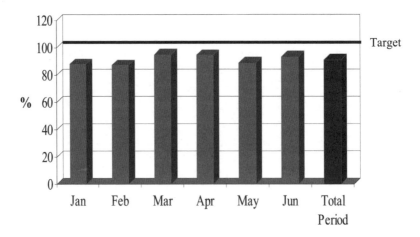

The above chart/graph, which shows a *billable hours ratio* of almost 91%, is interesting from three perspectives:

–   it shows reasonable consistency month-on-month

–   it shows a clear shortfall against the average norm (27.4) of 2.5 hours per
     person per week

–   there is a shortfall against the *norm* every month.

Together these tell you that there is an issue of over-staffing amounting to 25 hours per week; roughly equivalent to two-thirds of a person – or 7% of the staff.

That's not bad across a staff of ten – for a short time.

But with a *billable hours ratio* of 91% *across the six-month period* there will be a significant impact on the profitability unless the next six months show an equivalent over-achievement.

With less than a whole person too many, there's no opportunity to downsize, so the firm simply needs to fill the void as quickly as possible.

b. Staff utilisation ratio

This is the ratio between the recorded *billable* hours and the *total number* of hours worked.

In the calculation of the *billable hours ratio* above, we concluded that it gave us some valuable insight into the workload our teams were facing each month; and so it does. However, it doesn't tell us anything about how many hours they are working in total and what other pressures they might be under. Ultimately, we should want our staff to achieve their billable norm within a reasonable working week. Lots of overtime on a regular basis may get the billable work done, but isn't good for morale or health.

A good way to look at a more complete picture of their working week or month is to calculate their *utilisation* − the proportion of their **total working week** spent on *billable* work. So if an individual had worked a total of 45 hours in a week of which 28 hours had been recorded as *billable*, their utilisation would be calculated thus:

28 (*billable* hours) ÷ 45 (hours worked) x 100 = **62.2%**

The purpose of this ratio is to monitor the impact of non-billable time on your staff workload.

For the firm as a whole you should be aiming for utilisation of somewhere between 60% and 75%. It should be higher for the lower levels of staff and vice versa.

Used in conjunction with a) above, you will be able to see at a glance how your staff are spending their time, so as a check here are a few scenarios and how you should interpret them:

Scenario	Staff group	Billable hrs ratio	Utilisation	Comment
1.	Total firm	100%	75%	Perfect. Good mix of billable to non-billable time. No overtime.
2.	Total firm	100%	60%	OK for a while. High overtime. Too much non-billable time. Stress.
3.	Total firm	80%	75%	Perfect… for a four-day week! Time not being recorded onto timesheets
4.	Total firm	80%	60%	No overtime and low billable time. Over-staffed.
5.	Total firm	90%	55%	Worrying. Billable norms missed yet lots of overtime. Why?

Let me explain how I reached the conclusions in the 'Comment' column above.

First I looked at the 'Billable hrs' column and took a singular view that anything less than 100% was a problem. Unless the firm achieves its *billable* norms, the likelihood of achieving the income and profit targets is reduced.

Then I looked at the utilisation column. On its own it means little (just compare rows 1 and 3 to see this illustrated) but in conjunction with the 'Billable hours ratio' column, it tells you a lot. If the billable hours are okay and utilisation is high, you have staff working reasonable hours and spending most of them doing client work. If, on the other hand, the billable hours ratio is okay but utilisation is low, then your staff are having to put in long hours to get all their work done.

Finally, I did a simple calculation to work out the average number of hours per week being worked:

Average norm ÷ billable hrs % x utilisation % = average week

So, as an example using scenario 2 in the table:

$$27.4 \div 100 \times 60 = 45.67 \text{ hrs}$$

So, under scenario 2, we can see that the staff are achieving their billable hours but having to do a lot of non-billable work on top, maybe new business or staff management. As an occasional blip that's fine, but if it's a regular pattern, you need to investigate to see what's really happening here.

It's not an uncommon pattern and most often caused by one of two things: either the staff are deliberately staying late to avoid the rush hour transport problems, taking their time doing non-billable work (maybe even doing personal stuff for a while but calling it work); or they're over-loaded with too many new business pitches, internal management and/or administration. You need to ask them and if it turns out to be them former, remind them not to put anything on their timesheet that isn't real work. If it's the latter, consider spreading the internal demands over a longer period of time and, no matter how tempting, try to limit the number of new business pitches that coincide.

Remember, the purpose of this whole book is to show you how you can earn the profits you deserve, *without having to work your staff to the bone*!

c. Future capacity ratio

This tells you how well your **forecast** staffing levels compare to the predicted workload.

You will recall that when discussing capacity planning in Chapter 2g, each of the account directors was required to turn their income forecast into a capacity requirement by level. It was this that gave us the basis for determining the 'right' level of staffing for the business.

As the year progresses there will inevitably be changes in the forecast income as clients come and go, budgets change, new accounts open up and projects are won and completed.

In addition to re-forecasting the income stream monthly in the light of all these changes, you'll need to redo the capacity plan at the same time. This will highlight the number of billable hours required to deliver the forecast income.

Ideally this will *equal* the total of *billable norms* for your existing staff. In practice, though, there will be significant variations as the income ebbs and flows month-on-month.

By calculating the total of *billable norms* for your staff per month (and remembering that most accounting systems allocate a fixed number of weeks to each month of the year – either four or five weeks) you will have a clear picture of the available *future capacity.* Then by comparing this with your capacity plan per month and calculating the ratio of *required capacity* to *future capacity* you will be able to see, at a glance, in which months you have 'sold' all the available time, where you need more capacity and where you still have spare, unsold time.

You should be aiming to achieve 100% overall with variations of no more than 10% up or down in any one month.

The calculation of the ratio would look like this and is expressed as a percentage:

Required capacity (from plan) ÷ future capacity (from *norms*) x 100

Using XYZ Company and the norms we worked out per level earlier on, it might look like this for a six-month period:

XYZ Company	July	August	Sept	October	Nov	Dec	Total
Weeks pm	5	4	4	5	4	4	26
Required capacity	1240	870	1450	1310	1050	850	6770
Future capacity	1340	1072	1072	1340	1072	1072	6968
Ratio	93%	81%	135%	98%	98%	79%	97%

Future Capacity Ratio

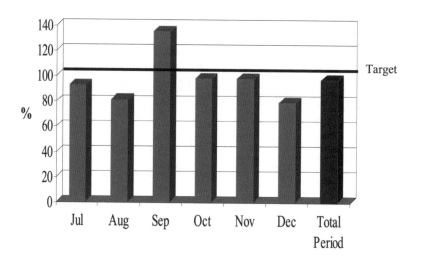

There are three very clear messages coming through from the table/graph above:

1. The overall picture for the total period looks pretty good; not quite 100% but close.

2.   September is going to be a hectic and stressful month where you may
        need some freelance help to get through. Ideally you would try to move
        some of the work forward and do it in July/August if possible and so
        avoid the extra freelance costs by using 'unsold' time in the earlier months.

3.   Staff should be encouraged to take holiday when there is spare capacity –
        July, August and December.

Just looking at the overall picture for the whole period would lead you to the conclusion that everything was fine, whereas, in truth, there are going to be some issues along the away. By knowing how busy September looks, in advance, you can take action to alleviate the pressure and save money. You can also let staff know early that September isn't a good time to ask for time off.

This flags up one other another important lesson – obvious really, but worth stating nonetheless – that unused time can never be recovered; if you don't 'sell' all the available time in one month you can never get it back. Unfortunately, time isn't cumulative and so you can't move it from one month to another, which means that heavy months (freelancers) and light months (unsold time) are nowhere near as profitable as consistently 'normal' months.

d. Billability ratio

This tells you how much of the firm's *billable* work is **actually** being properly paid for.

The ratios we have looked at so far have told us about the workloads of our staff; in particular, how busy they are, how many hours they're working and how much of that time is *billable*. What we need to know next is how much of that *billable* time we are actually being paid for – our *billability ratio*.

Just as with future capacity, this is best done monthly.

Fortunately, billability is easy to calculate as you simply divide the actual income for the period in question by the average hourly rate for the firm as a whole (calculated as a weighted average across all billable staff) to get the number of *billed* hours for the period. Then you divide that number by the total number of *billable* hours recorded for the same period.

You will be very successful indeed if you ever reach 100%, but you should aim for a billability ratio of at least 95%.

Let's look at an example:

XYZ Company	January	February	March	April	May	June	Total
Income	£85k	£87k	£98k	£78k	£82k	£92k	£522k
Theoretical average rate ph	£100	£100	£100	£100	£100	£100	£100
Calculated *billed* hours	850	870	980	780	820	920	5220
Recorded *billable* hours	1200	950	1040	1295	970	1020	6475
% billability month	71%	92%	94%	60%	85%	90%	81%

Billability Ratio

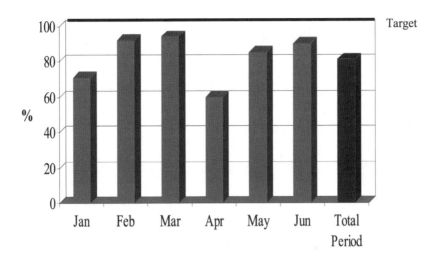

Here we can see quite clearly that over the six-month period in question, XYZ Company has achieved an average *billability* of only **81%** – which means that, at standard rates, it has been paid for only 81% of the work it has done for its clients.

The variations are considerable too, month-on-month; but seeing as how the workload hasn't altered that much (once you have allowed for January and April being five-week months), this seems to be the result of either planned or (more likely) unplanned *write-off*.

No wonder XYZ Company's profitability wasn't all it might be. By dividing the total number of *billed* hours (5220) by the number of *billable* staff (10) and the number of weeks in the period (26, minus 3.5 pro rata for holidays/public holidays and sickness), the average '*billed* hours per head' is only 23.2.

A lot of firms use a different measure when looking at this same information; instead of looking at *billability* as a percentage, they look at the actual rate per hour (or per day) achieved compared with their standard rate.

They do this by dividing the actual fee income earned for the month by the number of *billable* hours recorded onto the timesheets to get an average 'rate per hour achieved'.

Then they compare this to their rate card.

It's a perfectly reasonable way of looking at it and is totally consistent with looking at *billability*, except that it gives you an answer in £s per hour – and then psychology comes in to play.

Instead of seeing the *shortfall* in performance *implicit* in a ratio of 81%, they see a figure in £s – £80.62 in the above example – expressing what has been *achieved* rather than what has been lost and it is much easier to accept that as not too bad!

Let me make the point even more strongly: if the rate card averaged at £117 per hour and the actual rate achieved was £109, there is every chance that the management looking at the figures would see that as pretty close and therefore not really an issue. But, to my mind, that would represent a billability of 93% (a 7% write-off) and that's a loss of 7% of profitability. Given that most firms would consider 14% profitability as pretty good, the loss of 7 points equates to 50%.

That's 14% profitability instead of 21%. Or 7% when it could have been 14%.

See the point?

e. Write-off ratio

This tells you how much *billable* time you are giving away.

Having calculated *billability* in the last section, calculating write-off is simple: it is merely the inverse, ie 100 - *billability*.

So with *billability* of 81%, *write-off* would be 100 - 81 = **19%**

Earlier we discussed the different types of *write-off* and the figure above is the total for all types, so on it's own it isn't that useful in steering us towards the actions we need to take to minimise it.

To get really useful information we need to separate out the different types and develop plans to minimise each.

For *planned* and *legacy write-off* we need to convert the <u>discount</u> we are giving into the equivalent in <u>free hours</u>; in other words, the extra hours we are giving to the account compared with what we should be spending if we were charging our standard rates. These hours are effectively the ones we are knowingly giving away for free.

By adding these to the calculated *billed* hours we can 'adjust' the ratios to allow for these agreed discounts. After all these <u>are</u> *billed* hours – but billed at zero.

If we did, the *billability* chart we produced in the previous section for XYZ Company might look like this:

XYZ Company	January	February	March	April	May	June	Total
Income	£85k	£87k	£98k	£78k	£82k	£92k	£522k
Theoretical average rate ph	£100	£100	£100	£100	£100	£100	£100
Calculated *billed* hours	850	870	980	780	820	920	5220
Planned/legacy write-off hours	150	120	120	125	100	100	715
Adjusted *billed* hours	1000	990	1100	905	920	1020	5935
Recorded *billable* hours	1200	950	1040	1295	970	1020	6475
Adj. % *billability* month	83%	104%	106%	70%	95%	100%	92%

Adjusted Billability (Write-off) Ratio

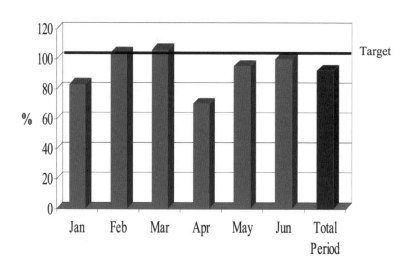

In the case of XYZ Company the adjustment made to take account of *planned* and *legacy write-off* is significant and has a dramatic effect on the *billability* of the firm. Instead of a *billability* of 81% we now have an adjusted figure of 92% — much better; and, in some months, *billability* has exceeded the 100% target.

This means that XYZ Company's unplanned write-off is only 8%. This accounts for the curious fact that even though it was only achieving about 23 billed hours per person per week, it was still making a 13% margin. If you've made it this far into the book, I suspect you were wondering about that too.

Now this is useful information because it suggests very strongly that the issues XYZ Company has with profitability are as much to do with the discounting it has been doing as with (what it would call) over-servicing. Yet without this analysis the firm would probably still be wrestling with how to eliminate its over-servicing problem.

In fact, in two of the six months above, the firm was actually paid for more hours than staff worked — a small *write-up*!

If I were running XYZ Company, I would focus more of my attention on clawing back some of the hefty discounts given, renegotiating some of the *legacy write-off* and/or replacing those accounts as soon as possible.

This is an excellent example of how the key ratios described in this chapter can steer you towards the right way of dealing with issues and prevent you from wasting time and energy trying to sort out the wrong problem.

f. Investment time ratio

This tells you how well you are controlling planned investment in the retention and growth of your accounts.

The really attractive feature of planned *investment time* is that by allowing for it in your *norms* for each staff level, you have taken it into account when planning your capacity and profitability. And that's really important because it means that when you do give away some investment time, provided it is no more than you have built in, it costs you absolutely nothing.

That makes investment time a fantastic tradable in negotiations with clients who want a discount. You can reject their request for a discount by offering to provide some free time instead – after all, it's the same thing in essence – provided that it's given **on top of the paid for time** rather than instead of. It costs you nothing because you have already budgeted for it but its perceived value to the client is at the full standard rate.

We defined investment time earlier like this:

> *Planned non-billable time spent on growing/securing existing accounts – by account. There is little doubt that clients want to see pro-activity from their agencies and nothing is more proactive than having unprompted ideas. It's all part of the service. However, there are occasions when either a client or an account has obvious growth potential or, sadly, when it may be under threat. In either case it makes sense to provide a little 'extra' service. This isn't over-servicing in the traditional sense but investment – planned investment.*

By setting a limit of 7.5% of total time against *investment time* and converting that into a number of hours per person per week, it isn't difficult to measure and control. Every (account) director should control the budget for his/her accounts and should monitor and approve its use carefully. The timesheets should contain a heading for *investment time* and the hours should be extracted and compared to 'norm'.

It is up to you what percentage you use and whether or not you choose to accept 7.5% of the total hours worked or 7.5% of the, say, 37 contractual hours per week. Either way, it has to be accounted for on top of the *billable* norm – not instead of it.

To calculate the *investment time* ratio, simply extract the information from the timesheets (for the individual, team, level or firm as a whole), divide it by the relevant norm, then multiply it by 100 to convert it into a percentage.

A monthly calculation for XYZ Company, based on 7.5% of 37 hours per person per week, might look like this:

XYZ Company	January	February	March	April	May	June	Total
Recorded investment hours	120	145	130	125	120	95	735
Investment hours norm	139	111	111	139	111	111	722
Investment time ratio	86%	131%	117%	90%	108%	86%	102%

Investment Time Ratio

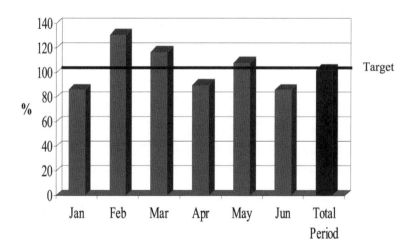

Whilst there is quite a lot of variation month-on-month, the overall picture is quite healthy with all the investment time being used. Nonetheless it remains close to the limit for the period in total.

This is a good result and doesn't need further investigation unless there is any suggestion that the allowance is being used improperly – and that isn't a ratio issue but a people management one.

g. New business ratio

This tells you how much time you are investing in *new business* and enables you to look at the investment/return equation.

It never fails to amaze me that agencies seem so smitten by the opportunity to win a new client that, when a new prospect walks in the door, all common sense seems to go out of the window.

Winning is everything and the cost of winning never enters the equation.

In itself that is bad enough, but when *new business* activity starts to affect the achievement of the *billable norms,* that is unacceptable.

That's why I have recommended that you put a *norm* to *new business* activity and why, earlier on, I suggested that up to 10% of the working week might be a good starting point. Once again, though, whether you choose to apply the 10% to the contractual hours or the actual hours is up to you – as long as it is all over and above the *billable norm.*

That probably means somewhere between 3.5 and 4.5 hours per person per week; and in cumulative terms that is quite a lot of time.

Think of it like this: for XYZ Company that would equate to around 40 hours per week or, put another way, equal to one of its ten people working full time on new business alone.

As with investment time, it is up to you what percentage of time you choose (and it may need to vary depending on how critical your need for new business is at different times in the year), but the important thing here is monitoring it and being in control. It will help you to judge whether or not to go for a particular opportunity and how much time to spend against it.

I have always found that setting a 'budget' for a specific new business pitch puts a fine focus on the things that really matter and helps the team to get to the heart of the issue quickly.

To calculate the *new business* ratio, simply extract the information from the timesheets (for the individual, team, level or firm as a whole), divide it by the relevant norm, then multiply it by 100 to convert it into a percentage – exactly as for *investment time.* Once again, you can do the calculation per head, per team, per level or for the firm as a whole.

h. Staff cost : income ratio

In Chapter 2, I introduced the concept of time *really* being money and explained that, no matter what we might like to tell our clients about expertise, capability or value, what we are really selling is time.

From that point on, almost every section has taken that for granted and worked on the basis that, by working with hours (a concept staff can understand and accept easily), we can manage our people more tightly and with greater focus than by working with money.

There really is no substitute, when managing people, than to talk to them in a language they understand and can assimilate easily. How much easier is it to ask someone to allow three **hours** for a task than to tell them that you've estimated £x for this job? They know what an hour is but do they know what £x is supposed to buy?

However, there is one weakness in this approach that needs to be addressed; monitoring hours versus the *norm* is fine as long as your *charge-out rates* and *costs* remain in kilter. And, as we all know only too well, costs tend to rise rather faster than our fees – especially salaries.

So it is good practice to keep a wary eye on the *staff cost to income ratio* to ensure that, even though all the previous ratios might look fine, you aren't losing profitability through allowing salary inflation to run ahead of your hourly rate increases.

However good your capacity planning, utilisation, billable hours and write-off statistics are, profitability can still be thrown off course if you allow salaries to inflate too fast or if you promote people ahead of business need.

It ought to be obvious (although it wasn't that clear to me when I started out in agency management) that, in the end, you do have to look at the money to be sure that all your ratios really are delivering the performance your firm deserves.

So look at your total staff costs – by which I mean include all their on-costs as well as the salaries themselves – and divide that figure by the total agency income and multiply the result by 100 to express it as a percentage. Anything less than 50% suggests that your staff costs are low (too few people, too many junior staff or low pay) whilst anything above 55% suggests the opposite.

By comparing your *future capacity* with the actual team in place, you should be able to spot if all (or part) of the problem is having the wrong mix of staff. This is simple enough to do because each monthly fee reforecast should also be converted into 'hours per level' and that will tell you whether or not what you have equals what you need.

Once you've eliminated this from the possibilities (or not as the case may be), it's relatively easy to spot if you have another issue – the wrong number of people overall or the wrong salary levels.

I know it's predictable, but the chances are that if your staff cost to income ratio is too high (ie above 55%) it's probably due to all three causes in combination: too many senior staff through unplanned promotions, some salaries too high because of unplanned salary increases and a few extra heads as well.

It isn't an easy issue to solve – at least not quickly – as it requires some turnover in staff to get there. That's why a 'healthy' level of staff turnover is to be welcomed. Maybe 10–20% per year?

i. Aged debtors ratio

Let me start off here with another obvious statement: that consistent failure to make profits leads, sooner or later, to the demise of any business. However, a much more common business killer is lack of cash.

Even profitable businesses can go bust through failure to generate sufficient *cash* to pay the bills.

Usually it goes something like this: your business is doing well, you're growing fast, winning new accounts, recruiting new staff and dealing with the issues as they arise. Everything seems to be on the up. However, the new accounts are only just starting to get going and you've agreed to a 'normal' monthly in arrears invoicing arrangement – which means that, at the end of month 1, you issue an invoice for the first month's fees and expect to be paid in about 30 days.

The new staff members are on a salary, of course, which has to be paid at the end of the month regardless, so at the time you're issuing the first invoices to the new clients, you're having to pay the salaries to the new (and existing) staff.

But, as so often happens, the clients don't pay on time and after 60 days you still haven't received their cheques. So, there you are, having now paid three months' worth of salaries with no cash yet received from the new clients.

On top of that you also have to fund all the extra costs of running the new accounts. There's pressure on the office space, too, and you had to buy new furniture and computers, mobile phones – the list seems endless.

If you started out with a substantial cash balance, the worst might be that your cash in the bank is rather depleted but that's okay because it will build up again as the new accounts begin to pay their invoices and the profits accrue.

But if you didn't have a healthy cash balance to start with, by the end of three months you could be up against (or over) your overdraft limit and trying to persuade the bank to increase it for you – which they may or may not do.

Then the worst happens, one of the clients you've been working with for years (and who has been very slow to pay recently) suddenly goes bust owing you five months' fees and costs. Terrible timing; couldn't have happened at a worse time; and its debt is only that high because you've been so busy getting the new accounts up and running that you haven't really kept on top of the cash collection.

Bang!

The bank says no more overdraft and what's more they're feeling nervous now and decide to call in the existing arrangement; you can't pay the salaries this month; suppliers are pressing for payment; you're chasing the cash in but it isn't coming fast enough… and in the end you accept the inevitable and go into liquidation.

The price of success?

Frankly, no!

Controlling the cash position is critical in any business but none more so than the professional services sector where staff and related costs account for such a high proportion of the total.

So what could have been done differently?

To start with, allowing clients to operate on a monthly in arrears basis doesn't help because it is always going to mean that you are funding at least the first two months of costs – and that means the amount of cash you have tied up in the business (your working capital) will always be rising.

You should endeavour to negotiate more advantageous invoicing and payment terms – but more about this in Part 2.

Secondly, you need to ensure that your clients pay you according to their agreed terms of business (or at least, close to). This means keeping a very close watch on the debtor situation daily and making it part of your director/account directors' jobs to ensure that the cash is collected promptly.

I've never come across a business where everything always gets paid on time, but vigilance and toughness do pay off.

I strongly believe in having debt collection as part of the directors' bonus criteria – to maintain their accounts to a predetermined aged debtors ratio. Directors have to meet targets like those suggested below at the end of each month if they are to accumulate the 'debtors' bonus for that month. Use your FD/CFO/accountant to suggest what the right mix is for your firm then, once in place, your directors ought to work with the accountants to ensure payments are received promptly.

Owing up to 30 days	Owing 30 – 60 days	Owing 60 – 90 days	Owing 90 days +
>70%	<20%	<10%	nil ★

★ This would exclude any notified debtors that were in the hands of lawyers or collection agencies.

Basically, the way I worked this was simple: the percentage figures above refer to the proportion of the total amount outstanding in any one director/account director's account group; 70% or more of the total amount needed to be in the 'up to 30 days' column or, in other words, not yet due; nothing was allowed to be owing for more than 90 days (60 days overdue) unless it had been notified to the FD and action agreed to either collect the money or resolve any dispute.

The two interim headings were a little more complex and, to a degree, flexible: the third (60-90 days) column could not exceed 10% whilst the second column could only exceed 20% by the amount that the third column was short, no more.

In other words 70:20:10 was fine as was 70:25:5 and 75:15:10 or 75:25:0.

However, 70:15:15 was not, nor was 65:25:10.

By approaching it this way and ensuring that the directors and account directors understand that collecting the cash is an integral part of their job, you can reduce the need for bank support and fund your own growth much more easily. It also improves profitability by enabling you to earn interest on cash deposits instead of paying interest on loans.

j. The key rules of thumb

There are times when it would be incredibly helpful just to be able to work out the answers to some of the most common questions about agency management without having to resort to detailed analysis and calculation – to have a few simple touchstones that enable you to check whether or not something makes sense.

Over the years I have found a number of these 'rules of thumb' helpful and somehow they always seem to work, regardless of the situation.

1. **The three times rule**: account handlers need to handle (bill) income equivalent to **three times** their salary.

2. Never plan for unknown new business to be more than **20–30%** of your total income for any year (except in very small businesses).

3. Keep the billable : non-billable staff ratio **in excess of 8:1**.

4. Aim for **>50% conversion** of pitches to wins.

5. Pay bonuses for the achievement of **specific, personal targets** – not just through 'grace and favour'.

6. Re-forecast income, costs, profit and future capacity **monthly**.

7. Talk to your staff **at least twice as much** as you think you need to – that's the only way to really understand what's going on.

But, and it is a big but, don't fall into the trap of using these rules of thumb *instead* of proper measurement – they aren't a substitute for knowing your real business ratios, but they are a useful double-check and, in some cases, just good practice.

Take rule 7 for example: we all think we're pretty good at talking to our staff, keeping them informed and up-to-date with what's going on; and we probably are. What we may forget though, is that when we were starting out in our careers, we were generally highly motivated by the MD unexpectedly dropping in just to pass the time of day for a few minutes; and if they seemed genuinely interested in talking to us (as opposed to checking up on us) that was a real boost.

I am convinced that, if you really want to know how well you are doing, you need to ask the junior staff what it's really like to work at your firm – but be prepared, they'll probably tell you.

k. Timesheet exercise

So you've reached this far into the book, which means you've read a lot of stuff about time, capacity, utilisation and so forth – things which, to be honest, are generally foreign terms to most of us in the marketing and communications sector.

But really taking on board what it all means and understanding how it can be used to help make better management decisions takes practice.

That's why this section contains a working example of how the timesheet data from our firm of ten consultants might really look – in the real world rather than just in theory.

Overleaf is a summary of the firm's timesheets for a complete quarter – all ten staff added together – and I've even calculated a few totals and percentages for you.

The main columns – with the 1–13 along the top – represent the weeks in the quarter and the figures below are the hours spent that week on the various activities shown in the left hand column. So you can see that, for example, in week 7 the team of ten spent, in total, 270 hours on billable work, 39 hours on new business and so on.

At the foot of the chart there are five questions, which, if you have followed all the logic so far, you should be able to answer.

Have a go and then ask yourself: if this was your firm, how would you feel about their performance and what would you want to improve?

Example Timesheet Analysis

Consultancy of 10 client facing people
Fee income for quarter = £250k
Rate card (average) = £100 per hour
Planned write-off = nil
Target average billed hours = 27 pp pw

Weeks	Quarter 1 (weeks)													Total	% of total	Ave pw	Ave pp pw
	1	2	3	4	5	6	7	8	9	10	11	12	13				
Billable work	240	270	320	220	245	260	270	255	325	260	250	220	265	3400	63	262	26.15
New Biz	27	33	5	21	14	27	39	15	12	9	21	12	18	253	5	19	1.95
Investment	9	12	1	22	13	10	17	15	2	14	16	12	12	155	3	12	1.19
Training	13	18	0	24	12	15	9	13	16	0	5	22	12	159	3	12	1.22
Int. Mgmt	22	26	21	25	18	14	14	12	6	22	18	15	14	227	4	17	1.75
Int. Admin	66	56	22	76	47	39	33	68	31	53	57	47	55	650	12	50	5.00
Sick	12	8	24	0	8	24	8	8	8	40	4	8	16	168	3	13	1.29
Hols	8	16	40	80	40	20	16	0	0	24	80	80	20	424	8	33	3.26
Total	397	439	433	468	397	409	406	386	400	422	451	416	412	5436	100	418	41.82

Q1 How many hours were actually billed?
Q2 How many hours did each person bill on average per week?
Q3 What was the utilisation for the quarter?
Q4 What was the billability %?
Q5 What was the unplanned write-off %?

The answers are overleaf.

<u>XYZ Company Limited</u>

Answers

Q1   Actual billed hours = £250,000/£100ph = 2,500 hours

Q2   Atual billed hours = 2,500. 2500/10 people/13 weeks = 19.23hrs

Q3   Actual billed hours = 2,500. Total hours recorded = 5436.
Utilisation = (2500/5436)x100 = 45.99%

Q4   Actual billed hours = 2,500. Total billable hours = 3400.
Billability = (2500/3400)x100 = 73.53%

Q5   Unplanned write-off = 100 - billability. 100 - 73.53 = 26.47%

Erratum

Amendment to Q3

Total billable hours = 3400. Total hours recorded = 5436.

Utilisation = (3400/5436) x 100 = 62.55%

Chapter 5

THE FD/CFO/ACCOUNTANT – FRIEND OR FOE?
(Friend or foe?)

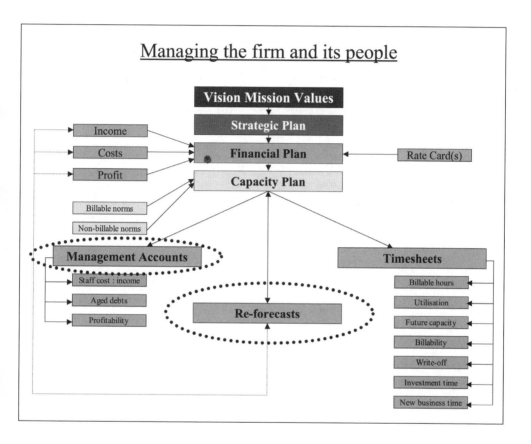

In the introduction to this book I described what I consider to be one of the biggest weaknesses of many of today's marketing and communications firm leaders – that they are professionally rather than commercially driven; they have grown up in the service sector and often reached the top by being good at delivering to clients and yet have little or no experience of business management.

It really is strange to me that, in the professional services sector, we accept this without any real challenge whereas if we look at almost any other business environment we would find a similar path to the top both unnerving and unusual. Imagine a pottery manufacturer where the best potter becomes the MD or pharmaceutical company where the most prolific research scientist is promoted to the top job. I am not saying that it doesn't happen, just that it is the exception rather than the rule.

However in PR, advertising and the other marketing communications services, it is the rule rather than the exception – as it is in all the 'professions'. All too often, the 'professionally' driven leader is more comfortable with *words* than with *numbers,* happier in the company of clients than accountants and more comfortable with Visions, Missions and Values than with financial spreadsheets.

As you will have realised by now though, getting good commercial results does require a grasp of (relatively) simple number crunching and if you have managed to work your way through Chapters 1 to 4 already, you will understand the level of numeracy that is required for strong commercial management. It isn't higher level mathematics but it is a little more than simple arithmetic.

We also have to recognise that many of the people attracted to the marketing and communications sector (and who might end up at the very top of their firms) may lack the confidence or ability with numbers to enable them to do everything themselves; that is why a strong finance director or accountant is an essential ingredient in the most (commercially) successful agencies.

In this, the final 'introspective' chapter in section 1, we are going to look at those areas where, in addition to supporting you with management information (and doing the number crunching that you aren't sure about), the FD/CFO or accountant can be a real profit generator not just an expensive overhead. They can, and usually do, pay for themselves in either added profitability or saved expenditure; they can and should be your right hand and party to everything that matters in the commercial management of your firm.

a. Revenue and capital expenditure

Often when talking to agency directors I find that they don't understand the difference between revenue and capital expenditure; they understand 'overheads' but when it comes to being able to vocalise why some costs appear in their 'accounts' whilst others seem to be consigned to the 'balance sheet', they struggle. I am not entirely surprised as there are so many accounting rules and regulations and accounting methods that it is confusing to say the least.

I have no accounting qualifications and so what I am about to explain here is by a layman for the layman – but it worked for me and gave me sufficient understanding to be able to talk sensibly to my FD.

Let's start with a simple explanation of each:

1.   **Revenue expenditure:**

These are the costs incurred by your business – generally the day-to-day running costs – which appear in your (monthly and) annual **accounts.** The full amount of each cost appears as an overhead in the month in which it was incurred (which may mean 'paid' or it may mean 'committed', depending upon the accounting method you use in your business – cash or accrual). Revenue expenditure reduces profits by the **full amount** of the expense.

2.   **Capital expenditure:**

These are the costs incurred by your business – generally for the purchase of assets – which appear on the **balance sheet** and are depreciated in value over time. Only the annual depreciation appears in your Profit and Loss accounts in any one year, not the full amount of the expenditure, and is usually spread equally across the 12 months. Capital expenditure reduces profits only by the **amount of the depreciation** in any year.

I always found that the easiest way to think about revenue and capital expenditure was by analogy to personal finances.

Every month you receive a salary payment, which you probably use to pay all your regular outgoings – mortgage/rent, household costs, utility bills and so on. With luck you may even have some over to pay for entertainment and luxuries (your 'free cash') and anything that remains unspent could be considered as profit. This is revenue income and revenue expenditure.

However, you may also have some savings or investments (unspent profit from previous times, one-off windfalls or whatever). If you need to buy a new car, for example, you probably won't have sufficient profit in any month to pay for it, so you may choose to spend from your savings to pay for the car. This is capital expenditure. It doesn't affect your ability to pay your regular monthly bills or your monthly 'free cash'.

So, in essence, we're talking about the difference between *income* and *wealth*. Buying the car from savings doesn't affect your *income* and at the moment that you make the purchase it doesn't reduce your *wealth* either because you have simply exchanged an amount of cash for an asset worth the same amount. However, as we all know, the car will begin to depreciate from the moment we drive it out of the showroom, reducing its value, and therefore your *wealth,* at the same time.

So think about revenue and capital expenditure this way: spending revenue is like spending your salary and a statement showing the sum total of all your income less your expenditure across a year would be your personal *accounts.*

If you've spent everything you earned, your profit will be zero; if you've spent more than you earned, you will have made a loss; and if you've spent less than you earned, you will have made a profit; and that profit could be considered as savings and add to your wealth.

Spending capital only affects your *wealth* by the amount that the asset you have bought **depreciates** each year and so spending capital has no *direct* effect on your profit; that said, you will need to put the amount of the annual loss in value of the asset back into your savings each year to cover the replacement cost of the asset in the future – and that is, in essence what **depreciation** represents – and it does come off your profit.

So your *accounts* show your revenue flows for the year whilst your *balance sheet* is simply a snapshot of your wealth (or net worth) at that point in time. In reality, they can tell quite different pictures: you could have a very strong net worth but be making a loss or vice versa. Only by looking at both can you get a picture of the health of a business (or an individual come to that).

Imagine an individual who has inherited wealth in the form of a large country house. He/she may now be considered wealthy in terms of the value of the property (a high net worth) but may not have enough income to pay the bills associated with it – often the case with the landed aristocracy across the UK and Europe. On the other hand, someone may have a very healthy salary, which they spend freely, but own nothing; so they appear wealthy as they have substantial disposable income but, in truth, are not.

Without the job they have nothing to fall back on.

You may be wondering why any of this matters and it comes down to this: your FD or accountant will understand all there is to know about capital and revenue but will always have choices to make about the best way to handle certain transactions.

For example, you may need new office furniture and the choice will be whether to rent it, buy it on hire purchase or buy it outright for cash; each approach has a different impact on your accounts and your balance sheet and so the FD will need some guidance from you as to what your objectives are for the firm's finances; and these will depend on the position you are in and what you are trying to achieve (and we'll cover more on this in the next section). You may, for example, want to maximise short-term profitability; or conserve cash; or minimise debt; or any number of other possibilities.

By understanding those possibilities and working with your FD or accountant, the same transaction can have very different impacts on the performance of your business – its profitability, cash flow, net worth and future value.

b. The FD/CFO – overhead or profit generator?

I suppose it depends to a degree on the size of the firm in question but during my career I have always found that a good FD or accountant contributes as much to the bottom line as any senior employee. In fact, it was always a running joke that the FD seemed to generate more profit than many of the full-time income generators. But it wasn't by selling time to clients; it was by working to a clear financial strategy and help-ing the firm to avoid much of the waste that pervades all larger organisations.

It is undoubtedly true that as an organisation grows so does the level of inefficiency; the chains of communication become longer and it gets increasingly difficult for the MD to keep everything under control. New structures and control mechanisms can (and usually are) devised and put in place but no matter how well it is done, there is always a loss of efficiency through the adoption of processes. The simplicity of having one person aware and in control of everything and operating to a singular style can never be replicated across a management team, however good they are.

Slowly, as a business grows it becomes less efficient and more wasteful and often it falls to the FD to identify the areas of inefficiency and develop ways of combating them.

Take cash collection, for example: when we start out in business, collecting the cash in is a top priority because we need it in the bank in order to pay ourselves (and our sup-pliers and staff). As the business grows and our cash position improves, the pressure to get clients to pay promptly decreases as other priorities take precedence. Before we know it we are allowing our clients to take longer and longer to pay.

It may not seem like a big deal, but look at it like this: if you allow an extra 45 days of credit over and above your specified terms (which, in reality, most firms seem to do), the cost in interest alone equates to around 1% of margin. In other words, you could improve your profitability by 1% simply by ensuring that you are paid to terms.

That takes no account of the fact that an extra 45 days of credit requires an extra 10% to 15% of your *turnover* in working capital – that is, the cash tied up in your business to enable you to pay the bills/salaries and so on whilst waiting for clients to pay you. It's an expensive mistake.

By taking control of cash collection, your FD could add 1% to the margin.

Another area that can avert disaster is credit checking and I am constantly amazed by how few firms bother with this simple and inexpensive safeguard.

I hear regularly about clients who build up significant debts with their agencies before, unexpectedly, going bust. The impact on the agency can be devastating as the whole of the bad debt comes straight off the profit line and can wipe out most, if not all, of the agency's profit margin in one go. It always seemed to me to be a risk that is better avoided or, at least, minimised. It's another task of incalculable value that your FD can do with ease.

A simple credit check will put you in a position to negotiate your terms of business much more strongly with a new client. If they haven't been trading long and have no real history the credit check will tell you so. Or if they simply have a poor credit rating, you need to know. Then you can at least take an active decision about whether or not to work with them; and if you decide to go ahead, whether or not to allow them credit or, instead, ask for payment in advance. In itself, doing a credit check won't make you extra profit, but it could prevent you from losing a whole lot!

So it's clear that a good FD can play a big role in making sure your trading profits go to the bottom line of your accounts rather than being lost in inefficiencies or bad debts. But that's far from all.

A clear financial strategy is pretty important too – and this is another of those areas where the words are easy to say (and every MD would generally agree with the sentiment) and yet many don't really understand what it means and how to determine what their strategy should be.

Take tax, for example. Certainly no-one likes paying it but there's nothing worse than realising that, if only you had done things differently, you could have paid much less. The same is true with bank charges and interest payments; and what about the choices you face when needing to acquire new equipment – leasing, hire-purchase, outright purchase... the list is almost endless. Speak to a leasing company and, not surprisingly, they will tell you why their approach is the best for you; and so it is with every supplier.

So how do you choose what to do?

The truth is that the approach you choose should be a reflection of your financial objectives and strategy. And you and your FD need to decide what that is.

For many smaller firms, the objective is often to maintain a positive cash flow. That means making sure that the cash balance in the bank stays positive and that the cash inflow/outflow is controlled to ensure that there is always sufficient cash available to pay the salaries, supplier invoices and other overheads on the due dates. To achieve that goal they need a strategy that sets out how they are going to manage the cash flow – their payment policies, credit control approach, charges for late payment, capital expenditure controls, leasing/hiring policies and so on.

For other firms it may be that cash *flow* is less important (particularly for those firms that are part of a larger, cash-rich group) and instead, they might aim for minimising working capital. This would mean setting policies specifically to avoid tying up their cash in assets by leasing or hiring instead.

A firm that is grooming itself for a trade sale might choose to focus on getting its balance sheet in good shape by minimising long-term debt and commitments. It really is a case of determining the strategy that is right for you at the time and that's where the good FD can make a big difference.

Although a good FD has only limited ways to generate profit, he/she has almost limitless ways to ensure that the profits you make through trading actually end up where they should – on your bottom line and available for re-investment or dividend payout.

If that was all that a good FD did in your firm, I suspect you would quickly see the justification for the cost; but there's more – and this is the extra bonus that he/she brings!

In most professional service firms almost all the senior staff are 'professionals' – client service specialists who have grown into their senior roles. They understand the world of the client and that is a huge benefit when providing their services. But it has a big downside; in my experience we all become so familiar with the ways of the client that we can't always step back far enough to see that what might be good for the client isn't necessarily the best for our firm. The biggest example of this is over-servicing (or unplanned write-off.).

The FD doesn't suffer from this myopic perspective nor do they lose sight of the firm's business objectives. It may be an irritant on occasions but the FD simply sees the numbers for what they are and doesn't carry the client service baggage that so many of us do. That gives them a big advantage – objectivity! And that's why it does us all good to listen to the FD.

Finally, one last thought.

Finance directors work with money all day every day. They are used to finding solutions to financial problems and they see the commercial success of the enterprise as their domain. That usually makes them pretty tough individuals. And when you add that to their lack of client service baggage you end up with a strong, dispassionate negotiator – just what you need when dealing with hard-bargaining clients or, especially, procurement officers.

And in my view, it always makes sense to separate the commercial negotiation of a deal from the team who will have to do the work – it avoids any undue tension in the client relationship.

c. Management accounts and re-forecasts

It may seem strange, at first sight, to include both management accounts and re-forecasts under the same heading as there is more than enough to say about each to warrant their own sub-sections. However, as you will see a little further on, the two are inextricably linked and it is only by looking at both together that the most accurate picture of the year as a whole can be painted.

Earlier on, in Chapter 1, I talked about the financial plan being the steps you need to take and the resources you need on the way to achieving the strategic plan objectives (and ultimately the Vision). This really spelled out that a financial plan isn't a target or an aspiration but a statement of what you really believe is most likely to happen during the financial year ahead.

But as we all know only too well, what we believe will happen is rarely borne out in fact.

It is inevitable that the real world will vary from our predictions, sometimes by a little, often by quite a lot. So you need a way to monitor your progress through the year and to flag up the differences between your plan and the reality; and you need to look in both directions, back over what has happened so far, as well as what has changed in your outlook for the remaining months.

It may seem blindingly obvious but the purpose of monitoring performance against the plan is not so much to see where you *are* as to be able to re-forecast where you will *come out* at the end of the year; in so doing you can decide upon any action that needs to be taken to either get things back on track or adjust to a new set of circumstances. That's why it's so important to produce the management accounts **and** re-forecast *every month* rather than quarterly (which many smaller firms do), so that actions can be taken promptly and have time to take effect.

Management accounts provide you with a direct comparison with the financial plan and so it is important that the format of both should be the same; that way any and all variations from the plan can be highlighted and easy to spot. The same is true of re-forecasts; they too need to be formatted exactly as for the financial plan because, in effect, that's what they are – the latest evolution of the plan for the year.

The key areas to concentrate on are those that you took so much time and trouble to forecast before the year started: income, costs, profit and capacity requirement. And you need to look at each one in detail. By looking at the month just completed and the year-to-date figures together you are better able to understand what variations are emerging and whether or not they are simply issues of timing or more permanent changes or trends. This understanding provides one of the key inputs into the re-fore-cast.

Putting a re-forecast together is much the same process as for the original financial plan. The (account) directors need to look at their income streams account-by-account, project-by-project and reassess the likely income for the remaining months of the year. In addition, you will need to reassess the allowances for *growth/shrinkage, unexpected account losses, new accounts from existing clients* and *new accounts from new clients*. Try not to be tempted into simply covering any year-to-date shortfalls by unrealistic increases in the 'unknown' lines. It will only lead to even tougher decisions later!

You also need to look at your capacity going forward in the light of any changes recorded or anticipated in the income stream. Given that staff costs represent the largest part of the overheads over which we have any short-term control, making adjustments to the capacity plan (and the implications that has for recruitment, redundancies and the use of freelancers) is probably the most important outcome from the management accounts and re-forecasting process.

We need to remember (and it is really easy during this analysis/re-forecasting phase to forget) that the purpose of this whole exercise is not simply to re-forecast the expected outcome but to decide upon the **actions** needed to ensure that (ideally) you achieve/exceed your planned *profit* or, where there are significant variations, maintain the profitability ratio.

Just as when you put together the financial plan in the first place, the aim is to fix your profit (or profitability) and adjust your cost base to ensure it is delivered – *not* the other way round!

This is when the key ratios that were explained in Chapter 4 come into play and are a major support and help. The ratios should be produced for the month just ended and for the year-to-date so that, at a glance, you are able to see what is really happening in the business. It is all too easy to overlook an emerging trend if you are trying to get a feel from the accounts or re-forecast alone. The key ratios will provide you with as clear a picture as you can get.

At this point it is important to draw a distinction between under-performance and over- performance. It may seem obvious but managing over-performance may be a 'better' problem to have but it can be just as demanding as handling a projected profit shortfall. The key requirement in both cases is to understand *why* the variation is happening: is it due to a variation in income or costs – or, most likely, both?

When dealing with an income shortfall the key need is to adjust the future capacity to ensure that, as far as possible, any excess, future capacity is removed. If the shortfall is small you may be able to make the necessary adjustments by delaying or cancelling planned recruitment. Generally, small variations in income can be adjusted for without too much difficulty and the planned profit maintained.

However, where the shortfall is substantial it simply may not be possible to maintain the planned profit (as a monetary sum) and so, in those cases, the fall-back position is to endeavour to maintain the planned *profitability* – the percentage of income that your profit represents.

Almost inevitably, in these circumstances you will need to make staff cuts.

This requires a steady hand and an ability to judge when to act and when to hold fast. It simply isn't possible (or wise) to make redundancies every month on the basis of the latest outlook – not least because it is extremely damaging to your firm's reputation but also extremely expensive and disruptive. The key here is only to act when you are confident that the outlook demands it; then act swiftly and decisively ensuring that you take enough action **in one go** to provide the cost savings you need.

In my experience (and I know I have been guilty of this on more than one occasion) we all want to minimise any redundancies and end up having to repeat the exercise a few months later. There is no doubt in my mind whatsoever that one bigger hit is far less damaging than two smaller ones. If in doubt always do more rather than less.

Upside variations in income are a much more pleasant problem to have and the only real question to be answered is whether or not you have (or can recruit) the necessary extra capacity.

The danger here is that, in the excitement of moving ahead of plan, the temptation to become over-generous and lose sight of the need for proper expenditure controls can be irresistible. Don't lose sight of the bigger picture – the Vision, Mission and Strategic goals – by awarding excessive bonuses or, worse, permanent salary increases that impact your profitability. Your business may be bigger than you anticipated, but your target profitability should remain. If you achieve more income, you should achieve more profit!

In looking at the scenarios above, the general focus has been on variations from plan caused by **income** change. Although this is the most common cause of variation, it isn't the only one.

Cost variation is a more difficult problem to solve, not least because it usually signifies one of two issues: an underestimation of the business costs in the plan or a lack of cost controls in the day-to-day running of the firm. Either way, the combination of the management accounts and the key ratios (overlaid with a modicum of common sense) should be sufficient to enable you to re-forecast your cost lines more accurately.

Perhaps not surprisingly the most common overspend is on staff costs caused by unplanned (or larger than planned) salary increases or staff turnover. Frequently within the marketing and communications sector (and particularly when the market is strong) there are more jobs than good quality staff to fill them. The effect is to put excessive pressure on employers to keep their teams together, often by giving higher than intended salary awards and/or early (and unplanned) promotions.

The impact on the bottom line can be dramatic.

I have always believed that salary increases are **not** the best way to reward and retain staff – far from it in fact. The truth is that if a member of staff is dissatisfied or considering a move, a salary increase will only have a short-term effect; within a month or so the impact will have gone and the dissatisfaction or itchy feet will return. And what's more, I have always felt a certain discomfort with the idea that just because someone is threatening to leave, they somehow become worth more than they were before.

Far better, I believe, to keep base salaries under control and to limit increases to reflect inflation, real experience and necessary promotions; then use both incentive and reward bonuses to ensure the most valuable and effective people are well remunerated.

This has two big advantages: first, it links the reward to the performance in an entirely individual way; it encourages accountability and implies, very clearly, that 'the firm appreciates me'. Secondly, it minimises the fixed element of the staff costs and allows a significant proportion to become variable – only being paid out if the individual/business is performing well enough. And that increases management flexibility.

In fact, the general concept of keeping fixed costs low and maximising variable costs is a good one and something to keep in mind all the time. The larger the proportion of your costs that vary with the overall ups and downs of the business, the easier it is to maintain the desired profitability.

It is worth remembering that staff motivation depends on much more than remuneration; training, career development, perceived opportunity and morale/culture play an equally large part. It may seem surprising but in all the staff surveys I have seen, provided that the financial remuneration elements are okay, the softer factors relating to future opportunity (training, career opportunity, international exposure etc) seem to have a bigger influence than any of us might imagine; we seem to forget, once we reach the higher realms of management, what it was like to be young, ambitious and aiming for the top!

But, once again, I digress.

Getting back to cost management, we already know from Chapter 2 that there are only a few costs we can really control – the discretionary costs.

So, once you have concluded that the issues with the firm's performance (the variance from plan) are due to cost overspend (and you have re-forecast all the lines as best you can), it's time to look again at the impact on the profit before tax (PBT). It's the same process as for the financial plan – calculate, adjust the discretionary spend and re-calculate until you arrive at the desired profit (or profitability).

Finally, having produced your monthly management accounts/re-forecast and compared them with your plan, there is one final job to do. You need to do the same comparisons with the *previous re-forecast* to identify any variations from that. There shouldn't be too many and they shouldn't be large because, after all, the previous re-forecast is only a month old.

That said, inevitably there will be variations (usually on the income lines). Where these are within normal operating tolerance you need do little more than keep half an eye on them to ensure they don't accumulate over the months to a significant amount. However, where they step outside acceptable limits you need to investigate – to discover whether or not any shortfalls will be recovered in the coming months of the year. Timing quirks will always be there but all too often so-called 'delays' quickly become 'postponements' and then 'cancellations' (or 'move into next year').

The only way to ensure you have a realistic picture upon which to build your latest financial outlook is to be confident in the optimism/pessimism balance of each of your (account) directors. Know how they forecast and make adjustments as you see fit to ensure that the numbers you are working with are as accurate as you can get. In the end, you will need to keep working on your teams' forecasting ability until you get from them what you want – a realistic picture of what they expect to happen, which is neither a best-case nor a worst-case scenario.

Once you get there (and it will take a lot of complaining, training and checking), you will have a solid method of forecasting the performance of the firm that is about as good as it can get. In turn, that will give you all the information you need to take early enough action to protect your bottom line – and, after all is said and done, that is what it is all about!

d. The audit, annual report and accounts

The audit

There are not many areas of management of a professional service firm where the practices vary with the size of the firm. However, when it comes to the formal aspects of auditing and reporting there is no doubt whatsoever that, the bigger you get, the more onerous these formal aspects become.

As I have stated before, I am no accountant so this is not going to be a technical appraisal of the processes involved – more an overview of what, as an MD or director, it's useful to know.

Let's start with the audit – and first the good news: in the UK (and this is generally true elsewhere, too) small firms do not need to have an audit and for the purposes of this regulation a small firm is defined (in the UK in 2005) as having:

–   Turnover not more than £5.6m
–   Gross assets not more than £2.8m
–   Employees not more than 50.

Within the marketing and communications sector this means that many firms are exempt. However, firms above these thresholds will need to be audited by a registered accountant and as the years go by, the process inevitably becomes more detailed. I have always looked on this as a positive support rather than a necessary evil and found that auditors generally approach the task in a collaborative rather than confrontational frame of mind. Provided you do the same, it should be relatively painless.

There will be occasions when they want you to change your approach or policy towards certain aspects of your accounting and mostly they will be right – but (and it is a big but) there are frequently situations where no clear-cut rule or answer applies. This is where it is valuable to have a good relationship with the auditors so that the flexibility they have can lean in your favour on occasion.

One of the advantages of an audit is that any errors or mistakes in your accounting stand a good chance of being spotted early enough to be put right whilst occasionally (but hopefully not in your firm) it can uncover fraudulent activities. It pays to remember that all the directors are equally liable for the activities of their company and ignorance of the financial situation is no excuse.

Auditors also play another useful role – as advisors on processes and methods. They see many companies and many different ways of operating and can offer valuable insight into better ways to do things. Taken into your confidence, they (like your FD) should be friends not foes.

Fundamentally, the audit simply assesses whether or not your record of your firm's financial performance is a true representation of the facts. Where there are differences they are generally down to different interpretations of accounting practices, although sometimes the audit will pick up a major error or omission.

Whilst this can be painful when it hits your perceived bottom line or balance sheet, just as often it can go the other way and identify profits or asset value you didn't think you had. Either way, and costly as it is, it's a check you should consider making even if your firm is below the legal threshold.

Annual report and accounts

The following comments are all based on UK practice and law, but are similar in many other countries across the world. However, if your business comes under the laws and regulations of another country, you will need to check their specific rules.

Just as for the audit, most small and medium-sized private firms in the UK (and many other countries) do not need to file a full report and accounts package but, instead, can opt for short-form accounts. To qualify for this dispensation (based on 2005 data from the UK) the firm in question must have:

—   Turnover not more than £22.8m
—   Gross assets not more than £11.4m
—   Employees not more than 250.

This puts most marketing and communications firms in the band for dispensation. However, a company may not file abbreviated accounts if it is or, at any time in the relevant year, was:

—   A public company – including a private PLC
—   A company carrying on an insurance market activity
—   A person with permission to carry on a regulated activity under Part 4 of the Financial Services and Markets Act 2000 (UK)
—   A member of an ineligible group – one in which any of its members falls into one of the three categories listed above.

Additionally:

–   A parent company cannot file abbreviated accounts as a small or
      medium-sized company unless the group itself qualifies as small or
      medium-sized in total. The size criteria must be met in this year and
      the previous year.

Where a firm does qualify for the short-form (or abbreviated) accounts, the minimum
submission must contain the following:

–   the name of the company;
–   its registered number;
–   the type of company it is, for example, private or public;
–   the registered office address of the company;
–   the address where certain company registers are kept if not at the
      registered office;
–   the principal business activities of the company;
–   the name and address of the company secretary;
–   the name, usual residential address, date of birth, nationality and
      business occupation of all the company's directors;
–   the date to which the annual return is made up (the made-up date).

If the company has share capital, the annual return must also contain:

–   the nominal value of total issued share capital;
–   the names and addresses of shareholders and the number and type
      of shares they hold.

Now I have to confess, this is about as technical as I get, so for more information I can
only refer you to your accountants. That said, and whilst I am all for the minimisation
of bureaucracy, I believe it is good practice to behave as if your firm were bigger than
it is – in other words, to report in a fuller and more complete way.

In my view, this has a number of benefits: it is a good discipline to examine your business from the perspective of someone who is used to looking at bigger firms, as it
makes you appear more thorough and professional; it forces you to look more closely
at how you are operating; and finally, I found that writing a Chairman's Report helps
you to step back from the day-to-day and see the bigger picture more closely, after all,
the report should be about progress towards the achievement of the strategic plan as
well as the financial plan – which takes us full circle back to where we started out – in
Section 1, Chapter 1.

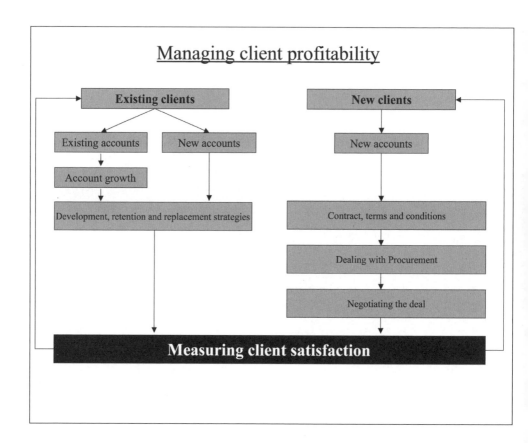

Part 2

MANAGING CLIENT PROFITABILITY

Chapter 1

BUILDING PROFITABILITY THROUGH GROWTH

(New business – the life-blood?)

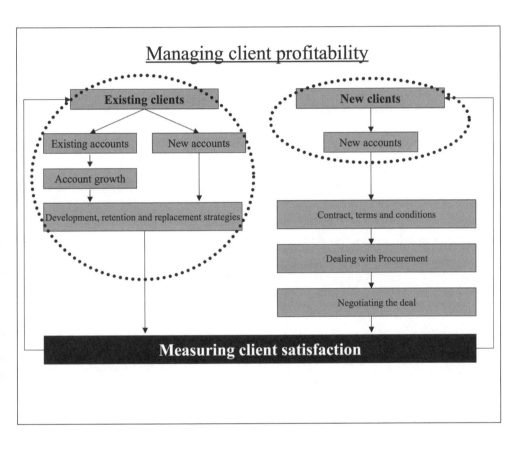

a. Clients and accounts

During the past couple of years I have had the opportunity to see inside and talk to staff from quite a large number of different firms – from PR to advertising and from design to executive-search – and I continue to be struck by the haphazard way in which most of them go about acquiring new business. For some it is a very personal process, all about networking and who you know; for others it's a process – a numbers game if you like – with hundreds of mailers leading to tens of leads, which, in turn, deliver a handful of pitch opportunities – maybe!

Irrespective of their general approach though, there always seems to be one thing missing – structure.

We all know that new business can come from a variety of sources and, if asked, we all could identify a number of them – referral, previous contact, new staff… the list is quite long. But few of us break this down analytically so that we can really understand where our new business opportunities originate.

As if to illustrate the point, not long ago, working with the senior team of a large PR firm, we got on to talking about new business and their (and I quote) "…exceptional conversion rate". They told me that they averaged 70% conversion of pitches to wins, which I had to agree was stunning. They also told me that it was becoming more and more difficult to maintain the rate as the number of firms pitching was often four or more. That got me thinking…

So I began to ask other firms about their conversion rate and the number of competitors they were generally up against.

From what they told me I was able to conclude something pretty amazing.

They all told me that their conversion rate fell in the 40% to 70% bracket and the number of firms pitching was usually three or four and often higher.

So, let's look at what that tells us; firstly it is clear that firms at the lower end of the conversion scale claim to win one in every 2.5 pitches and those at the top end reckon they win two out of every three.

It seemed to average out at about 50% or one in two.

However, if there really were three or four (or more!) competitors pitching, the average win rate *ought* to be between 25% and 33% (or less). Something didn't add up here.

How could this be? What was going on?

Either, I concluded, there are dozens of 'anti-matter' firms out there that only ever lose business or someone wasn't telling the truth; and without much more thought I concluded that it could probably be explained by exaggerated claims for conversion rates and/or a gentle massaging of the statistics to ensure that they said what the firm wanted to hear – sort of 'human nature, not wanting to hear the truth' sort of stuff.

And maybe I was right…but it was far from the whole picture.

What became clear and surprised me hugely when I went back to the firm with the claimed 70% conversion rate was that they hadn't exaggerated at all.

What they had done was to include all the new business that they won, non-competitively, from their **existing** clients; and it was quite a lot.

You can do the maths for yourself, but clearly non-competitive wins both raised the conversion rate and reduced the average number of competitors at the same time – which distorts the picture rather!

All of which leads me, in a rather roundabout way to the point of this story; that conversion rates, percentages and statistics are worthless unless you know *exactly* to what they refer. And that leads me on once again to my favourite rant: precise terminology.

This section is headed 'Clients and accounts' because, as you will already know from Part 1, Chapter 1, the two terms are often confused or misused and are, when properly understood, critical to the analytical approach to business development that I am proposing. I consider this to be so important that I have chosen to repeat here what I described in outline in Part 1.

CLIENT:

An **organisation** (be it commercial or charitable, profit-making or not for profit, governmental or NGO, private or public) for which your firm works. In some cases the organisation may be a single individual, for example a celebrity or sports star.

ACCOUNT:

The **specific area** of the client's business that you support.

Clearly, in the above definitions, a CLIENT may have many ACCOUNTS. It is this specific fact that enables us to take the analytical approach to business development that I am about to propose.

You will have gathered by now that I am less than impressed by the way many firms go about business development and earlier I suggested that it was haphazard and lacking in structure. Well let's see if we can put that right.

Let's start by looking at what we mean by 'business development'. For some it is a way of referring to all business that they have won since the start of the year; that could include increased budgets or fees for existing accounts as well as completely new accounts. For others it refers to new *accounts* only; for a few, it seems to mean only business won from new *clients*.

You may be beginning to see already why being clear about the definitions can avoid confusion. For me, business development falls into three distinct categories, each of which requires a different approach and has a different set of barriers to overcome:

1.   Growth of existing accounts

2.   Additional account(s) from an existing client

3.   New account(s) from new clients.

In the next few sections we'll look at how to deal with the different challenges that all three categories pose. To make it simpler (and because many of the considerations are similar) I have linked categories 1 & 2 under the heading 'Growing existing *clients*'. Winning new clients is very different and so has a section all to itself.

b. Growing existing clients

Few statistics seem to be true across the whole of our professional service sector but one seems to hold out – more or less – across most: that is that the bigger, more successful and stable firms seem to generate about half their growth each year from their existing clients.

Now, of course, there are variations year on year and firm to firm, but it's a very telling statistic nonetheless.

And yet when you analyse how much time is invested in 'winning' additional business from *existing* clients, it amounts to only about a third of the time that we are prepared to invest in pitching to *new* prospects. In fact back in Part 1, Chapter 2 you may recall seeing this chart of how staff tell me they spend their time in a typical week:

Typical week	
Billable client time	27 hrs
New biz	6 hrs
Investment time	2 hrs
Training	2 hrs
Internal management	4 hrs
Internal administration	3 hrs
TOTAL	**44 hrs**

You may also recall that an analysis of timesheets shows a slightly different picture:

Typical week		
Billable client time	27 hrs	21 hrs
New biz	6 hrs	5 hrs
Investment time	2 hrs	3 hrs
Training	2 hrs	2 hrs
Internal management	4 hrs	4 hrs
Internal administration	3 hrs	9 hrs
TOTAL	**44 hrs**	**44 hrs**

Regardless of which one is the best representation of reality, the fact is that 'New biz' always accounts for much more time than 'investment'.

Maybe that is because we allocate time working on a pitch for an *existing* client as 'New biz' or maybe it isn't. It really doesn't matter because in most firms there isn't a timesheet category for 'Investment time' and I have had to extrapolate those figures from talking to them and asking them to break down their figures into my category descriptions.

The fact that usually there isn't even a category for 'Investment time' says it all!

However, when I ask senior account handlers about the source of 'New biz' they all tell me (or at least agree when I suggest it) that winning additional business from *existing* clients is much easier than winning business from entirely *new* clients.

So we have a mystery; why, if winning additional business from existing clients is easier, do we devote more of our (limited) time to the more difficult task of winning *new* clients?

It makes no sense.

Now I can't prove this point but I have a very strong suspicion that most firms simply assume that it's the account director's role to search out and develop additional opportunities from their clients (and that they do it). They assume that if little additional business is forthcoming, it's because it isn't there.

How wrong they are.

Account directors are much like the rest of us in professional service firms – not that good at selling. They assume that their primary role is to deliver against the existing brief and ensure that the account isn't lost – and they're right, it is their **primary** role; but it isn't their whole role. Once again the extreme lack of confidence of our profession comes to the fore and instead of hunting out fresh, additional opportunities we take the safe route of sticking with what we know, considering that modest, inflationary increases in budget year on year constitute success.

In my experience, few account directors really develop their clients as well as they could or should.

Now, I am not advocating a heavy selling approach to existing clients; I am suggesting we look at our existing clients in much the same way that we look at new prospects and begin investing some structured time aimed at developing additional business, much as we do when preparing a pitch. When there is a new client on the horizon we think nothing of throwing time at it even when there is only a one in three or one in four chance of winning. Yet with our existing clients we would call that time over-servicing and get over-worried about it.

Did I not say much earlier on that over-servicing was the killer of profitability? Am I contradicting myself here? Well no, I am not!

What I am talking about here is structured, planned investment in selected existing clients, to generate a multiple return.

Back in Part 1, Chapter 2e, I defined investment time as:

> Planned non-billable time spent on growing/securing existing accounts – by account

I suggested that a budget of up to 7.5% of every account handler's time should be set aside for this specific purpose – and you should expect it to be spent. Not using the investment time budget should be as big a sin as over-spending it.

So where should the investment time be spent and what sort of things should we be doing?

Well if I may, I'll deal with the 'where' question in a couple of sections time. First, let's look at the 'what'.

To do that we must first understand the key factors that influence clients and make them well disposed to award us more business. Whether it is growing an existing account or winning an additional one, the fundamental principles are the same. We could all list many factors that come into play, but the three below encapsulate them all:

1. The *client's perception* of the quality and breadth of work we do (and are capable of doing) on the account(s) we already hold.

2. The level of senior, decision maker exposure we have.

3. The fact that, regardless of anything else, people do business with people (not firms or brands).

Pretty much all of the other influencing factors can be categorised within one or other of the descriptions above.

How many times have we read that one of our client organisations has awarded an account, unbeknown to us, to one of our competitors and, when asked why, claims it didn't realise that we could do that?

How often do we find that our day-to-day contact at the client end doesn't have the authority to award another account to us or increase the budget?

How often have you experienced or heard of an account following the account director (or main contact) to a new firm?

We need to work on all these factors to ensure that we are in the best possible position to exploit any opportunities that arise or that we may help create.

It mustn't be left to chance; we can't assume that every account director is doing all the right things because most of the time they're not – they're preoccupied with delivering results against the brief

How do we avoid being pigeonholed as the 'consumer agency' or the 'newsletter people' or the 'b2b specialists'? How do we get exposure at a senior level? How do we get noticed?

Well the truth is that it isn't that difficult but, sadly, we mostly 'forget' to do the things that make it all possible. We don't all forget all of them but none of us does them *all* – *all* of the time!

I've called this:

THE NINE THINGS WE ALL FORGET TO DO!

And here they are:

1.   **Tell clients about successes and high-profile work for other clients**

     More times than I care to recall, when I mention this to account directors on one or other of the training programmes I run, they explain to me why they don't do it very much. They give me all sorts of reasons (I tend to think they are more likely to be excuses or post-rationalisations) ranging from "clients like to think that we only work for them" and "they don't like to be reminded that they aren't our only client" or "if I told a client about a success we had for someone else, they'd want to know why we hadn't done that for them – it only leads to problems".

I have to say, I simply don't buy that at all.

Sure, you need to be selective and diplomatic in the way you introduce such a conversation – and make it subtle – but in the main I have found that clients like to be reassured that they are working with a successful firm that achieves notable results. It also gives them material to talk to their bosses about to ensure that their agency/consultancy maintains a positive profile within.

Think about all the advertising that car manufacturers do, the millions of dollars being spent every month. There is a widely understood truth (which I am sure is not just a myth) that a substantial part of the rationale is to achieve a very specific goal.

Is it to sell more vehicles?

Is it to take greater market share?

Is it to announce new models?

Well yes, probably, to all those things, but it is also to achieve one even more critical thing – to reassure those who have already bought or decided to buy their product, that they made the right choice.

After all, purchasing a car is one of the three biggest decisions we make during our lives – after buying a property and getting married. We can get cold feet pretty quickly and the manufacturers know this. So they help us through reinforcing our decision continually by telling us what a good choice it was.

Telling your clients about successes that other parts of your firm have achieved is much the same; it makes them feel warm about working with you.

2.   Re-present your 'Credentials' at regular intervals

This one is really a no-brainer and yet so many firms simply don't do it. The fact of the matter is that if you don't tell your clients about the changes and developments in your business – however small and insignificant they may seem to you – they will continue to think of you as being the firm you *were* when they first hired you.

That means you will be pigeonholed and not considered when an opportunity comes up that isn't what they believe is within your area of business.

I learned this lesson the hard way many years ago, when I read about one of my firm's clients appointing one of our main competitors to handle an internal communications programme. They simply weren't conscious of the fact that we had recruited IC specialists and developed a thriving unit in the couple of years since we were appointed to handle their consumer/brand accounts. But by the time I asked the client about their decision it was too late and our competitor had established a seat at 'our' table! To make things worse, they would naturally try to chip away at our hold on the brand accounts. Potentially doubly dangerous.

The rule here is very straightforward: always keep your clients up to date on the latest developments in your firm, no matter how irrelevant they may seem. You never know when it will pay you back through additional opportunities. It doesn't need to be done formally and probably is better done casually in conversation, but however you choose to do it – **do** it! And that leads me on to the next in our list of nine things we all forget to do…

3.   **Introduce all new recruits to all clients, even specialists outside the area of your remit**

It's a cliché, I know, but we do live (and especially work) in a very small world indeed. The longer you spend within any business area, the smaller it becomes. This inevitably leads to a gradual reduction in the number of degrees of separation between any two individuals.

On many, many occasions I have been introduced to someone and within seconds we have discovered something (or someone) in common. It may be from school or college, membership of a society or club, maybe both worked for the same firm at some time and have friends in common – who knows? But what *is* for certain is that once discovered, they have probably moved a little closer together, and as I have said before, people do business with people.

It may not bring you any more business today, but making these extra connections between the client and your firm will strengthen the bond between you – and that cannot ever be a bad thing.

4.   **Perform regular health checks**

You already do this one – right?

Well, we all believe that; or most of us anyway. The problem here is that we, in the marketing/communications world, like most service firm professionals, don't want to hear bad news. We love to hear the good stuff about how well we've done, the exceptional results from our latest campaign or project or whatever.

But when it comes to issues, we don't always feel like taking them head-on; we prefer to skate over them in the hope that our 'relationship' and future performance will make it all well again. I'm sure it isn't deliberate avoidance, more our naturally optimistic character and positive outlook.

That isn't to say that we don't ask for feedback, we do. It's just that when we ask "How are things going?" we only want/expect to hear the positives and so the "Okay I guess" response is taken to mean that everything's fine. "Great," we say. And we move on. The issue under the surface is left to fester.

And then we're faced either with a much bigger problem later or a client that quietly starts to look around for a new firm.

I know that this happens from personal experience; but I also hear about it quite frequently when discussing account losses with my consultancy clients. Almost everyone, it seems, has had some experience of losing an account completely without warning – a bolt from the blue so to speak. Of course, it isn't always down to festering issues, sometimes it can be for completely unavoidable reasons – like a change of personnel at the client end, a merger or a change of corporate strategy – but I would guess that the most frequent cause is an underlying and unaddressed dissatisfaction.

That said, it really can be avoided: but it needs a more structured approach to overcome our natural reticence to look for issues. We need to keep our antenna tuned in; we need to check and double-check and ask for clarification when a client says something was 'fine' or 'okay' or makes some other non-committal comment.

Checking with others at the client end is often a good way of getting insight, as is asking your client how his/her colleagues feel about a particular outcome or event. It's always easier for them to tell you that *someone else* wasn't entirely happy than to admit that *they're* not.

The state of the relationship between you and your client is worthy of a more formal review from time to time. Put it on the agenda at your major review meetings and ask direct questions about how they feel about the way things are going. Structure the questions into groups and lead the client gently through the team, processes, budget control and so on.

Take note of any issues and deal with them!

I will cover this subject in much more detail in Chapter 5, 'Measuring Client

Satisfaction'.

5.   Make working together enjoyable

I have to confess – I feel like I'm stating the obvious. But with the ever-increasing demand for more 'professionalism' and less and less time for the human touches in business, we are in danger of forgetting what it is that we, as people, find rewarding and motivating. I see people working in our industry at a breakneck pace with a packed diary and stress levels far higher than can be healthy.

To a degree that is the nature of the business and that can be part of the enjoyment, but there is an increasing tendency these days to assume that the best measurement of 'professionalism' and 'business-like behaviour' is the apparent efficiency and speed with which we conduct our meetings. We judge our importance by the back-to-back nature of our diary; we haven't the time for the niceties and touches that mark out a real relationship between *people* as opposed to a working relationship between *positions*.

Of course, everyone is different and we all need to modify our style to ensure that we 'fit' the client we are working with; but, for most clients, taking a little time to get to know them and making the effort to indulge them a little isn't asking too much, is it?

Put yourself in their shoes [stand by for another exaggerated and sweeping generalisation] and imagine their daily life. Their business is mundane and their office 'corporate' and grey. Because their firms are often much bigger than yours, you may find their norms are quite different from yours – plastic coffee from machines, small work stations, strict reporting lines and hierarchies, boring décor and an uninspiring working environment.

Believe it or not, coming to see you is probably the highlight of their week!

You see, we can easily become desensitised to the trappings and nature of the environment in which we work – young, vibrant, dynamic, casual… – and very different from the client's.

So don't make your business like theirs. Stay aware of the creativity and the youthful exuberance you bring and make the experience as enjoyable as possible. Provide chocolate bars or other 'naughties'; pass on samples from other clients that you have; brew great coffee and do lunch when you can; make the client believe that they really matter; it makes all the difference.

Remember, people do business with *people*, not firms or brands.

6. **Provide solutions not problems**

This is another one of those tired clichés that has lost most of its meaning in the rush to introduce it into everyday-speak. But it still says it all; it is the very foundation of professional service; it's what the client is paying for.

But surely, I hear you thinking, everyone knows that?

And you'd be right, everyone does know it. But not all of them do it.

I think it's time for another short anecdote.

During my latter years as a European CEO, I spent a huge amount of time (too much probably) travelling to the firm's offices throughout Europe. The pattern of the day was always much the same – up early, airport, flight, taxi, meet MD for chat about numbers, meet a few staff, chat, lunch, more chat, taxi, airport, flight…

Now I don't want to make out that these trips were unimportant – they were not – but they weren't exactly inspiring and I only ever got to see what they wanted me to see.

So I developed a plan.

I would always ask if I could have a desk somewhere for an hour as I had some urgent business I needed to deal with there and then. I would always engineer it so that I could sit somewhere amongst the general office and overhear a few client conversations. Admittedly there were occasions when I couldn't understand a word of what was being said but most times there would be a few that I could or, better, that were in English.

On those occasions, I was staggered by the number of times I heard something like this:

> *"Yes, I know, it's a real disappointment that we won't be able to use that venue for the conference but I've been there and it really won't hold the number of delegates we're expecting. I was hoping we could use a different layout and squeeze them in, but it's going to be really tight if we do. So under the circumstances I needed to come back to you for your opinion; what do you think we should do?"*

Now once again, I'm exaggerating a little and generalising a lot but the truth isn't that far away. We always assume that our more junior employees are well guided and schooled by their managers, but often they aren't.

Clients really do get very frustrated when we ask them for a re-brief when we should be advising them of what we are proposing.

The biggest single issue that clients tell me they have with professional service firms is lack of pro-activity and I have to confess, I agree. It's totally unacceptable and can only lead to a falling out.

So next time you get the opportunity to eavesdrop a little, do so and maybe you'll prove me wrong…or maybe not!

7.   **Think about the client's *business* (not just the account)**

I suppose that getting older and yet still retaining strong links into the professional services world has one big advantage – perspective. The old cliché that there is nothing new in this world has never been truer than here: no matter how well you deliver against the client's brief, the real value is, and always has been, in delivering something that is unexpected, something 'over and above'.

Look at it like this: no matter how well you deliver against the brief, that is what the client is paying you to do and so it is expected. It still leaves the client feeling that they have had to come up with the brief in the first place and so they feel, naturally enough, that it is they who came up with the ideas and you that executed them – however well. It is the buyer/supplier relationship in microcosm.

Not surprisingly, they consider it normal that you should deliver well and it is a condition of continued work that you do. Fail here and the only outcome is a loss of the account. So delivering brilliantly isn't the route to more business, it's only a route to retaining what you already have.

What I hear time and time again from clients is that their very best agencies deliver pro-activity. When I probe to find out what they mean, they tell me that they get the feeling that their account director/team is really thinking about their whole business and not just the account they are paid to work on.

It may seem blindingly obvious but thinking about the client's whole business and being able to set your account(s) in that context leads to observations and ideas that simply won't arise any other way. The conversations you have with the client will reflect your understanding and have greater value – and the buyer/supplier relationship has a real chance of becoming a true partnership between colleagues.

But that isn't the only benefit – far from it.

Thinking about the client's whole business needs to have a tangible output – has to lead to something the client will see as true added value. And the next few paragraphs deal with exactly that!

8.   **Have unprompted ideas**

Imagine the call: "Hi John, I was thinking about your business last night and something occurred to me; have you ever considered..." or "Hi Sue, I don't suppose that you saw the article in [FT, Wall Street Journal... whatever] yesterday about... It prompted me to wonder whether we could take that a little further..."

These are the calls that generate the added-value perception.

Now it almost goes without saying that nine times out of ten the call will only lead to a rebuff of some sort – something like "Interesting thought but we had a go at that a   couple of years back and it wasn't great for us – but I appreciate the thought."

But just occasionally, maybe once in ten calls, it can lead to something much more positive: "Interesting idea, it's not something we've ever considered before. Why don't you work up that thought and I'll see if we can get a test budget together..."

You see, just having interesting ideas – regardless of whether or not they are taken on board by your client – generates a huge perceived value. It says that you are really involved and providing value above and beyond the brief.

Having an idea accepted opens the door to new business – a project, say, or a new account.

Having new ideas isn't easy, though, and it's not something that you can do every week; but you do need to make a habit of it and deliver something to the client, unexpected, *every month*. The issue is how to do so without generating loads of write-off.

So let's deal with that now and close the loop on another element of client service that will, I hope, provide another 'Eureka' moment...

9.   **Invest in client growth and retention**

Much earlier on we looked at the concept of *Investment time* and I defined it like this:

> *Planned non-billable time spent on growing/securing existing accounts – by account. There is little doubt that clients want to see pro-activity from their agencies and nothing is more proactive than having unprompted ideas. It's all part of the service. However, there are occasions when either a client or an account has obvious growth potential or, sadly, when it may be under threat. In either case it makes sense to provide a little 'extra' service. This isn't over-servicing in the traditional sense but investment – planned investment. Each account director needs to have some flexibility to allocate some time to this – but in a planned, controlled way.*

This is why it is so important to 'budget' for investment time in all your senior (and junior) staff's working week.

I am frequently told that 'having unprompted ideas' and 'thinking about the client's whole business' are well-understood concepts that every professional service firm understands. And that is probably true.

Unfortunately, I hear just as often that 'we just don't seem to find the time to do as much of it as we would like' or 'we agreed to set up an internal programme to review our clients and generate ideas but after the first meeting most people were too busy to attend'.

It comes down to this: if we needed to put a pitch together for a new prospective client, we'd all make the time. It's just a question of priorities. Why can we make the time for new prospects but not existing clients? What is **important** here – and what is merely **urgent**?

Keep getting the important and the urgent mixed up and you're putting your existing accounts at risk as well as not exploiting the opportunities they afford.

c. Winning new clients

It's possible you could conclude from the previous section that I believe most professional service firms spend too much time looking for new clients and not enough time developing their existing ones – and you'd be dead right, I do.

That isn't to say that new clients aren't critical, because they are - we all need new business and new clients are an important part of that – it's just that a sensible balance needs to be struck between the two sources of new business.

We could all benefit from being more selective about the new clients we pitch for and from recognising early on just how much a new business pitch really costs, both in terms of time and money. Analysing how much it really costs to win a new client can be quite a shock.

Often, when I've done this after the event, I found that the real cost of winning was significantly more than the first year's potential profit on the account. With a conversion ratio of, say, one in three that means that, on average, the true cost is three times what we've calculated – or three years' profits.

What's really scary is that we often don't retain accounts much longer than three years; so that means we ought to never make any money out of new clients!

Of course, that isn't strictly true because we 'budget' to spend an amount of our working week doing non-billable work and new business is one of the ways that we spend that time. But if we don't keep it under control, it can eat into the time we have determined ought to be billable (or we simply work longer weeks) and so, either way, our utilisation falls. And that's not really what we are trying to achieve!

Throughout this section you will find pointers to when to walk away from an opportunity. There aren't any hard and fast rules other than to say that an application of good, common sense can save you from a lot of work and a lot of disappointment – if you're brave enough to do it. I can only urge you to think ahead very carefully about the so-called 'opportunity' and ask some pointed questions:

– Is this account really for us?

– Does this opportunity really fit with our business and strategic plan?

– Does the client understand what they are looking for?

– Is the brief clear and concise?

–   Is the budget stated and appropriate for the task?

–   Can we meet all those involved in the decision about who to appoint?

–   Have they short-listed us for good reason – our expertise, our experience, through a recommendation?

If the answer to any of the above questions is no, then consider very seriously *how* and *if* you want to take this forward. One no may be okay, especially if you can resolve the issue through discussion with the prospect; but if you have more than one no or if the prospect isn't prepared to engage in a sensible discussion about the issues, then walk away; you probably won't win it and, even if you do, you may quickly wish you hadn't!

But we mustn't get all negative here; after all, new business can be the most exciting part of the job. Winning provides the high that keeps us hungry and alive! It's motivating for the staff working on it and good for morale.

So let's take a look at the factors that will help us attract and win *more* than our fair share.

At this point, I am going to do something that I said I wouldn't do, namely get all 'clever-clever' and 'management-book' with a mnemonic. I defend myself with the excuse that it isn't my invention and that I have unashamedly stolen it from somewhere.

However, it is the **only one** that I have ever remembered and, to be fair, it's quite good and useful.

It is:

AIDA

And it stands for (in my interpretation at least):

–   Awareness

–   Interest

–   Desire

–   Action

It's a useful way at looking at how we, as consumers, end up doing or buying the things that we do:

- First, we need to be **A**_ware_ that something exists.

- Then we need to find it **I**_nteresting_.

- That interest needs to be developed into a **D**_esire_.

- And then we need to turn the desire into **A**_ction_ – to do or to buy!

At each stage, there needs to be some sort of input to move us on to the next one.

Consider this simple example.

A friend asks you whether or not you've heard a new album by XYZ; you've never heard of XYZ (although you are now _aware_ of their existence) and so you tell your friend 'no'.

He/she goes on to tell you how amazing it is and, given your respect for (and similarity to) your friend's musical tastes, you find it _interesting_ to hear more about the artist and the style.

Your friend plays you a couple of tracks as a result of your expression of interest and you agree with his/her assessment – it is very good – and your interest is turned into a _desire_ to own the album. You decide to get a copy at the next opportunity. And that thought gets logged away with all the other things you plan to do when you have a moment.

Then, a few days later, walking in town you see the album in a record store window and that prompts you to _act_. You go in and buy the album (or go home and download it to your MP3 player).

Job done.

At each stage in the example above there has been a stimulus and a response; and the response could have been either positive (and moved you on to the next stage) or neutral/negative (and stopped the process).

The same is true of pretty much everything we do and, especially, buy. And that applies to clients looking for professional service firms, too:

- If they aren't aware that your firm exists, you will never get any business from them.

- If they aren't interested by who you are/what you do the same applies.

- If their interest never grows into a desire to work with you, the relationship will be nothing more than a passing acquaintance.

- And if their desire never gets the stimulus it needs to convert it into action, it will fade into oblivion.

Your job is to build the awareness and then provide the necessary inputs to generate the momentum to move through all the stages. You could even compare this to the development of a relationship between two people – but I'll avoid that analogy!

So let's get back to winning new clients and apply the logic to that process to see what we need to do at each stage to generate the initial connection and the momentum to drive it forward.

Awareness

It has been my experience – and I'm frequently told that it is generally true – that most new clients are introduced to professional advisors and service firms through some sort of referral. It may be a direct recommendation from an existing or past client or it may be a little more distant. Either way, there is no doubt that a referred prospect is a much easier convert than a 'cold' one.

We all seem to know this fact too, judging by the acknowledgements I get whenever I mention this in conversation. And yet, even though we know it to be true, many (dare I suggest 'most') of us don't make the most of the opportunity it affords.

So let's take a look at what generates a referral.

The first necessity is that the referrer knows a bit about your business and judges it to be a good quality firm – or, more likely, knows *you* and judges *you* to be a good operator.

Then they need to know someone who might be a potential client.

Finally, the referrer needs to be motivated to make the referral.

Sort of obvious stuff I'll admit, but it does bear breaking down a little to see where and how we could help the process along and improve our referral rate.

We'll start with referrers. If we had more of them there is a reasonable chance that the number of referrals we receive might go up. And so to increase the number of referrals we receive, we first have to increase the number of referrers.

And that's all about building and maintaining a contact network. We all have a network but the question is how well do we develop it and do we really use it?

So ask yourself these questions:

- How many of my ex-clients, previous colleagues, suppliers and advisors am I still in regular contact with?
- Do I keep them abreast of what I/my firm am/is doing?
- Do I keep abreast of what they/their firms are doing?

The likelihood is that the list of contacts is much shorter than it could be and that the frequency and regularity of contact is less than ideal.

Now I know that we're not all natural networkers, but all it takes is a little discipline, structure and effort to be pretty darn good!

When I first started out in the communications business I met a man who for 27 years had held one of the top jobs at Cadbury. Then he 'retired'.

He then moved to one of the top advertising agencies in London to be deputy chairman. After another eight years or so he 'retired' again.

Then he was tempted back into an interim post at another big agency for another couple of years before 'retiring' for the third time.

Finally, after a little coaxing, he joined our firm as a part-time, non-executive director. He was probably 70 by the time he joined us, but was the finest networker I have ever met.

And he did it all by handwritten notes and a little black book – really. No e-mail in those days. He knew everyone and everyone knew him. The introductions he made were invaluable and it enabled us to get in to see potential clients that would never have even considered us because they didn't know we existed.

Because of our non-exec we not only raised our awareness but generated interest too – after all, if he had chosen us then we must be worthy of him, or so they assumed.

Today it takes so much less effort to keep in touch – so lesson one is: do it!

Stage two in the referral process is to ensure that your potential referrers actually rate you. This isn't too difficult because we can safely assume that if you are in regular contact, the respect you hold for them is likely to be reciprocated. If it isn't, the chances are that the regularity of contact will quickly diminish to nil when your e-mails aren't answered and your calls ignored!

So, assuming you have a good(ish) network and your contact is regular and positive, the next step is to tap into *their* network.

Like you, they may not be the best networkers in the world, but without doubt, they do have contacts – within their own businesses, within their trade and professional bodies and amongst their friends. And some of those contacts might be potential clients for you. So how do you get to meet them?

Okay, at this point I'm going to get a bit obvious again because the answer is blindingly simple – ask!

Very few of us actually ask direct questions, preferring the subtle approach, which, quite frankly is a waste of time. We think that asking for something in a direct, honest way will reflect badly on us or make us appear desperate. On the contrary, in my experience, many people find that sort of directness refreshing and reward it with equal directness.

Tell your chosen contact that you are looking for a new client in the 'xyz' field and ask them if they know anyone to whom they could and would refer you. They might say 'no', but you've lost nothing; they might say 'yes' and you're away into a new potential client. If you never ask, one thing is for certain – they won't do anything.

Stimulating referrals through your cultivated network is one way to build awareness and begin the AIDA process, but it isn't the only way.

All the marketing and communications professions have trade bodies and many of these have a referral service. In addition, there are often a number of commercial referrers or 'marriage brokers' who link up clients with appropriate agencies/consultancies. If they don't know you exist, they are never going to refer you to anyone.

So make sure you know who *they* are and that they have your latest credentials; that way you stand a chance of an unexpected referral. And don't just leave it there – try hard to get to know them; invite them to your offices for an update and add them to your 'network' to ensure that they hear from you regularly.

Now, right at the start of this section on awareness, I indicated that 'most' new clients arrive through some sort of referral and that seems to be true; but it is 'most' not all.   Others arrive because you've identified and targeted them or they've identified and targeted you. So let's look at each of these routes to see how we can maximise the chances of success.

Finding new clients from a cold start is a long and difficult process, which most of us would prefer not to do. Almost everyone I talk to tells me that 'cold calling' is the bit of their job they dislike the most. I always respond in the same manner, that if they are really 'cold calling' they aren't doing it right!

Stick with me here because I want you to follow a logic that may seem a little counter-intuitive on first sight – but it really isn't.

I'm going to assume that we all have some basic marketing collateral in place – a website, some sort of credentials presentation, case studies, that sort of thing. But when it comes to getting more proactive, we often look to some sort of mailing to try to generate initial awareness and interest.

The problem with that route is we do it pretty poorly, often targeting too many prospects and not following up effectively; we turn it into a numbers game a bit like the telesales organisations we all seem to hate (at least when we're the target)! And that's why we all hate doing it so much.

It is far better to target a *small* number of prospects and to approach them *individually* and in a *relevant, pertinent and interesting* way. Remember we are trying to build awareness (and a little interest) here.

I have often thought there is nothing worse than being approached by a potential service provider where the only content is a poorly veiled "we're looking for more business, how about you give us some?" Instead, we need to have a reason for making the contact, a purpose for the call or e-mail or whatever. And the purpose needs to be sufficiently relevant to the prospect to stimulate some intrigue.

It might be that you have some specific sector experience or specialist knowledge; you may have done some research or read a relevant technical article; you may have done some high-profile work for another client that could strike a chord with the prospect – it doesn't matter as long as it is pertinent.

Then find a way to present that to the prospect; ask for a meeting; and explain why; because, as I said earlier, it does no harm to be direct and up front.

Making a small number of properly thought through, purposeful contacts like this and continuing the dialogue on a regular basis is much more likely to lead to a new client than a shotgun approach to mailing.

Remember, we aren't looking for hundreds of new clients so we shouldn't use mass marketing techniques. We only need a few, so select those that you really want to work with and where you have something special to offer them and make it personal.

Finally, within this section on awareness, think about this: potential clients are also on the lookout for you. They know there are lots of firms out there, but not who they all are. My old firm did some research a few years ago to identify how well clients knew the consultancy/agency sectors in which they were working. Perhaps not surprisingly, the answer was 'hardly at all' in many cases.

Simply naming five advertising or PR agencies was beyond most until prompted and even then, awareness of anything outside the very biggest was extremely patchy. I think it is safe to assume that far fewer potential clients know about you than you would wish or hope to be the case.

So make absolutely certain that when a prospect does make contact as a result of their own research, you respond in the way you know you should. That means covering every eventuality and not assuming anything about any call.

Let me explain.

Some years ago I received a call from a mobile phone company (actually my secretary answered the phone even though I was in the office because I was in discussion with a colleague at the time). She asked all the 'right questions' about who was calling, from what company and what it was in connection with (how I hate being asked those questions now!) only to conclude that it was probably someone wanting to sell us mobile phones or network services.

She summarised this to me and I agreed that she should pass the call on to our IT director, who was out of the office on that day. So she told the caller that he really needed to speak to our head of IT and because he wasn't around today she would get him to return the call.

Needless to say he didn't return the call because he was led to believe that it was probably someone wanting to sell something and he had 20 calls a day like that!

It was only by chance, at a conference a week or two later that the potential client sought me ought and told me the tale "for my benefit"!

Lesson learned methinks!

I heard a statistic a while ago that over 50% of unsolicited calls from potential clients never connect with the person they need to speak to. I don't know that it's true but I suspect it is and it's totally avoidable by thinking ahead and thinking it through. Is a prospective client trying to reach you right now? Would they get you? If not, would your colleagues do the right things?

Think about it.

All too often, even today, I hear phones ringing out unanswered in professional service firms. But if the call isn't answered personally, callers may not leave a message, preferring to ring back later, by which time their stimulus to act may have gone.

The irony about all of this is that generating awareness all comes down to *communication* – and we ought to be good at that, shouldn't we?

Interest

There is a very fine line (or more of a blurry edge) between generating awareness and turning that into interest. That's because it is almost impossible to generate awareness of someone or something without at least beginning to stimulate interest (or boredom) at the same time.

As human beings, we already have such a wide experience that we can't help but begin to judge new people or things almost immediately we come across them. That's not necessarily a bad thing, but first impressions are hard to shift and that's what we're talking about here.

Only rarely, when, for example, we are introduced to a completely new technology that we simply have no understanding of, do we remain open-minded for long enough to absorb the messages and make a judgement as to our level of 'interest'. In other words, even then, we have to 'behave interested' in order to determine whether or not we really are.

Given that a prospective client is unlikely to be completely ignorant of the services that you offer, the chances are that you have only a few seconds to make the first, favourable impression.

In many ways, the dangerous analogy I rejected earlier between AIDA and the dating game remains true.

Turning *awareness* into *interest* needs a number of things to go right. Appearance is important, of course, but so too are personality, intelligence and style. All too easily the process of wooing a new prospect can fall down at this early stage simply because there isn't enough about you or your firm to make it *interesting*. So, we all need to work at it a bit.

You could say it all comes down to difference.

During the research I commissioned a few years ago to look at *awareness,* I also wanted to know whether or not the differences that I perceived between well-known PR agencies were significant enough for prospective clients to be aware of, and use, in their selection of possible 'partners'.

The results were very telling. In the PR field, with the exception of the firms the respondents were currently working with, they had very little knowledge about **any** of the others with the most common statement being that they were all 'much of a muchness'. There was almost nothing that provided differentiation between the bigger firms and even amongst the smaller firms the only points of difference seemed to be the sectors they served – and that wasn't generally understood except by those in that sector!

The same was true for advertising agencies. Even though they work hard to try to establish a clear positioning and point of difference, the end result is very fluid and unclear.

The point is this: none of us in marketing and communications services is big enough to afford the sustained and substantial marketing programme necessary to turn our firm into a brand.

And perhaps, even more importantly, we just aren't very different!

So-called points of difference have to be manufactured and are often so esoteric as to be either unbelievable or irrelevant.

So, when I said a few paragraphs ago that *'You could say that it all comes down to difference'* I was lying; well not lying exactly because you could say that – but I wouldn't, because it simply wouldn't be true.

What it *does* come down to is people; our people and how well they come across to potential clients; their intelligence, personality and style. Because (and even though this is the biggest cliché in our industry, it is no less true) people are our only real asset.

Remember, people do business with people!

So how then do we turn *awareness* into *interest*?

The answer is to front-up only the people in your organisation who are best at selling; those who are the most sensitive to the signals they are receiving; those who are flexible and can adjust their style to attract a wide range of personality types.

Every organisation has some. They are the ones who are confident but not cocky; generate sales without selling; have instant rapport and find it easy to mix in new company.

Some might call them the Hunters whilst the rest of us are the Gatherers and to an extent that is true. They are usually great at opening new opportunities but often lousy at keeping up a sustained level of interest; because before long they are hungry for something new.

Look for them in your organisation and keep them well fed with new opportunities to 'be interesting'. That's what turns *awareness* into *interest*.

But there is a problem here.

People move around from firm to firm and to a large degree that explains many of the ups and downs in fortune that our sector experiences. If people do business with people, then keeping your Hunters is a critical necessity. They are the key players in the business development role and to a very large degree form the personality of your firm.

Being reliant on these few, key people can be worrying so it makes sense to do everything we can to keep them happy and loyal. However, there is one other thing we can do which, although a little superficial and shallow, does help to create differentiation in the prospect's mind – create a style for your firm that reflects its personality and **values**.

Do it by presenting your people and your offices in a way that expresses those attributes. Do it well and keep it maintained and up to date. Nothing says more about a firm than a faded, jaded look that was once funky and young but is now nothing more than a grubby and uncared for reminder of how you used to be.

Review every aspect of your firm's contact with the outside world regularly and, ideally, through the eyes of a third party, so that you get to see it as a prospective client would. It may seem trivial and over-controlling, but small failures or dis-appointments at this stage can easily stall the process and the prospect may cool off for good.

Small things like the way your telephones are answered or the friendliness of your voicemail messages can be significant. The stacks of boxes or papers in the corner of the office tell a tale, too – you're not very tidy or concerned with detail.

Although I'm no advocate of an empty desk policy, there is little worse than the sight of piles of paper that clearly haven't been moved for weeks (or months). Keep the place clean, tidy and looking efficient.

And so back to our dangerous analogy – you wouldn't go on a first date with-out thinking about your appearance, would you? So why do it in business?

Desire

Turning interest into desire is really not too difficult and it all comes down to three things, the first of which is listening.

In my experience there is nothing prospective clients enjoy more than talking about their organisation or job with someone intelligent, understanding and interested; someone who asks lots of questions and who listens, actively, to the answers.

When I first started out in this business I thought that a credentials meeting was all about telling the prospect about our firm and impressing them with how experienced, clever and creative we were.

How wrong can you be?

Pretty quickly it became clear that the most successful meetings were those where we never got beyond a couple of slides or charts because the prospect started to talk. We went way off the agenda into the areas that were the burning issues for the prospect and were able to demonstrate that we had something to contribute to their thinking.

There is no magic formula here because every prospect is different, but there is a general rule: question, listen, and question again; ask for clarification; propose a few 'what ifs' and let the prospect make the running.

Remember, no matter what they tell you they are looking for, they will think they've found it if they see you as a like-minded individual, intelligent, friendly and supportive – but also challenging. And that means asking lots of questions, not from a checklist but from your head, relevant questions prompted by the content of what is being said, not what you've prepared earlier.

It's dangerous I know, but let's return to the analogy (even though I am bound to end up in hot water) and consider a couple's first date.

Imagine the man spending the first 20 minutes telling the woman all about him, what he likes, what he does for a living, all about his hobbies and sports. Sure, it's all relevant information that his date may want to know eventually, but I suspect the date could be the first and last! So much better to ask the other person a few well-chosen questions and provide short answers. That way you stand a chance of finding some common ground pretty quickly and maybe turn interest into something a little stronger.

But, as I said earlier, there are no rules.

Every meeting will be different and the real secret is to be flexible and adaptable enough to gauge whom you're dealing with and respond appropriately.

I remember a credentials meeting with a major prospect where, during the whole session that lasted well over an hour, we hardly spoke at all. We nodded at times, looked interested and quizzical where appropriate and made a few supportive noises. We asked a few questions but in the main the prospect made all the running.

At the end of the meeting the prospect made it very clear he liked what he saw and invited us to pitch.

The second critical factor is highlighted well in the example above – to be what they want you to be. By this I don't mean that you have to act out a role trying to present yourself as something you are not; the chances are that you will fail dismally if you try that and you'll end up looking pretty stupid. No, what I mean is that you need to adapt your style to match that of the prospect.

If he/she is a 'driver' – the sort of person who likes to be in control, take quick decisions and be very direct and active – then be similar; give short direct answers, don't beat around the bush, get to the point quickly and say what you think.

If, on the other hand, the prospect is very 'analytical', then offer lots of 'data' to support any claims you make, ask for evidence from them, show interest in reading the full research report not just the executive summary and so on.

You get the picture.

People do business with people, sure enough; but the implication is that they do business with people *like themselves*.

Finally, keep those dreaded case studies to a minimum. There is nothing worse than an endless stream of 'what we have done for other clients'. Prospects may well like to feel reassured that you have addressed similar issues to theirs before and operated in their sector, but that's about it.

Don't be tempted to put in all your favourites just because they won awards or demonstrate high creativity if they aren't directly relevant. It does more harm than good.

If the prospect is an 'analytical', then give them the full methodology and analysis of results; but if you have a 'driver' in the room, keep it to headlines only. Simple.

Action

Remember the story about a friend telling you about a new album from someone you hadn't heard of? Well the final part was when a specific stimulus (seeing the album in the record shop window) turned 'planning to' into 'doing'.

That's what this final section in AIDA is all about – providing the stimulus that causes the prospect to act and either brief you to do some work or ask you to pitch.

Once again, there is no secret; it just comes down to finding the right reasons to remain in touch and never being afraid to ask for the business.

It can go one of two ways: either the prospect remains open to your calls because everything has gone well up to this stage or they might simply 'disappear'. If they do, it is because something went wrong previously even though you may not have noticed.

Often I am told that the prospect is 'on hold' because things have changed their end. That may be true occasionally but mostly I believe that to be self-delusion. If the prospect doesn't want to stay in touch with you, the chances are that they have gone cold and no amount of stimulation is likely to reverse that.

So what sort of stimulation is likely to prompt that final step into action?

Well there is no doubt that everything that has gone before still holds true here. You need to remain efficient and accessible if/when they call you; you need to maintain the warmth and empathy that you have created.

Most of all, you need to maintain the challenging approach and demonstrate your real interest and desire to work with them through pro-activity.

Even though I hate the term 'pro-activity' we all know what it means: making the time to take some unprompted action that will impress the prospect and make them realise what they would have if they were working with you.

It means having ideas to talk to them about; making suggestions and asking more questions; it means showing real interest.

I have always found that a regular but varied selection of small actions on your part can be just the stimulus that's needed here – a phone call with a thought; a cutting sent through with a question or comment; asking for their advice… the list is pretty long.

Don't make yourself an irritant, though, or you'll quickly undo all the good work you've done to date. Keep the activities moderate and don't be afraid to ask the prospect where they are in their process. Ask for the business or the account and maybe, just maybe, they'll give it to you.

So, here we are, with a new prospect ready to give us a brief to pitch for their business. It's what we've been working towards for some time. Now you're probably expecting a long and detailed section on how to pitch and win.

Well, you're going to be disappointed because that's been done so many times and whilst everyone has some good ideas, the truth is nobody really knows, because every pitch is different.

What is clear is that there are plenty of ways to pitch and **lose!**

So here are my nine things to remember if you don't want to pitch and lose:

1. **Never accept a brief at face value...**

    ...there is almost always something else behind the brief, which you need to discover and address. And if they ask you to field the actual team that will handle the account, only do so if they are the best pitchers and presenters. Don't be tempted to take along poor presenters and find them something to present – it won't work. There's always a way to explain why your best [business winners] people are there.

2. **If the brief is clearly off the mark...**

    ...address it head on as requested but allow time to share your 'additional ideas' as well so that they can see the 'other way'. You need to be subtle here to ensure that you don't insult the client(s) but skilfully done it can be a real winner.

3. **Do everything in your power to meet ALL the decision makers before the pitch...**

    ...because there is nothing worse than preparing a presentation for people you have never met and don't know. If you really can't meet them, then the chances are that at least one of the prospect's team will give you some personality or hierarchy information that could be critical. After all, how can you *pitch* your presentation if you don't know whether you are presenting to Drivers, Analyticals or whoever?

4. **Ask lots of questions...**

    ...right through the build-up and preparation period. Be noticeable by your level of involvement and the amount of checking you do to ensure you have fully understood.

5. **Match their styles...**

    ...by ensuring that your team balances well with their team in personality types and style; try to use a one-to-one marking approach.

6. **Pitch first or last...**

    ...as the prospect will remember the *first* presentation because they were looking forward to it. They'll remember the *last,* too, because they'll be relieved that it's all over. Those in-between will blur into a forgettable melee of 'who was who?' and 'who said what?'

7.   **Make your presentation at least 90% about them...**
...because there is nothing more likely to turn the prospect against you than too much background and introduction, methodology and planning. Get to the first BIG idea quickly and deliver against what the prospect is hoping to see – what you are going to do for them.

8.   **Remember that pitches are about losing not winning...**
...because if you do all the build-up to the presentation well, the prospect will already have you way ahead on their mental scorecard – you'll have won already, provided that you don't blow it on the day. So don't be too rigid about your presentation, remain flexible and look for the prospect's signals that tell you to move on (or vice versa). Be ready to adapt what you say to the circumstances.

9.   **REHEARSE, REHEARSE AND REHEARSE...**
...because there is nothing worse (and more guaranteed to lose on the day) than an unrehearsed presentation with too many 'Jack-in-the-boxes' jumping up and down to present their bit. Nor is there any excuse for the obvious handover of *"er, well, that's it from me so, er, now I'd like to hand over to er... John"*; handovers just aren't necessary so when you've finished, stop and the next person starts.

A well-rehearsed presentation means that everyone in the team knows **exactly** what they plan to say and could do it with no visual aids or cues at all. The only way to do that is to ensure that everyone writes their own part. NEVER try to present something you haven't written yourself – it won't have the necessary conviction and passion.

Before closing this section on winning new accounts, I can't resist allowing my cynical side just a little release. A while ago I took a little time to try to analyse what it was that clients were looking for when selecting a marketing or communications agency to work with.

So I scanned all the trade papers and asked around and finally came up with *my* definitive list of what clients *say* they are looking for. Here it is:

1.   Knowledge of their business
2.   Creativity
3.   Good people
4.   Pro-activity
5.   Effectiveness

Looks sort of familiar doesn't it?

Seems to match with what you've heard over the years.

Yes?

No!

In my experience it may be what they say but it isn't how they behave. It's too rational and we all know that choosing a professional firm to support you isn't a wholly rational decision – it is heavily influenced by emotion, by the feelings you have about the firm.

How many times have you been told that "your presentation was really excellent and really addressed the brief very well; it was an extremely tough decision but unfortunately..."? You know the rest. When you find out who has been appointed, you can't understand it...

Well here's why: because the winners presented an *idea* that was so captivating it overrode all other considerations.

That's why it's so important to meet all the decision makers ahead of the pitch because it's the only chance you have to check out the likelihood of that circumstance.

Clients may *say* they want the list of attributes above but in my experience a lot of them actually react to a different set altogether:

1.   GREAT'BIG IDEAS
2.   Impressive results
3.   Confidence that you will deliver them
4.   Recognition for them (with their peers and bosses)
5.   Low risks or, preferably, guarantees.

It's ironic I know but there simply is no perfect solution to winning new accounts. It is all about how sensitive you are to what will attract the client and whether or not you can deliver it.

d. Reviewing your client list

At this point (and thinking about the primary aim of this book – to help firms like yours to achieve the profitability that they deserve), having looked at developing existing clients as well as winning new ones, there is one more job to be done before we move away from the general area of your client/account list – to review the clients you *have* in the light of the profit opportunity they represent.

Every firm I talk to seems to have a few legacy clients – clients you've held for a long time but which haven't really grown with you either in terms of scale or, more likely, hourly rate. These accounts hold back your average profitability and you need to decide what to do about them.

Unfortunately, it isn't necessarily an easy decision as it will depend on a number of factors, including your values, but if you are to achieve your desired profitability you can't ignore it as you may need to 'pass them on' if you are to achieve your aims.

We've touched on *legacy write-off* already and talked about the process for improving the financial return but, as I said then, there are no guarantees and it can take a long time.

So what should we do?

Start by drawing a grid like this.

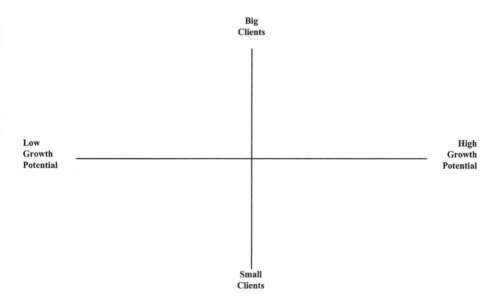

Then plot your *clients* into the grid, with the small ones with little growth potential in the bottom left quadrant and so on. I am using *clients* rather than *accounts* here as a large *client* might well have one or two small *accounts,* which, although potentially not very profitable in isolation, may be critical to holding on to the whole portfolio.

That said, within your firm, the allocation of clients into the grid will always be open to interpretation and to a degree all that really matters is that you get most clients into the correct quadrant. You don't need to fit each client into its quadrant *relative to every other one* as this process doesn't need that level of precision.

Once you've put your clients on the grid, you need to consider each quadrant individually and develop your objectives for each of the groups.

In all cases most of the objectives will be fairly obvious and largely the same – high-quality service, results, minimising write-off and so on – but the priorities will be different. The grid below shows the key priority for each segment:

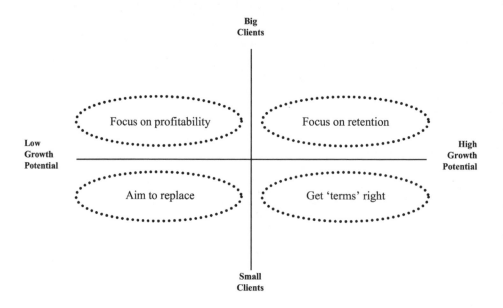

Let's examine the key priorities for each segment in detail:

1.   **Bottom left:**
      Here we have the legacy clients where there is little or no opportunity to improve the profitability or to grow them. You should aim to pass them on to another 'more appropriate' firm and use your experience to win a bigger or higher potential client in a similar business.

2. **Bottom right:**

    These are the clients where, although not yet *major* clients for you, there is significant growth potential – either from bigger budgets or additional accounts. It is critical to get the terms right now, otherwise you could be highly successful in turning a small, unprofitable client into a large, unprofitable one.

3. **Top left:**

    Both here and in the top right segment is where you earn most of your profit (and pay the overheads). These are the key clients you need for the future. However, they differ significantly left to right. Here, top left, the growth opportunities are limited so you need to focus on optimising profitability.

4. **Top right:**

    This segment presents you with a dilemma: the clients are already big but could be bigger still. The temptation is to go for the additional opportunities but I suggest a moment of caution before you do. Ask yourself what proportion of your total revenues this client represents; if, as a percentage, it is already close to (or more than) your overall profitability percentage then think very hard. Should you lose that client it would wipe out all your profits or worse.

The level of exposure you have to any one client needs to be a deliberate policy not an arbitrary occurrence. The temptation to continue to build business with one 'favourite' client has led to the downfall of many firms. If you decide to invest for growth do so in the knowledge that your exposure to this one client needs to be balanced; if you decide not to seek more business from them, then invest for *retention* and focus on building a high-quality service reputation.

e. Client development, retention and replacement strategies

Having looked at the client list and determined where our clients fall in the grid, we have been able to determine the key priority for each segment. Now we need to consider how we make that happen; what our client development strategies should be.

To do that you need to take a look at the final grid below and this should provide another of those 'Eureka' moments when so much of what has already been discussed in previous chapters comes together.

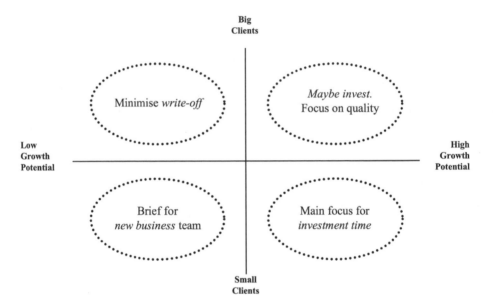

There is no reason to do this too often; I have always found that an annual review is enough and that achieving the right strategy for most of the clients is a big step forward from leaving it to fate.

So, without wishing to become too repetitive, and just in case that 'Eureka' moment passed you by, it's worth taking just a few paragraphs here to understand how the strategies for each segment fit into the bigger picture of our Vision, Mission and Values and top-level strategic plan.

Let's look at each segment in turn once more:

1.   **Bottom left:**
      Earlier we looked at winning new clients and concluded that a focused, person-

al approach was best. We also concluded that approaching prospects needed to be more than just a shot in the dark – there needed to be a reason for the call. What better reason is there than having a team with directly relevant experience ready, willing and able to devote themselves to a new challenge?

It may seem callous to simply walk away from a long-standing client because they're small, not growing or simply not profitable enough (and then, worse, approach a competitor) but that isn't quite what I am proposing. I'm suggesting that when a client becomes too small or too unprofitable for your firm, it is also likely that your firm is no longer the best one for them. Handled with sensitivity, a change (aided by your knowledge and experience of the industry) should be seen as the best for both parties.

Then you have free rein to seek out a bigger (or more dynamic) client for you. Before you think that I'm suggesting any breaches of confidentiality, far from it. I am not suggesting that you pass on such information to a competitor, merely that you use the general, public domain intelligence you have gained over the years.

2.   **Bottom right:**
Right the way through Part 1 of this book there were references to *investment time* and it was defined as:

> Planned non-billable time spent on growing/securing existing accounts – by account

Here, with the small but high potential clients, is where you should spend a large part of the *investment time* budget you have created for your team. This is where the glorious triad of the *client development strategy* meets the *existing client development* process meets *investment time*. It's quite a gathering and goes a long way towards bringing all the previous chapters together.

Think of it like this: by spending a large part of your planned *investment time* here, you are securing the big, profitable clients of tomorrow and going a long way towards curing the constant feeling of insecurity that dogs our every move.

3.   **Top left:**
The few large clients that, if the 80:20 rule applies (and it usually does), make up 80% of our revenue are all above the horizontal line in our grid; they are the solid earners that provide us with most of our overhead recovery and profit potential. We simply can't afford to lose clients from either group and so we must ensure that our *development strategy* reflects the need to keep these clients secure

as well as profitable.

So, yes we need to spend some of our *investment time* budget here, but fundamentally we should be using our knowledge and experience of working with them to minimise *unplanned write-off* and maximise the profit potential.

4.   **Top right:**
The dilemma of to grow or not to grow has already been covered and the risks exposed. There is no doubt at all that growth is tempting and hard to resist. After all, delivering high-quality service and building a strong, proactive reputation with a client is exactly what opens new doors. So, if you can't resist the temptation or if the client doesn't yet represent too high a proportion of your revenues, then go ahead and invest for growth but use the opportunity to improve your contractual security – your length of contract and/or notice period.

After all, the bigger the client, the harder they are to replace and the longer it takes.

All of which leads on very nicely to the next Chapter which is all about contracts and how to get good security as well as good remuneration!

Chapter 2

CONTRACTS, TERMS AND CONDITIONS

(The legal bits for non-lawyers)

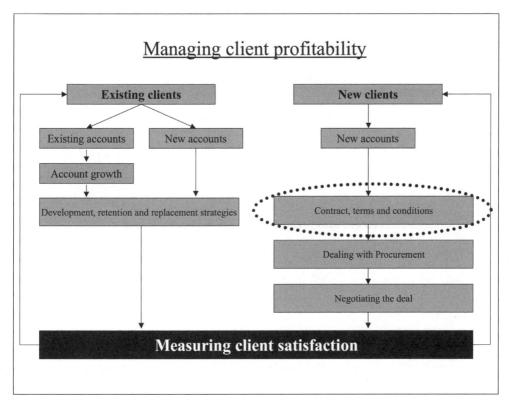

Given the title of this chapter, there is a very strong likelihood that it will become the least read part of the book – which I can understand being neither a lawyer nor an insomniac – but to skip it would be a big mistake.

Not convinced?

Okay, then here's a promise:

> The concepts described here have the potential to improve your profitability as much as all the other concepts in this book put together – really!

Still want to skip on?

Thought not – good decision I'd say.

Just stick with it through the boring bit and the rewards will be there at the end. You see chapters 3 and 4 all rely on a good understanding of the boring bit and without that you're lost.

So here's another promise to keep you with me: I'll keep it simple without a single 'heretofore' or 'party of the first part' in sight.

If I do that, do we have a deal that you'll keep going?

And just to keep your interest up, that was an example of what we're going to touch on in the coming pages – trading; the sort of trading we need to do if we want a good deal with a client; the 'if I do this, will you do that' sort of trade. Exciting isn't it?

Okay, enough of the 'trading' let's get on with the boring bit.

It seems to me that over the years, the importance of having some sort of contract for the work you undertake for a client has become more and more important. Yet many marketing and communications firms aren't as disciplined in this area as they should be. Often a client is taken on with nothing more than a tacit agreement and the important details about expectations, payment and the nature of the relationship are left unclear.

Worse, both parties might not even recognise the lack of clarity, both thinking it *is* clear, even though they might both have quite different takes on things. In such situations, you can be pretty sure that, as the buyer, the client's take on the deal will generally prevail as our insecurity about retaining the account kicks in.

In recent times, it has become common for clients to appoint agencies and consultancies on a purchase order basis, with no contract as such, just a purchase order to cover the agreed work and payment.

Safe enough one might think as a purchase order is generally a contract in itself – except that purchase orders always have a set of *Terms and Conditions* in small print on the back and they determine the rules. For example, a purchase order may specify 60 or even 90 days payment terms and once you've accepted the purchase order you are bound by those terms.

It's so much better to have a proper, negotiated contract where both parties are clear about and happy with the arrangement (and the art of getting a 'win/win' contract is covered in Chapter 3).

It also distresses me to hear of so many occasions when a contract has been intended, maybe even drafted, but never finally agreed or signed, often many months after the work has begun. Then something unexpected happens and the 'contract' is terminated only to lead to a major disagreement on the terms of the termination – something which happens more often than you might think and which is so easily avoided.

In my view that is just laziness and totally unacceptable.

I suppose the reason for contracts taking a back seat to the work up-front in the driving position is fairly simple: few if any of us are lawyers and contracts are a bit boring. After all, they only matter at the start of a relationship and at the end and getting on with the work (and earning the income) is really what it's all about surely?
Well, frankly, that's utter rubbish! And if you still believe that to be true then this book has failed in its first priority, to focus on improving the profitability and commercial success of your enterprise and reduce the ever-present insecurity we all feel. It's just another example of the professional taking priority over the commercial.

Contracts ensure that we have reasonable leverage when it comes to being paid and set out the standards we expect of each other. They provide security in a world where insecurity is the norm and allow us to take decisions in the knowledge that, for a while at least, our income stream is predictable.

This chapter is really all about stressing why having a contract and an agreed set of terms and conditions is so important; and why, with the ever-increasing presence of procurement on the client side of things, being familiar and at ease with 'Contracts for Services' is more important today than ever.

So let's take a closer look at what a 'Contract for Services' really is.

a. What is a contract and what is it for?

Once again here I find myself needing to be precise in the use of terminology and language because, most of the time, those of us outside the legal profession interchange the word 'contract' with 'terms and conditions' (or vice versa) without either recognising that they are different or, in most cases, even caring.

And I guess it doesn't matter that much because there are always lawyers around to unscramble any mess in the unlikely (?) event that it causes a problem – provided that we were happy to pay their fees!

So let's look at the differences between the two.

In the professional services world, the agreement between a client and a service firm usually takes the form of a 'Contract for Services' (not to be confused with a Service Contract, which is the form that a typical *employment* contract takes).

Basically a Contract for Services is the agreement between the parties that sets out what the service provider is going to provide, when they are going to provide it and how much they will be paid for it. In its simplest form, such a contract only has four elements (the four essential ingredients of any contract):

1.   **The offer and acceptance**
     This is the bit where you specify what service(s) you are going to provide and the client agrees.

2.   **The consideration**
     It is accepted within a contract that the provision of services needs to be undertaken in return for a 'consideration'. Generally speaking this is the amount that you are to be paid for providing the service. Interestingly, if the consideration is nil then generally the contract is invalid – that is why you often hear of deals being done for a nominal amount of, say, £1 or $1.

3.   **The start date**
     It's sort of obvious this one, defining, as it does, when the arrangement comes into force. However, it isn't necessarily the same as the contract date, which is when the deal is signed.

4.   **The finish**
     Equally obvious - this specifies when the contract ends. This isn't quite as

simple as it seems though, because whilst many contracts might specify a partic- ular date when the contract expires (as in a fixed-term contract), others, espe- cially in our world of marketing and communications, only specify a process for determining the end date – the giving of a period of notice, for example.

Interestingly, no contract *has* to be in writing for it to be legally binding, nor does it *need* to be signed; it's just a lot easier to prove if it is. So, verbal agreements *are* contracts provided that the four elements above have been agreed. The difficulty with verbal or unsigned contracts is that they are really only worth anything if both parties adhere to them or, if the worst comes to the worst, they can be proven. A signed, written docu- ment is much harder to deny than the spoken word.

Given the simplicity of a basic Contract for Services, it ought to be an easy task to get one in place for all clients. But, it isn't that simple because every contract has addition- al elements that need to be specified if the contract is going to work well – the terms and conditions that are applied to the contract – and we're going to look at those in the next section.

Before we move on to look at how we refine our contracts by adding terms and con- ditions to them, let's finish off the contract basics. It is highly desirable to get the con- tract in place and signed *before* starting the work to which it refers. All too often we *mean* to get the contract signed but are in such a hurry to get on with the work that it takes second place and once that happens it's not entirely surprising that we never quite get round to it.

Sometimes, though, it can be difficult to get all the 'to-ing' and 'fro-ing' done before work needs to start; this can be because of a looming deadline or, more likely, because the client takes his/her time or needs to run the details through the legal department – and that can take forever.

In my firm we had a solution for this eventuality, which we called the 'Understanding of Terms Letter'.

Basically it worked like this: if the contract proper was likely to take a while to finalise, we would write down, in a letter to the client, the basic elements of both the contract and the terms and conditions that were clear.

Typically, it would include the four key contract elements and those additional terms and conditions that were unlikely to need negotiating. Sometimes it was a very simple letter, other times it was more complicated. It wasn't embellished with legal jargon and, in all likelihood, it contained loopholes that could provide lawyers with months of debate; but that wasn't the point, it was simply a way of getting a temporary set of rules in place that were sufficient to make a good case should things go wrong.

The danger with the Understanding of Terms letter was that, once written and sent to the client, it could (psychologically) relieve the pressure on getting the proper contract, terms and conditions in place and so you need to put a time limit on it – no more than three months – and specify that in the letter. That way, the pressure to keep the discussions moving on, remains.

So what does such a letter look like?

Here's an example of such a letter:

Sample letter not for reproduction

Date

John Smith
Marketing Director
ABC Company

Dear John,

First of all let me say how much we are all looking forward to working with you and the team at ABC.

Whilst the detailed terms and conditions of the contract between our firms are being worked through I thought it would be sensible to put in writing what we have, so far, agreed, so that we can get the work underway without any further delay. The terms stated in this letter will only apply until the formal contract is put in place or for three months from today, whichever is sooner. Hopefully, the formal contract will be finalised and signed long before the three months is up.

What we have agreed so far is:

1. You have accepted our offer to act for XYZ as [insert professional service] consultants.
2. We will undertake the programme as defined in our proposal to you in return for which you will pay our fees of xxx.
3. We will commence work on dd-mm-yy.
4. We will invoice you on the start date for our initial three months fees and you will pay the fees within 30 days.
5. Any expenses incurred by us on your behalf will be billed to you monthly in arrears and paid by you within 30 days.
6. At the end of three months from today, should the formal contract not be in place (and in the absence of any further temporary agreement between us), we reserve the right to cease work.

I am sure that we will work well together and look forward to a long and mutually beneficial relationship between our firms.

Kindest regards.

Yours sincerely

As you can see from the letter, there are many elements left unspecified and so it should never substitute for the formal contract, terms and conditions, but it is better than nothing and, in essence, provides for an 'up to three month fixed-term contract' on basic, agreed terms.

Does it work?

Well yes and no.

In the main it provides the sort of cover that gives a measure of comfort during the period of negotiations and allows work to start without too many worries – provided you use it! The problem is that even with a standard format available, it can be difficult to get the senior team to use it consistently; it often gets forgotten.

To get round this problem, I strongly suggest that you make 'contract cover' another of the bonus criteria for your senior team to ensure that they are well motivated to do it.

Another problem is to ensure that the people who do eventually sign the contract have the authority to do so. It is often assumed that, provided the signatory works for the organisation in question, the organisation will be bound by the contract. This is often not true and organisations have been known to claim a contract is invalid because the signatory was not authorised to commit the organisation to that level of expenditure (usually when they are trying to get out of a long notice period and after the signatory has 'left').

So it's well worth checking whether or not the proposed signatory for the client has the necessary level of authorisation. Generally, a director or equivalent outside the UK, would be recognised in law as representing their organisation and so would be deemed to have authority.

Finally, it is also worth making sure that you are contracting with an *organisation* that is recognised as such – a company, partnership or registered charity, for example. Brands are not generally recognised and, to be honest, it's hard trying to sue a handbag, a software package or a pharmaceutical for breach of contract! The same is true of dot.coms; so always ensure that your contract is with the legal organisation and not a nonexistent (in law) 'name'.

b. Terms and conditions – what are they and what do they do?

As you will have gathered by now, a contract comprising only the four essential elements is not really much use for the majority of services that the marketing and communications sector provides. That is why we need a set of *Terms and Conditions* appended to or included within the contract itself.

Typically, the terms and conditions (we'll refer to them as T&Cs from now on) contain all the details that make the contract work for you and your client and define the *way* in which the contract will be operated – in a way they are a bit like the *values* that relate to a strategic plan.

The nature and extent of the T&Cs that you apply to your contracts may vary from contract to contract, but it's probable that, even throughout the variations, many will remain pretty similar. That is because we need to plan for largely the same circumstances and eventualities.

In many ways T&Cs evolve from the four key contract elements and (although far from an exhaustive list) typically cover:

– The length of the contract.
– How and when the contract will end.
– The work to be undertaken.
– How the work will be performed/administered.
– The charging basis.
– *How/if 'expenses/disbursements/bought-in costs/account costs' will be charged.
– Whether or not mark-up will be applied to the above.
– What mark-up percentage will apply.
– How and when payment will be made.
– How late payment will be dealt with.
– How disputes will be resolved.
– The protection of both parties from damage.
– Confidentiality, intellectual property and copyright.

As you can see from the list above (let alone from all the other possible T&Cs not men-

---

You will notice here that I have used four different terms because, once again, there is no consistency in how we refer to the costs we incur on behalf of clients either in carrying out the programme or administering the account. For clarity I have always used the following definitions: Expenses – out-of-pocket costs incurred by the team in the management of the account, eg travel costs, subsistence, generally not marked up; disbursements – I never used this term but, technically, it is another way of referring to bought-in costs, generally marked up before invoicing to the client; bought-in costs – the programme implementation costs incurred with third parties on behalf of the client, generally marked-up; account (or sometimes 'house') costs – the internal share of office costs incurred on behalf of the client during the administration of their account, eg telephone calls, photocopies, postage etc.

tioned), the opportunity for variation is almost limitless. That is why most firms have a standard set of T&Cs that form the basis for the deals they do with clients. In many cases this is based on a guideline set by the appropriate trade association for their area of business. In the UK for example, the PRCA (Public Relations Consultants Association) provides a 'standard form' contract and T&Cs to its members. Many firms simply adopt it as it is whilst others adapt it to their specific requirements.

More and more, though, clients are rejecting their agency or consultancy standard contract and providing their own version instead. Frequently, in my experience, these contracts and T&Cs are quite different from the service firm's own and are heavily biased in the client's favour.

Yet again, our insecurity shines through and we often simply accept the client's contract (sometimes without even negotiating it) as we feel that the client has the upper hand in the relationship. We feel that *we* need *their* business more than *they* need our *expert help*.

And that can be really bad for our profitability!

Ideally we want to use *our* standard contract and T&Cs as the basis for the relationship because it has been developed specifically to deliver the commercial performance we want.

This highlights the first lesson in negotiating deals with clients (which we will look at later in this chapter) that the first issue to resolve is whose agenda will drive the negotiation, yours or theirs? Put in simple terms, whose contract and T&Cs will be used as the basis for negotiation because if it's yours, then they have to negotiate you *away* from it; if it's theirs, then you have to negotiate *them* away – and that is the hard part.

The secret to establishing whose contract and T&Cs will form the basis for any negotiation is to provide them *as early as possible* in the process.

When you meet for the very first time in the AIDA process it is worth providing a set of T&Cs in any handout or document you provide. Point out that it's there 'in case they are interested', but without dwelling on it or drawing too much attention to it.

Then do the same thing again at the pitch. Put your T&Cs into the document or hand them out at the end – whatever you feel more comfortable with. By so doing you are stating up front that, if they choose to do business with you, it will be on this basis.

It will rarely preclude a client from wanting to negotiate changes, but it does make it more likely that *your* T&Cs will form the basis from which *they have to negotiate* rather than the other way around – and that's the best starting position you can get.

c. What should be your 'standard terms?'

Across the whole marketing and communications services sector there seem to be three basic approaches to working with clients – project by project, fixed-*term* appointment and *ongoing* appointment. Each has its strengths and is appropriate for certain types of relationship and work.

Sadly, all too often, the type of contract chosen isn't the right one for the nature of the work.

So let's look at this in more detail starting with the approach that, often at the agency's cost, is gaining in popularity amongst clients.

1.   The 'project-by-project' basis

It is hardly surprising that this way of working together is becoming increasingly popular amongst clients as it is the one that requires the least commitment on their part. In some cases the work is literally briefed project by project with the briefs being spread amongst a number of 'rostered' firms.

In other cases, there is a hollow commitment to an ongoing relationship but with a project-by-project approach. They appoint a firm on this basis, promising a regular stream of projects, but there are no guarantees. Normally that means no contract, just a purchase order per project.

Under this arrangement you could be fooled into believing that you have an ongoing client, but in truth the work-flow can start, stop, increase or decrease at will and, generally, has to be done under the terms and conditions of *purchase* defined by the client. This usually means accepting *their* billing and payment terms as well as many other, often quite onerous, obligations. These will be spelled out in the small print on the back of their purchase orders so it is worth taking the time to read what it is you are accepting.

Sometimes the arrangement can work well, but it depends entirely on the goodwill of the client and his/her integrity. More often it is simply a way for the client to maintain complete flexibility at your expense.

It isn't a very attractive proposition for the agency as it provides little security and is usually totally unpredictable. This creates its own problems for both income forecasting and capacity planning.

Most frequently, the solution to this unpredictability is to assume that there *will* be a regular flow of work and to staff up to meet it. However, when, inevitably, the flow is interrupted or delayed, the over-capacity erodes the firm's profitability very quickly.

So project-based accounts are potentially much less profitable than contracted accounts.

This is precisely why it is important to have **two** rate cards for your services (see Part 1, Chapter 3b) – your standard rates (calculated in the way shown in Part 1, Chapter 3a), as well as your discounted contract only rate.

Standard rates, which have an extra premium built in, should be used for all project-by-project accounts so that the profitability of the work *done* is enhanced sufficiently to allow for occasional erosion.

Your contract rates should only apply to properly contracted work where the level of protection provided in the contract merits the reciprocal discount to the client.

Fundamentally, the standard rate card plays two important roles: to provide the additional profitability to offset the inevitable unpredictability of the account and, probably more importantly, to provide you with the opportunity to offer a discounted rate in return for a more secure relationship. It's a strong trade and one that often succeeds.

Either way is fine.

However, if you do settle for a project-by-project basis you don't have to also settle for the client's terms of purchase. It is well worth trying to negotiate an umbrella contract and T&Cs that, whilst not offering all the protection of a full rolling contract, can provide some important protection.

So much here depends on the client's attitude towards the relationship (and it's clear from the fact of the arrangement on offer that the client isn't looking to be tied down), but it is at least worth asking (or trading for) some or all of the following:

1. Formal appointment as an agency/consultancy of record.

2. Minimum fee income – per month/quarter/year as appropriate.

3. Appropriate notice period with payment (or work) during notice period based on average (or agreed minimum) revenues during previous

3/6/9/12 months…

4. No work for 'x' months triggers notice period at your discretion.

5. Account costs at your standard rate.

6. Mark-up on bought-in costs.

7. Invoicing timing (50% upfront?)

8. Payment terms – 30 days.

9. Interest on overdue payments.

The likelihood of getting much of the above will depend on what you have to offer in return and the reality is that, if you succeeded in getting most of the above (especially the minimum payment and notice period), you would, in effect, have a rolling contract. So be prepared to trade some, or all, of your 15% standard rate premium – another reason why a standard rate card is an essential weapon in the battle for profitability and security.

2. **The 'fixed-term' approach**

This is a big step up from a straight project-by-project arrangement. First, it provides a period of security and, secondly, it should enable you to forecast revenues and capacity requirements fairly accurately.

The big problem with fixed-term contracts is that they expire and even with the best of promises, there is no guarantee they will be renewed.

Now here I need to make another (!) confession because for many years I considered that a long fixed term of, say, two years or more was, on balance, about the same as having a regular rolling contract with a minimum term and notice period (see below). After all, a fixed two or three-year period provides a lot of security and that goes a long way towards offsetting the downside of expiry.

In many ways I was right, but I hadn't taken into account other downsides: that clients generally want to peg the hourly rates for the period of the contract and that, in the same way that the client is tied in to you for the period, so are you to the client – and with a difficult or unreasonably demanding client that can be quite damaging.

So the message for fixed-term contracts is this. Accept them by all means but take into account the downsides when negotiating the deal. Don't be lulled into accepting that longer periods are necessarily more attractive unless you are confident that the relationship will be a good, solid one. Don't be talked into fixing your rates for a time period beyond what you consider to be commercially fair – in most cases 12 months.

And one more thing – and I know it will be a little controversial – but think of any fixed-term contract that is for less than 12 months as a project and set your rates as such.

No-one would argue with the claim that a fixed-term contract of one month is, in reality, just a project; and I suspect that at three months the same would be true. So at what point does a project become a fixed-term contract? Six months? Nine? 12? You'll need to decide for yourself and draw a line somewhere. My view? Well 12 months always worked for me.

Use the same argument about standard/contract rates to try to get a rolling contract or a longer fixed term if that's appropriate but don't just agree to your contract rates for, say, a six-month contract without a fight. After all, don't your long-term clients with rolling contracts and notice periods deserve some benefit for their commitment?

Assuming you've accepted a client on the basis of a fixed-term contract of 12 months or more (because anything less would be a project, wouldn't it?), what contract, terms and conditions would be appropriate?

1. A formal written and signed contract with start date, end date, defined services and defined fees.
2. How additional work will be charged.
3. How any requested changes will be agreed.
4. Invoice timing and period – advance or arrears, monthly or quarterly…?
5. Account costs definition and billing rate – flat rate percentage or ad hoc?
6. Mark-up on bought-in costs.
7. Payment terms – 30 days.
8. Interest on overdue payments.
9. Confidentiality, intellectual property and copyright.

And probably the most valuable of all…

10. A date by which termination must be confirmed, in the absence of which the contract is automatically renewed for a further 12 months.

Given the negotiable nature of T&Cs, you are unlikely to end up with everything you want, but if you don't ask, you won't get, if you'll pardon the cliché.

The trick is in knowing that the best way to get what you want is by offering something the client wants in return (we'll look at the art of trading later).

3.   The 'ongoing' relationship

For most providers of professional services, this type of relationship is ideal – a client who is committed and intending to continue working with us indefinitely. Even if/when the relationship does reach the end of the road, there is still a period of notice to work through (or be paid for in lieu), which gives us time to replace the business or, at worst, to adjust our future capacity.

This gives us the best we could realistically hope for – long-term commitment *and* reasonable security. What's more, it is relatively easy to forecast revenues and capacity requirements.

The key considerations to take into account when setting up a rolling contract are not that different from the fixed-term version, except you need to specify the period of notice to be given and, ideally, the minimum contract period before notice can be given. This is important because a rolling contract without a minimum term could be little more than a project. Imagine a rolling contract with three months' notice where notice is given after three months; that is simply six months' work and, in my view, shouldn't qualify for contract rates.

So use the project/contract rates argument to negotiate a minimum period of, say, 12 months, which must be completed (or paid for) before notice can be given.

Clearly there can be no absolutes here because every relationship will be different but that shouldn't stop you from having a standard set of T&Cs from which to negotiate an agreement.

A standard rolling contract and T&Cs would normally contain:

1.   A formal written and signed contract with start date, defined services, defined fees, minimum period of contract and the length of notice period to be given (either way) prior to termination.
2.   How additional work will be charged.
3.   How any requested changes will be agreed.

4.   Invoice timing and period – advance or arrears, monthly or quarterly…?

5.   Account costs definition and billing rate – flat rate percentage or ad hoc?

6.   Mark-up on bought-in costs.

7.   Payment terms – 30 days?

8.   Interest on overdue payments – usually 3% above base rate per month or pro rata.

9.   Confidentiality, intellectual property and copyright.

In addition (and this applies equally to any type of contract, whether an umbrella project-based arrangement, fixed-term or rolling) you may well want to include a few 'restrictive covenants' – legalese for things that you and/or the client agree **not** to do. Breaching of confidentiality is an obvious one but others, perhaps less obvious, can be equally important.

For example, it is quite common to agree within the T&Cs that neither you nor your client will poach each other's staff during the period of the contract, nor for an agreed period after termination.

Although this is quite a good deterrent, it is extremely hard to enforce because when the worst happens and your account director resigns to take up a post with the client it will inevitably be positioned that he or she applied for the job and wasn't poached. That said, many clients do take the clause seriously and wouldn't behave that way anyway.

Just in case, this can be addressed through the employees' contracts of employment by including a clause that binds staff to not applying for a job with any client organisation – but again, it is difficult to enforce.

A slightly more powerful way of addressing the same issue is by specifying that if either party does recruit from the other, a recruitment fee will be payable, perhaps equal to, or higher than, that of a commercial recruitment consultancy – 30% to 50% of the remuneration maybe. That way, the cost of finding a replacement is borne by the 'poacher'- which seems fair doesn't it?

The other major area of restriction is usually conflicting accounts and this one can become a minefield. That's why the next section is devoted to this one issue and how to avoid the excessive restrictions it can sometimes impose.

d. How to deal with conflict and/or exclusivity

Let's consider a lawyer being asked to represent a client in a claim against his/her employer. No-one would expect to find that same lawyer also representing the employer would they? It would be like having an argument with yourself – ridiculous and frankly impossible to conceive.

Or is it?

What if the lawyer concerned wasn't an individual but a small firm and had two separate teams working, one for the claimant and one for the employer? That could work couldn't it?

Or if the firm had two offices in different cities?

Or different countries?

At some point, surely, the distance between the teams would be sufficient to ensure complete confidentiality?

Well, to be blunt, even if that is true, it really doesn't matter; because the issue is not one of distance but of *conflict of interest*. No matter how far apart the two teams are *the firm* has a competing and conflicting interest in their briefs from their clients.

Given that none of us is perfect, there will inevitably be occasions when choices have to be made that will advantage one party at the expense of the other; and that simply cannot be right. That's why it is accepted that law firms may only ever represent one side of a case.

Now of course, the marketing and communications sector isn't quite the same and the rules are much less clear.

However, what is clear is that it's *another* area where we allow a lack of precision in *meaning* to infect our business. We don't fully understand what client conflict is, and sometimes issues of supposed conflict are really no more than clients seeking 'exclusivity'.

We can't blame the client completely because we have gradually allowed the meaning of 'client conflict' to morph into a much wider encapsulation of anything 'competitive' and it's time to get back to somewhere much closer to the original intent if we are to avoid yet another drain on our potential profitability.

That said, there is a critical clue to solving the issues of client conflict hidden in the above legal scenario: when we refer to 'client conflict' what we really should be describing is a 'conflict of interest' that would prevent us from delivering integrity and total support to a client; and understanding that point is essential to unravelling how we should behave.

Once we approach the issue this way, the solutions to many of the situations in which we find ourselves become easier and much more obvious.

It is generally accepted that agencies and consultancies will not accept briefs from clients for directly competing products or services and that seems perfectly right and proper. That would create a real conflict of interest – imagine, for example, a creative team have come up with a brilliant idea, which client would get it? The one who pays the most? The one you like the most?

It simply would be unethical (and lacking in any integrity) to work this way. And in all likelihood no client would accept it either.

But that is the simple-to-solve case; the straightforward one; the no-brainer.

What about being asked to work for competing brands but in *different market sectors*? Or for competing companies but on *different product types*?

This is where having a clear understanding of the difference between a 'client conflict' and 'client exclusivity' is critical.

Let's look at each in turn:

1. **Client conflict**

    This is where working for two clients of competing brands would/could lead to a conflict of interest for you as the professional service provider. You could find yourself in an untenable position where you would have to give one client preference over another or do something for one client that was potentially damaging to another.

    This is simply unacceptable.

2. **Client exclusivity**

    This is where a client requires you not only to avoid conflicts of interest (which you would) but a bit (or sometimes, a lot) more. Often this can be an undertaking not to work for a competitor even though it may be in a different market sector or on a non-competing product. This is not client conflict as there can be no real conflict of interest for you as you do not represent both clients in any head-to-head competition.

Imagine, for example, that you work for a drinks company supporting a brand of whisky and they ask you not to do any work for any competing whisky brand; that would be a completely reasonable request on the grounds of a direct, head-to-head conflict of interest. And I suspect there would be few if any disagreements.

However, if that same drinks company were to ask you not to work for *any* drink brands from *any* other drinks companies, that would seem to be asking for your services *exclusively* and would, to my mind, be unreasonable.

The question, though, is this: at what point between the two relatively clear scenarios above does a request for no conflict of interest turn into a request for exclusivity?

What if they asked you not to handle any other *spirit* brands?

Or any other alcohol brands?

Or any other drinks at all, including soft drinks?

Or tea?

Or coffee?

Or soup?

I found myself in exactly this situation some years ago when a major drinks distributor (of spirits) proposed contract conditions that included a clause asking that we agree not to work on any other drinks, be they spirits (reasonable), wine or beer (somewhat tenuous), soft drinks (clearly unreasonable) or even tea, coffee or water (a non-starter)! They argued that every decision to have a drink could, theoretically at least, be a decision between one of their spirit brands and anything else. We disagreed and argued that, because they also had wines and beers and soft drinks in their portfolio, all handled by other agencies, we could only agree if they also gave us all that business, too.

They didn't; but at least they saw the logic of the argument and finally we settled on a reasonable 'no conflict of interest' basis that included all other spirits (even some for which they did not have a brand) but excluded everything else.

As with so many issues in business, the answer is rarely the same twice because every situation is different. It requires a certain amount of judgement and negotiation to reach an acceptable compromise.

But at least the argument can be logical and powerful if you are clear about the difference between client conflict and exclusivity.

The argument goes something like this:

1.   You wouldn't handle any competitive whisky brand because it would represent a conflict of interest.

2.   However, where there is no such conflict of interest – for example, with the slightly ridiculous suggestion of soup – then the client is asking for the *exclusive* use of your services. It won't prevent the so-called competing product from being supported by someone else; it will simply block you from a potential income stream.

   So if the client *insists* on this restriction on your business, you should ask for compensation, something equivalent to the potential loss of trade, in return. It's a simple trade – if we do this, then will you do that? The premium ought to be substantial enough to make the client reconsider the validity of their request so maybe something around +100% on the fees might do the trick.

But where do you draw the line?

For me, the answer is straightforward: immediately after direct, head-to-head competition. So in the case above, anything more than another whisky brand would represent some measure of exclusivity and would need something in return.

The question is what?

And here, I leave that decision up to you with the advice that it should have broad 'equivalence' to the level of market restriction you suffer. You may choose to use an 'exclusive rate' argument or look for much greater security through a longer contract or notice period. You could ask for additional 'spirits' business from them if you agree not to work for anyone else…

What is clear is that when a client asks for exclusivity under the guise of conflict, don't be taken in and don't agree without getting something in return…fair's fair, after all!

e. Trading – the basis of negotiation

So far in this chapter about contracts, terms and conditions, there have been a number of references to trading and you will have begun to get the picture. Fundamentally, the concept is based on the principle that if two parties want to agree to work together, then each and every additional benefit that one party wants to secure ought to be off-set by an equivalent benefit for the other party – the principle of equivalence or, as I prefer to call it, fairness.

As we will see later, negotiating a deal really isn't about winning or losing (as many seem to think – and behave!) but about finding the middle ground where both parties feel like winners – the true win/win situation.

So, in theory at least, negotiating the T&Cs of a contract ought to be relatively easy – simply a matter of ensuring equivalence.

Unfortunately, it's rarely as simple as that and all sorts of other factors come into play: psychological games of dominance, macho posturing, natural competitiveness, wanting to beat the other party... and so on.

By far the biggest difficulty is working out the 'equivalence' between two completely different requirements. For example, imagine that your client has asked for extended credit terms of 60 days; what would you ask for in return that provides you with an 'equivalent' benefit? A longer contract? Longer notice? Retention of copyright?

The most equivalent trade would be for earlier invoicing – 30 days earlier – as the cost of 60 days credit would be exactly offset – the invoice would become due for payment on exactly the same date as it would have originally. And this may work because the client may simply be looking for a longer period to administer payment rather than the cash-flow benefit of later payment.

The difficulty is in knowing what is in the client's mind and so you need to ask! Often when faced with a request from a client, we respond to the request at face value rather than asking what is behind the request. Why are they asking for that?

Years ago, one of my bosses used to say that behind any question is another – the real one – and that is what we need to discover. It seems he was right, certainly in this type of situation anyway. In the case above, the front question is asking for extra days of credit when in reality the question behind that is about extra time to administer payment. If the real question had been asked, we could have responded with a 'yes, we'll invoice you 30 days earlier'.

If we knew that the client was looking for more time for administration of the invoice, the above trade ought to work – they get what they want and we do too (the win/win).

However, if the client was really looking for the cash-flow benefit of later payment, then our suggestion would be unlikely to succeed; and we would need to find a different trade to provide us with equivalence. That might be by withdrawing another client request from the negotiation by saying that 'if we agree to the credit terms, then we couldn't accept your request for a lowering of the mark-up percentage', for example.

This raises another important point about trading: that to succeed in getting equivalence, it is essential that *all* the requests for variance from the standard T&Cs are revealed *before* you commence the negotiation. That way you stand a chance of being able to trade acceptance of one request against the rejection of another.

Eureka! The logic for starting with *your* T&Cs as the basis for negotiation becomes clear. By ensuring that your standard T&Cs have a certain amount of room for manoeuvre built in, you can usually meet enough of your client's requests for 'improvement' and still retain your desired profitability.

On the other hand, if you are using the client's proposed T&Cs as the basis, the chances are that they will start out offering low profitability and you will have to trade your way up – which is much, much more difficult.

So, the principles of trading and equivalence are pretty simple and easy to understand. The difficulty is that underlying each and every trade is the equivalence judgement or calculation. That can be very difficult especially when trying to match two completely different items. It requires that you start with a set of proposed T&Cs for which you can judge or calculate the potential profitability; you then need to be able to assess the impact of each and every trade on that profitability.

That is not easy.

When you then add into the mix other *non-financial* elements, such as contract longevity and security, the task becomes even harder, requiring good judgement at every stage.

As will become much clearer in Part 2, Chapter 4, the traditional way of doing this requires experience, skill and a lot of courage, risk taking and brinkmanship.

This is why I decided a few years ago to develop a much simpler way of assessing trades, which would not only be very much easier but more consistent, more accurate and faster. And which would make negotiating a more pleasant and confident experience for everyone.

So, did I succeed or was it another fruitless crusade in pursuit of the Holy Grail?

Well you'll have to wait until Part 2, Chapter 4 to find out – unless you skip straight to there now, in which case you'll miss out on a critical prerequisite to successful negotiating – knowing who you're dealing with; because dealing with 'Procurement' is what the next chapter is all about.

Chapter 3

PROCUREMENT – THE NEW ENEMY?

(The client's new face)

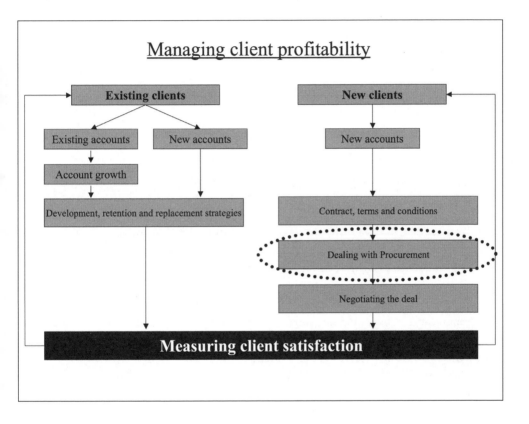

It's all well and good discussing contracts, terms and conditions but, before negotiating a deal, it is always wise to try to understand who you are dealing with.

Historically, the deal for marketing and communications services was negotiated between the senior client contact and the lead director from the agency. It was always tense – a bit like a prenuptial agreement – as it was the final hurdle to be overcome on the path to a great, long-term relationship.

If all of us could be unemotional, objective and dispassionate it would be easy; but in an service sector overflowing with emotionally driven, passionate professionals, it is hardly surprising that contract discussions are often tense, difficult and the source of a lot of anxiety.

Which is precisely why they often end up overly favourable to the client, are frequently left uncompleted and occasionally even become the source of a major falling out before the relationship has even begun to bloom.

Fortunately, we all now know that negotiating the deal is often best left to someone who is less emotionally tied to the relationship than the parties who will be working together; and that is a great step forward.

Except for one thing.

It really isn't true!

Now don't get me wrong here, the bit about being best left to less emotionally involved individuals **is** true, but whether it's a great step forward is debatable.

More and more clients have adopted it and put it into practice. But as the service providers, most of us understand the *logic* but few of us seem able or prepared to *do* it. I still hear regular tales of 'how difficult it is to do the deal' from agency and consultancy directors who headed the winning team; how 'being tough in the negotiation undermines the start of the relationship'; how 'easy it is to upset the client'.

Actually that is a great step backwards because it provides clients with another advantage – they can be dispassionate, objective and even disconnected, whilst we are often still desperate to ensure we really have won the account and to get started. So we are tempted to give away more than we should.

It results from our lack of confidence and insecurity brought about by our inexperience as negotiators and, frequently, our lack of training.

That's where the client often has a big advantage; not only do they train themselves better (especially in commercial skills), but often they have specialists who do nothing other than negotiate deals – they're called procurement officers and they are invading our space with devastating effect.

So where have these specialists come from?

Well the truth is that they've existed for decades in various guises. Their roots are in manufacturing where, as 'buyers', their role was to source and buy the raw materials needed for the factory. They worked to a specification provided by the engineers and their brief was to buy the necessary materials at the best prices and to ensure that the production process had all the required materials, of the right quality, in the right quantities, at the right time.

Initially the function was more one of relieving those responsible for manufacturing from one of the more tedious parts of their job, but it quickly evolved as the potential for cost savings became clear. Buyers began casting their nets wider and using basic competition to drive prices down.

The general pressure on costs hit the suppliers, so they too learned to use the same approach on their suppliers – and so it all began.

Much like the rise of any new concept, the buyers gained power through their ability to improve the margins (and competitiveness) of their firms and as they became more sophisticated and knowledgeable, the Buying Department evolved into the Purchasing Department and, most recently, into its current incarnation – the Procurement Department – where their sphere of influence is wider than ever.

Okay, time for another small diversion – but one that is relevant as you will see.

Economists rarely agree on very much at all, but on one thing they do seem to agree: that there is an economic cycle; a period of time during which the economy seems to go full circle and then start repeating itself (to a large degree at least). Many say the cycle is about 12 years and that seems to have some evidential support.

I have my own theory on this (unlikely, I feel, to get much expert support) – that the cycle is driven by each new generation of 'C Suite' executives recognising that to change the way their predecessors operated, they need to invent a new approach (usually reversing their predecessor's philosophy), which turns out to be exactly what their predecessors two generations before did. They probably don't know that's what they're doing because, all too often as humans, we assume that everything we work out for ourselves is new, whereas it is usually just reinventing the wheel.

You see this in every aspect of life where fashion or trend has a part to play. It might be relatively innocuous as in this season's colour or the height of heels, but it can equally apply to rather more impactful areas such as management philosophy and social/political leanings.

One of the most obvious cycles seems to be related to the level of optimism in business and it goes something like this: when times are good, CEOs spend their time looking at how marketing and sales can add to their firm's profitability and profit growth through increasing the top-line revenue stream. This is when the marketing staff have the CEO's ear and hold the strongest hand.

However, when the outlook is less favourable CEOs switch their strategy away from the top-line and onto cost control. They aim to improve profitability and deliver profit growth through improved cost-efficiency. The marketing team no longer have the power to deliver and their place at the top table is taken by Procurement. So does the cycle drive the action or the action drive the cycle? Who knows?

As I write this, in the middle of the first decade of the 21st century, we are in the middle of a phase of heavy cost control and this is borne out by figures from the US that suggest that the average life span in the job for a VP-Marketing is at its lowest ever – about a year or so – whilst the VP-Procurement seems to have many times the security.

This is a long-winded way of saying that the rise in the power and scope of Procurement is hardly surprising and likely to be with us for some years to come.

Will Marketing come to the fore once again?

Inevitably it will, when the cycle demands, but in the meantime we need to deal with what we have today – a powerful pressure to buy goods and services for less than was paid last year.

And that's exactly what procurement is all about.

So far, in *our* world, they have focused mainly on the big-ticket items – advertising both above and below the line – resulting in a complete change in the way the major advertising agencies are remunerated. Media commissions funding creative services and research are gone (or going) and, instead, agencies have had to separate out the media and creative functions. Media independents have taken over from full-service agencies whilst 'creative' is now essentially a fee-based service.

The change has been dramatic and down, in most part, to pressure from Procurement to buy a la carte from wherever they can get the best deal.

That isn't to say that the influence of Marketing is dead, it isn't; they still have the final say on the main areas of creative service but no longer alone.

Having done advertising, Procurement are now moving on to the other marketing and communications services – PR, sales promotion, direct marketing…

Many of the larger clients already have full-time PR procurement officers whose sole function is to ensure cost-efficiency in the supply of PR. They understand the market, and how it works, better than anyone and there is nothing harder than to argue a point with someone who really does know as much (probably more) than you.

Over time, the approach filters down the chain to the smaller clients and that is already underway. It may never reach the lowest levels, but that is hardly any comfort is it?

So who are these Procurement professionals and how should we deal with them? Let's take a (slightly tongue-in-cheek) look at the four types[*] that seem to make up the Procurement universe – The Dominator, The Poker Face, The Student and The Professional.

---

[*] *The descriptions that follow are based on my personal experience and can only be a rough guide but if you've ever had dealings with Procurement you may recognise one or two.*

a. The Dominator

There is one factor that makes Dominators easy to recognise – they are bullies.

Their approach is straightforward enough: tough, pushy, rude, relentless and determined. But they're crafty too as they will use every trick in the book to make you feel that the only way out is to accede to their demands.

Typically they will tell you that your firm is way out of line with the rest of the market – too expensive, poorer quality, less professional, arrogant… they have no shortage of ways to put you down. They will inflate their own importance by telling you how influential they are within their own organisation and how getting on the wrong (or right) side of them can impact your future opportunities.

Their whole philosophy is that, by putting you down and forcing you to hear all the faults with your firm, you will recognise that you need to do something in return to 'put this behind you'; you will succumb to the pressure and accept that you need to accept less remuneration and security in compensation for your firm's flaws.

So how do you deal with a Dominator?

Well it isn't easy and requires a toughness and thick skin.

The critical part is to remain aloof whilst all the damning criticisms are being made. Show interest by asking how they have reached their conclusions and ask to see the evidence before agreeing to anything.

Whatever you do, don't be suckered into becoming defensive.

The best response to The Dominator is facts.

Know exactly where your firm fits into the market, why your hourly rates are what they are and how they compare to the market. Understand why your minimum contract and notice period are set where they are and be able to explain it clearly.

And use this one too: 'At XYZ Company we never…' or 'At XYZ Company we always…'

Present it as an absolute, a policy that would need board approval to vary. Be strong and remember that Dominators are full of words but are not decision makers. They, like all procurement executives, are simply aiming for the best deal that is available. If you don't make it available, they can't get it.

In the end it will come down to a negotiation and to trading. The sooner you can get past the 'wearing you down' bit and start talking about specific requests, the easier it will be.

b. The Poker Face

Perhaps another name for 'The Poker Face' might be 'The Accountant' because these types always want lots of information. They believe that it provides them with the opportunity they need to analyse what you've told them and use it against you – and it often works!

Frequently these days, tender documents request so much information that it can take days to assemble and for some reason, probably because a tender looks so official, we feel obliged to complete all the boxes – even when the request is completely unreasonable. It's a try-on.

I've seen documents that ask for detailed salary and benefits information for all the agency/consultancy staff. It's quite outrageous and should not be provided. It breaches all confidentiality.

Many procurement departments continue to ask for this information even though they know they have no right to it; they also preface the requests with bold statements like: 'all questions must be answered or your firm may be eliminated from the process.'

The truth is that you do not have to provide any information that would be a breach of company confidentiality. Instead provide generic data, *average* salaries, for example.

The reason that The Poker Faces want all this data is that, by applying the ratios *they* believe should apply to a perfect marketing or communications firm, they can demonstrate to you how far off you are and how inefficiently you operate. By doing that, they can justify to you why it is that what they're asking for is perfectly reasonable.

They, unlike you, have the time and motivation to analyse the data you provide from every angle and it is this 'understanding' that gives them the authority in any negotiation – they will probably know your business statistics better than you, which is, to say the least, unhelpful.

So how do you deal with The Poker Face?

The answer is to be just as knowledgeable as they are. It isn't enough to simply get your FD or accountant to provide all the data without understanding what it is telling you.

Nor is it necessary to provide all the answers. Think carefully about what you will and won't provide and use company confidentiality as the reason. That isn't to say that you shouldn't be helpful; provide average or generic data instead of specific where confidentiality dictates.

Then, when you get into discussion or negotiation with The Poker Face, listen with real interest to all their analyses, but don't get drawn in to defending your firm unnecessarily. Just as with The Dominator who uses abuse to get you on the defensive, The Poker Face uses analysis and conclusion to achieve the same result.

Be interested for sure, but don't be afraid to cut to the chase and simply ask what they want. Then you can adopt similar techniques as you would for The Dominator and use policy or trading to settle for something reasonable.

Be prepared for the unexpected because just when you think you've reached an agreement The Poker Face will raise another piece of analysis aimed at achieving a further move in their favour. Be sure to agree, *before* you begin trading, that what is on the table is everything and that nothing else will enter the equation.

c. The Student

Yet another technique is employed by 'The Student' types. They offer a, seemingly, much more friendly face and it's quite easy to be lulled into a false sense of security. They seem fairly gentle, even helpful, in their approach and freely admit that they aren't really to 'up' on PR, direct marketing or whatever.

They really want to learn, they tell you, and hope that in return for your openness and help, they can assist you to get a great deal from their organisation.

Don't believe a word!

This is just a great way of getting you to provide useful ammunition and to admit to things that they can use against you later on – and believe me they will.

They may appear to be lacking in the understanding department, but it will amaze you how quickly they get the hang of it all and begin to beat you at your own game.

It's critical to remember that, despite all the suggestions to the contrary, Students don't have the power to provide you with lots more business or even, necessarily, to get you in to new areas of potential. They just want you to believe they do. That way you'll do them a favour in the belief/hope that it will be returned.

It won't.

So how do you deal with The Student?

Start by appreciating their predicament and be friendly. But don't make the mistake of believing that you are fast becoming friends – it's just an illusion.

Play the same game in reverse with lines like: 'I'd like to help you but...' And 'I'm sure, once we are working together, we will be able to help you understand our industry better...'

Be patient with The Student but remember, it will end up in the same place – negotiating a deal – so don't get lulled into 'helping'; it will only be at your expense.

d. The Professional

I strongly suspect that, by now, you may be asking yourself if it really can be as bad as I've been suggesting and wondering if I am just being overly cynical.

Maybe I am a cynic but I can assure you that I have had dealings with all three types described above. Some were just tough, some downright unpleasant and some merely tiresome. But they all had one thing in common: to try to 'win' through a clever style or technique that gave them an edge. To begin with, some did win as I sat, inexperienced in these things, on the opposite side of the table.

But being trained in negotiating helped a lot as did getting older and wiser!

All of which might lead you to conclude that The Professional must be the most difficult and wily of them all.

But you'd be wrong, very wrong. Give me a Professional to negotiate with any day.

You see, Professionals aren't out to win by beating you down because they too have been around the block and know that the best deals come from a win/win situation. They understand that, if they push you further than you want to go, they may get the best *financial* deal for them but you will feel demotivated and disappointed by the outcome.

And that isn't the best basis from which to get excellent work.

The reverse is equally true; if you refuse to meet The Professional half way, then they may well be left with the impression that your firm is overly focused on the revenue stream and not sufficiently interested in the work.

Neither outcome is ideal for a long and rewarding partnership.

The diagram that follows shows clearly that aiming for the small area of overlap – the middle ground – really is the only way to get a true win/win.

Negotiating the middle ground

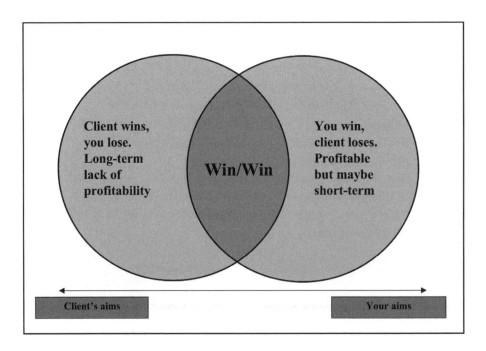

Don't assume that dealing with The Professional is a walk in the park; it isn't. They are tough, straight talking and direct. They may well have identified issues with your firm that are true – so don't deny it, admit it and accept that there may be some consequences.

Recognise that the aim of The Professional is a fair outcome. So let them know when you consider that they are pushing too far. Remember, you don't have to agree to anything you don't want – but you do need to find the middle ground.

Remain respectful and factual. Try to avoid emotional responses and stick with logic – and that means know what your facts are and how far you are prepared to go. Negotiating is like an auction – if you don't set yourself a limit, you could well end up seriously out of pocket.

Chapter 4

NEGOTIATING THE DEAL

(Why what you and your client value are different)

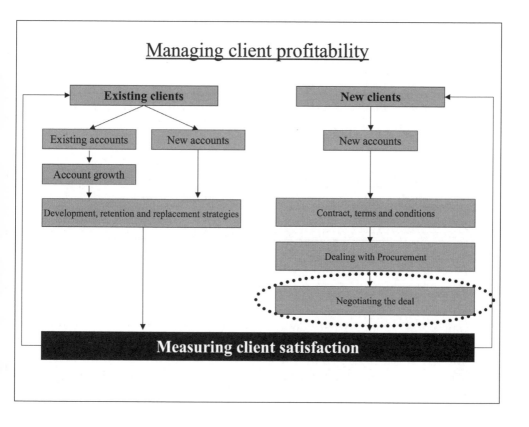

First, one golden rule that applies to any negotiation – get trained!

Negotiation skills can't simply be absorbed through the ether; you need to learn them and practise them regularly. If you do, they will serve you well, not just in business but in your everyday life too. There is almost nothing that can't be negotiated if you have a mind to do it and it can save you a lot of money.

Most of us simply don't have the nerve to ask for a discount; but it never ceases to amaze me how many times simply asking results in an offer.

Recently I was in a shoe shop and couldn't decide between two colours of the same shoe; so I asked what discount they would give me if I bought both pairs (a simple trade of 'if I do this will you do that') and the response was instant – 25%. I didn't want to push my luck so I accepted gratefully.

Similarly, this lesson was reinforced only a couple of weeks ago. I wanted to buy a mandolin (don't ask!) and was talking to the shop on the phone. It was priced at £425 but immediately I expressed interest I was told that 'they'd do it for £299'. I said I also needed a case, a strap and a new set of strings fitted and the instrument set up to my specification – all of which brought the (discounted) price to £362.50 + delivery.

Always being one to try for a bit more I decided to ask if they would do the lot, including delivery, for a round £350. The salesman explained that he would need to check with the boss and would call me back. Only then, after he'd rung off, did I realise that I hadn't said £350 but, because I was still taken aback by the £299 offer, had by a slip of the tongue, actually asked if they would do it all for £250!

When the salesman called back, he said they *would* do it for £250 with a no return clause or £300 if I wanted that security. Frankly I was a bit embarrassed by my mistake but nonetheless opted for the £300 option and did the deal.

I never cease to be amazed by the deals that can be done if you're prepared to try. That said, there are no guarantees except that if you never try, you'll never succeed.

So this chapter assumes that you at least have the spirit to want to negotiate and that you either have had, or plan to get, proper training. I can think of no other skill that will repay the cost of learning in so short a time – and then deliver return on the investment year after year.

That said, there are two rules that apply to contract negotiations and that you break at your peril.

The first is to negotiate only at the highest level. In other words, to make sure that the person (or people) with whom you are negotiating has the authority to agree the changes that you settle on. There is nothing more frustrating than to expend a lot of emotional energy and thought negotiating and finally settling on a deal only to find that the 'client' casually says: "Well now that we've settled that, I just need to run it by my CEO and legal team to check that they're happy with what we're proposing."

That can only lead to one thing – a renegotiation *starting* from where you thought you'd *finished*. That, in turn, means further concessions from you. It's a tried and tested technique that keeps you away from the real decision maker – after all how can you negotiate with someone in another room, whom you can't see, hear or talk to.

This is a technique employed successfully by car sales people. You know how it goes; you enter the glamour of the showroom and the smart young salesperson checks you out to see if you are in buying mode. If they sense that you are, they become your best friend for the duration. Once you've been through the proper process of discussion, presentation, test-drive and so on, you get down to business. For some that means simply agreeing to the 'sticker' price, whilst for others it's to negotiate the deal.

After all the protestations that 'they don't really offer discounts' are out of the way, you finally get to offer time and propose what you feel is fair. Only then does the reality of the situation become clear: that the person you are dealing with doesn't (apparently) have any authority to agree 'that level of discount'. So off they go to 'negotiate' with their sales manager on your behalf to see what they can get 'for you'. How one-sided is that?

Then, of course, they re-appear saying that the sales manager won't approve that level of discount but that they have been able to get agreement to a (lesser) discount of x – 'which is really unusual and has *never* been offered before; must be because the sales manager is in the middle of a meeting and hasn't got time to mess about.'

All of which is designed to tell you that 1) you can't talk to the sales manager directly and 2) further interruptions aren't a good idea. It's a 'take it or leave it' offer. It's probably not true, but it's a pressure many can't resist.

So you can see why it's important, in our type of negotiations, to avoid this situation by checking, upfront, that the person or people you are talking to have the necessary authority to agree any amendments and that no-one else has to ratify or check them before signing. If others need to give approval, ask (read 'insist') that they are present.

The second rule is never (read 'never, ever, ever') negotiate alone.

There are many reasons why this rule is important, but none more compelling than this: in the pressure of a negotiation there is no way that *anyone,* not even the most experienced, professional negotiator, can listen, clarify, make accurate notes of what is being said, think logically, prepare arguments and counter-arguments and handle the negotiating on their own.

As a minimum you need someone else there to clarify and note down what is being said and agreed. Ask any lawyer!

In addition, it allows you to take time out to consider what is being said by simply requesting a short break to consult with your colleague over a point.

The chances are that, over a lengthy discussion, things will be said that contradict one another or provide choices. You need to spot these and use them where appropriate to help your case. You can be sure that, if the client has been trained, there will be more than one of them and they will be noting everything you say and using it to help their case.

At this point you may be thinking that a negotiation is nothing more than a horse trade; a simple bartering. But there is more to it than that when dealing with a contract for services.

Generally the contract elements are fairly simple; it is the T&Cs that create the points of debate.

Critical to this is understanding that what *you* consider to be important and valuable might be different from what the *client* thinks. This is precisely why negotiation is possible – because you can trade something that you judge to be of relatively low value for something that you judge to be of higher value and the client can do the same.

The reason that this incongruity exists is that clients will always see the relationship from their perspective not yours – an obvious statement, but more relevant than might, at first, appear.

Consider this: the client particularly rates the director that you have proposed as the leader of the account and wants to have some 'guarantee' that the said individual will remain leading the account (with a significant time input) for as long as he/she remains at your firm. The director is happy to agree (on the understanding that it can always be renegotiated at a later stage in the relationship if something changes). It is clear that the client sees this as a critical part of the relationship.

Here we have a situation where something that costs you little is perceived to have very high value by the client.

So what could you negotiate in return?

First you will need to ensure that the client doesn't poach the director, so you will need some form of restriction to prevent that from happening – that should be straightforward. In addition, you may be able to use this request for a specific individual to argue for a longer contract term or a longer notice period. You would do this by arguing that, since this director is a key member of your team you would be losing considerable flexibility from your business by this commitment and so would need some extra security to compensate.

In the example above the differing value perceptions are reasonably clear, but even there the choices of trade are numerous. You could, for instance, have asked not for more security but for additional fees, or a higher hourly rate for the individual; maybe you could have proposed a minimum overall fee level per annum (as protection against future budget cuts); or perhaps a rolling contract instead of a fixed-term. The list of options is pretty long.

And that leads into the next section, which looks at how a typical contract negotiation unfolds.

a. Agreeing a contract – the traditional way

As can be seen from the examples above, the process of agreeing a contract and the accompanying T&Cs is a challenge.

Negotiating is a skill that anyone can learn and, with practice, become reasonably proficient at.

The problem we face, though, is not only *how* to negotiate but *what* to negotiate. Even if we succeed in getting our standard T&Cs accepted as the starting point, the chances are that the client will want to make some amendments. Some may simply be minor changes of wording that, frankly, don't have much (or any) impact. Others may be much more substantial and affect your potential profitability and/or security.

(I have never been able to understand why, but lawyers of all types seem fixated with ensuring that their words not the opposition's are the ones that finally appear in a contract or T&Cs. It's as if it's some sort of game, a lawyer dominance thing.)

The real difficulty is being able to judge what impact the client's proposed changes will have on your relationship, account security and profitability. It's worth bearing in mind, too, that some amendments can have an impact beyond the commercial and knock on to individual or team morale.

For example, some of the larger PR clients consider that they should get their annual strategy and programme planning work for nothing (unbelievably their PR firms often agree to this). Clearly there is an impact on the profitability of the account as it builds in a significant amount of *planned write-off* (see Part 1, Chapter 2j); but, more importantly perhaps, it can also demoralise the team who have to do their best work for nothing. It doesn't feel very good knowing that you're spending your time coming up with a strategy and plan for a client who is only going to pay for the, lower level, implementation work.

Setting aside the negotiating skills for a moment, how does a typical deal get done?

Well, regardless of all the 'rights' and 'wrongs' it almost always seems to start with the client. Either they send you a contract and T&Cs 'to sign' or else they respond to your documents saying that they'd like to have 'a discussion' around a few of the points.

(In the past couple of years I have come across more than a few occasions when a negotiation has been conducted over the phone. I think this is a really bad idea as it strips away one of the key dynamics of negotiating – the eye-to-eye contact. It is fine for simple deals but negotiating a contract, T&Cs is much better done face to face, when you can see the body language and where neither party can hide behind the semi-anonymity of a voice-only discussion.)

So whether the client wants to discuss your contract, T&Cs or wants to start afresh with theirs, it is best to set up a meeting where all the points can be clarified and the differences discussed.

The strong negotiator will always want to see the complete picture of demands before getting into any discussions other than clarification but, all too often, the contract meeting is led by the client and the points of difference are dealt with *one by one*.

This is a big mistake because it prevents you from having control over where, ultimately, this deal is going to end up. As each point of difference is discussed there are three possible outcomes: you agree to the demand, you reject the demand or a compromise is found. But the probabilities are that, as each point is raised and concluded, you will have to compromise or accede more than you will get the client to back down. That means you are building up a cumulative reduction in the desirability of the deal.

The problem is that you don't know how many more points there are or how big they might be. Some will be small, but others might be deal breakers and if you have already 'given' as much as you want to before one of the deal breaker issues comes onto the table, you have a big problem; because it's nigh on impossible to go back and withdraw a previously agreed point just to create a little headroom for the new one.

So you end up giving rather more than you intended – because you 'had no choice'. That is how so many agency/client deals end up weighted in the client's favour.

That is, provided that you have been able to keep a running balance of what you have already conceded and been able to work out the impact on the desirability of the deal as you've been negotiating.

Which, unfortunately, doesn't always happen. And that leads to deals being done first and the cost calculated later.

Oh dear.

But I concede that it is extremely hard, even when a client is generous enough to provide you with a list of all their demands ahead of the meeting, because putting a value onto each demand is difficult – as we've already seen.

So let's examine how this is done in the traditional way and then move on to how it could be done much, much more simply.

b. Valuing the 'tradables'

Let's start this section with an example which, although a little simplistic, is fairly representative of the type of requests that a procurement officer might make. I've chosen to use a typical PR contract here, but the principles are the same for any fee-based arrangement.

Imagine that you've just won a new account from a new client. You've done everything right so far – included your T&Cs in the original credentials pack; included it again in the pitch document; pointed them out to the client – and now, before negotiating (or even hinting that they might want to negotiate) the client has appointed you.

So you're in a strong position.

You draw up your contract and T&Cs and send it off to the client for signature and, in summary, it looks like this:

1.   Starting on [dd.mm.yy] ABC will undertake work for XYZ as per the attached [defined] programme. The cost for the year one programme is estimated at £150k of which £100k is likely to be fees and the balance for expenses and implementation costs. The contract will run for 12 months fixed after which it can be terminated by either party on six months' notice. This equates to a minimum initial period of 18 months.

2.   Additional work over and above the [defined] programme will be charged as incurred at the hourly rates specified on the attached rate card (contract rates).

3.   Any requested changes to the [defined] programme will be assessed and the fees adjusted accordingly.

4.   Fee invoices will be issued quarterly (representing one quarter of the projected total annual fee plus any agreed adjustments) on the first day of the period to which they relate.

5.   Account costs (as defined in the attached list) will be charged at 8% of the fees and added to the quarterly fee invoices.

6.   The costs of all 'bought-in' items required for execution of the [defined] programme will be invoiced monthly in arrears including an agency mark-up of 17.65%.

7.   All invoices fall due for payment 30 days after the invoice date.

8.   All overdue invoices will be subject to an interest charge of 3% over bank base rate, pro rata to the overdue period, which will be invoiced monthly.

9.   Copyright in all work developed by the agency will remain the property of the
        Agency.

10.   Neither party will solicit any member of staff from the other party to join their
        organisation during the currency of the contract or for 12 months thereafter.

Only then does the client say that there are one or two points that they'd like to discuss with you and could you come to a meeting to talk them through and agree the final T&Cs.

You sound a little surprised, of course, but agree to talk through any points 'for clarity' and ask if the client could tell you what they are so that you can come to the meeting fully prepared with answers and, obligingly, they list them for you.

The list of points looks like this:

1.   All annual programme planning to be done free of charge.

2.   Invoicing to be monthly in arrears.

3.   Account costs to be discounted to 5%.

4.   The margin on 'bought-ins' to be 10%.

5.   All hourly rates to be discounted by 10%.

6.   The notice period to be three months.

7.   The minimum initial period to be 12 months.

Clearly the client is looking at the contract mainly from a financial perspective and wants to negotiate a better deal with less commitment.

So how are you going to respond?

Clearly there are lots of choices ranging from 'sorry, nothing doing' through to 'fine, no problem'; but which is the right one?

Without knowing the client it's hard to say, but let's assume that you're prepared to give a little to show some goodwill. How do you work out what to give and what you want in return?

Let's look at the potential value of each of the client's requests:

1.   **All annual programme planning to be done free of charge.**

        Having looked at the work involved in producing the annual plan you estimate that it will take about 3.5% of the time that you have allowed for the year to do the plan.

That equates to about £3,500 per year at average rates – from next year on.

But it is also the higher rate work, requiring senior input, so adjusting for that raises the cost to £4,500 pa. You should consider this as planned write-off as it is effectively a discount on the fees of 4.5%.

There is also an impact on the team who don't like to see their best work being given away for nothing.

2. **Invoicing to be monthly in arrears.**

If you were invoicing quarterly in advance as proposed, you would invoice a quarter of the fee (£25k) on, say, 1st January and expect to be paid 30 days later.

So you would have all the cash in the bank on or around the first week of February.

If you were to agree to invoice monthly in arrears, then you would invoice £8333 on 31st January, the same on 28th February and again on 31st March and expect to receive the cash 30 days later.

In effect, you would receive cash during the first weeks of March, April and May; which, in interest terms, is equivalent to receiving it all during the first week of April.

The difference between the two scenarios is that, for however long you hold the account, you will always have two months' worth of fees *less* in the bank if you were to accept the proposal to invoice monthly in arrears.

So with an average of £16,667 less in your bank, you stand to lose (or pay) interest on that; which, at 7% over a full year, equals almost £1,200.

3. **Account costs to discounted to 5%.**

Fortunately the cost of this discount is relatively easy to calculate. The discount requested is 3% (from 8% to 5%) of the fees – which are estimated at £100k.

Should you agree to the requested discount, it would cost you £3,000 pa.

4.   **The margin on 'bought-ins' to be 10%.**

This, too, is quite straightforward. With a cost and expenses budget of £50k at a mark-up of 17.65%, you would expect to 'earn' £7,500. At 10% rather than 17.65%, your margin would be reduced to £4,545, a reduction of £2,955 pa.

5.   **All hourly rates to be discounted by 10%.**

Here the client, in effect, is asking you to reduce your fees by 10% – from £100k to £90k; a direct loss of £10,000 pa.

6.   **The notice period to be reduced to three months.**

Whilst this is not too hard to quantify, the real impact is in the reduction in security that it brings. Three months is not a very long time when compared to the time it might take to find a replacement client and you may be left with excess capacity for a lengthy period whilst you do.

You could choose to reduce your future capacity by removing staff but that has a significant cost attached and, as we all know, it is completely unrealistic to adjust staffing levels every time there is a change in the future capacity requirement.

The financial impact, of course, will only be felt in the year of termination and will be the equivalent of losing three months' income. In today's money that equals a one-off loss of £25,000 that year plus the loss of mark-up during that same period – between £1,136 (at the 10% rate) and £1,875 (at the full 17.65% rate).

Assuming that the average life span of an account is, say, 3.5 years you could argue that the cost of agreeing to this request would be between £7,467 and £7,678 pa. Say £7,500 pa.

7.   **The minimum initial period to be 12 months.**

Having already accounted for the reduction in notice period, the concern here is in reducing the period before notice may be given from 12 months to nine months. This is another one-off event which may or may not happen.

Assuming the account stays with you into a second year, the impact is nil.

However, if the client decides to issue notice at the first opportunity (after nine months) the cost to you is a loss of three months' income. That equates to £25,000 in fees plus mark-up of between £1,136 (at the 10% rate) and £1,875 (at the full 17.65% rate).

Using the same logic as above, that the average life span of an account is 3.5 years, you could argue that, on balance, the chances of being terminated after nine months are relatively small. Without going through a lot of tedious statistical analysis of normal distribution curves and standard deviations, take it from me that the likelihood is probably at most one in ten.

That means that the cost to you of accepting this request is about a tenth of the full three-month revenue loss, which equates to between £2,614 and £2,686, a one-off hit of, say, £2,650 for year 1 only.

So, putting all that lot together, what is it exactly that the client is requesting?

Adding it all up gives a picture that isn't too encouraging:

Item	Year 1	Year 2 on
1 – Prog. Plan. F.O.C	£0 *	£4,500
2 – Invoice timing	£1,118	£1,167
3 – Account costs	£3,000	£3,000
4 – Bought-in margin	£2,955	£2,955
5 – Hourly rate disc	£10,000	£10,000
6 – Notice period	£7,500	£7,500
7 – Minimum period	£2,650	£0
Total	£27,223	£29,122

* Done for the pitch

Admittedly, some of these costs are only risk assessment costs and may never materialise, but they have been averaged or spread to take that into account; so the figures in the above table do represent, in financial terms, what the client is asking of you.

It says, without any doubt at all, that unless you are making a very healthy profit margin of 25% or more (before any discounts or concessions), this account is going to be unprofitable. It will lose you money even before any unplanned write-off. Factor that in and you could be looking at an account that doesn't even recover the costs of the staff servicing it.

Scary isn't it?

The big-ticket item is clearly number 5 – the discounted fees of 10% – but you may be surprised to see that number 6 – reducing your notice period – also carries a high potential cost. Of course, the longer you keep the account, the lower this figure becomes but would you want to gamble on keeping an account for a long time these days?

Let's put these 'requests' into cost order and look at what that tells us (I've used year 2 for this):

1. All hourly rates to be discounted by 10%.

2. The notice period to be three months.

3. All annual programme planning to be done free of charge.

4. Account costs to be discounted to 5%.

5. The margin on 'bought-ins' to be 10%.

6. Invoicing to be monthly in arrears.

7. The minimum initial period to be 12 months.

Surprising isn't it?

I can't say what order I would have put them in by judgement alone but I can say this: that when I run training courses on this subject, I ask the delegates to rank the same requests either by their judgement or by calculating the cost.

The results are only notable for their inconsistency!

So how should we respond to the client?

The first thing to come out of this analytical approach is that we now have an order of priority for our negotiation. We know that it would be much less costly to 'give' on the low order items and to negotiate hard to keep the higher order intact.

Secondly, we know what each item costs and so, by setting our bottom line for the negotiation, we can conclude how far up the list we can afford to go.

Setting the bottom line really is a question of judgement. And it begs a few more questions. Here are some of them:

- What is the growth potential of this account?
- Will this account add significantly to the firm's profile or reputation?
- Does the client control other accounts that we could win?
- Would this account give us new experience that our strategy demands?

I suspect you can see where I am coming from here.

You need to judge whether or not to 'give' based on something more than just being asked. You need to consider what benefits the whole package on offer might bring. Then you can make an assessment about how much you are prepared to invest in the account.

What is clear is that it would be rather unwise (but disappointingly not that unusual) to decide to give more than your profit margin; and that suggests that, for most firms, the maximum ought to be something less than 15%; maybe 2.5% to 7.5%?

So let's work this through.

If you gave nothing, you would expect the account to generate revenues of £100k in fees and a further £7.5k in mark-up. (I am ignoring the account costs here because they don't count towards 'income' as they are a direct recovery of costs.)

That gives us a total Gross Profit (or Income) of £107.5k for a full year.

If we were prepared to 'give' 2.5% in our negotiation, that would equate to £2,688; if we considered that it was worth going to the maximum of, say, 7.5%, then we would have a little over £8,000 to negotiate with.

The next step would be to try to assess whether or not any of the client's requests seem disproportionately important; because those would be the ones which, maybe, have a higher perceived value than the real cost. The only way to do this is through discussion.

So, maybe, we can identify what is most important to the client and use that to our advantage – maybe not. Either way, what is clear is that one of the client's requests is, quite simply, unaffordable – the request for a 10% discount on the rates.

This is where I would use the policy argument in an attempt to remove that item from the list:

*"At XYZ we have a policy that we **never** discount our rates. I appreciate that you are looking to get a better deal from us and I am happy to discuss other ways we might achieve this, but I'm afraid that one is a non-starter."*

The approach may or may not succeed but it will achieve one thing – clarity that you are not going to give the requested 10%. It may go away completely or it may turn into a negotiation over the percentage but your position has been made clear – that if you do end up giving it will need board approval and isn't likely to be anywhere close to 10%.

So how would you approach the rest of the trading?

Once again it depends to a very large extent on your ability to assess what really matters to the client and how far you are prepared to go. But there seem to be four of the requests that offer some room for manoeuvre:

1.   The timing and period of invoicing

2.   The level of account costs

3.   The margin on 'bought-ins'

4.   The minimum period of the contract

Any one of these would be affordable at the 2.5% level and any three of the four at the maximum 7.5%. So it makes sense to trade these against the ones you don't want to give.

That said, you don't necessarily need to trade the whole of the request, but aim to reach a compromise or middle-ground position where, for example, you offer to move on some or all of the above in return for keeping the notice period at six months, the programme planning included in the fees and no hourly rate discounts.

You might suggest, for example:

- – To invoice monthly in advance rather than quarterly
- – To reduce the account costs to 6.5%
- – To reduce your margin on 'bought-ins' to 12.5%
- – To reduce the period before the six months' notice can be given to six months (achieving the 12 month initial period that was requested)

One excellent technique is to introduce another offer altogether – one which the client hasn't requested, but which goes some way to addressing one or more of the points.

One way to do this you could consider using some of the *investment time* budget that has been set for the team. You will remember that this is *non-billable* time that you are *planning* to spend on existing accounts to help grow and/or retain them and for which you have budgeted over and above the billable norm. So it is time that you are expecting to give away anyway. It costs you nothing.

This means that the client gets some extra time, free of charge, say for the first year, which can be used for additional activities outside the main programme. This time can be allowed to accumulate over the months and then drawn down for use when needed – a bit like a savings account.

An offer of a couple of free days per quarter, for example, might just swing the deal and enable you to get away without having to discount your fees. It costs you nothing, but the client will see it as worth two days at your highest hourly rate (a real win/win).

The permutations of possible outcomes are almost endless and each negotiation will be different but provided you do the work ahead of time, the approach you take can always be the same.

But as I've said a few times already, it isn't easy; in fact, it's extremely hard frequently the client's 'requests' can be nigh on impossible to cost.

So what happens in practice?

In my experience, many negotiations happen in an unplanned way, on the hoof, with the agency giving far more than they should. Another major reason why profitability across the industry is so poor.

So it seems there is a choice, do all the hard work and negotiate well and maybe get a good result, or fly by the seat of your pants and, unless you are exceptionally intuitive and quick witted, probably do rather less well.

But are they really the *only* two choices?

Surely there must be a simpler way to assess the cost of client 'requests'?

Well, there is.

It's an approach that takes much of the hard work out of the preparation because it's all done for you and available as a simple 'look-up' guide. And that's what the next section is all about.

c. 'The Good, the (not too) Bad and the Ugly' – an easier way to better deals

Having struggled with the traditional way of negotiating for many years, it occurred to me that many of the costs needing to be calculated before responding to a client's request for changes to the standard T&Cs, were very similar to previous calculations done for other negotiations.

It seemed to me that it ought to be possible to identify the frequently requested items and produce a look-up table of the costs. That would at least make it quicker and maybe add some much needed consistency when different directors undertook negotiations – after all, not every director was as good with the calculator as they should have been.

So I began by listing all the possible requests that I could recall (and a few that I couldn't). Then I started the first calculation and immediately ran into a big problem: to do any calculating, I needed to know the likely budget for fees and costs, otherwise I couldn't work out very much at all.

My first thought was to try to work out costs per £1,000 of budget (which was possible) but proved messy and over-complicated; and that sort of defeated the object of what was supposed to be a simple and foolproof look-up table.

So I thought again.

What I *really* needed to know was:

> – What was the *rank order* of the various requests, from most to least expensive?
> – Where would *the line need to be drawn* to ensure that a deal was profitable?

That led me down a different route entirely.

I still used the 'cost per £k' approach, but instead of listing everything in monetary terms, I assigned a simple score to each item; the more costly the item, the higher the score.

Then, by carefully drawing lines at various score levels, I was able to suggest scores that would deliver *excellent* profitability, *acceptable* profitability or that were simply *non-starters* – the Good, the (not too) Bad and the Ugly!

The scoring approach had another major advantage that I hadn't counted on: that even non-financial requests could be scored by applying experience and judgement and added into the mix. It wasn't ever going to be perfect, but it looked like it could be substantially better than treating every case as a one-off.

In the end it turned out to be a lot better and more user friendly than I ever imagined.

So how does it work?

Well, before going into the detail and revealing the scoring system, I need to set the scene and make a few observations and assumptions.

First, it is important to recognise that most clients operate against a *budget* for the service you are going to provide. We all know this, yet we always seem to respond to the client's budget by breaking it down into sub-sections – typically fees and costs. This has the effect of reducing our flexibility to switch between fees and costs.

Frankly, in my experience, many clients really don't care about how the budget is going to be split, all they are concerned about is that it isn't over-spent (often they don't even understand the difference between fees, account costs, expenses and 'bought-ins' anyway).

So the scoring system I developed makes the assumption that it is the *budget* that is fixed, not the fee/cost proportions. Gaining understanding and agreement to this point with your client is critical if you are to have the opportunity to 'earn back' unspent 'costs' in additional fees. I probably need to explain this point a little more in a moment.

However, even if the client wants to fix separate fee and cost budgets, all is not lost. The principles still hold true, but you'll need to re-rank one or two of the items. It will all become clearer as you read on.

The concept of a fixed budget is easy enough and I suspect that most clients operate this way. A few clients prefer to split fees from costs and control them separately, but even some of those are, in my experience, open to the notion of a single budget if it is 'sold' to them on the basis of flexibility to adjust the programme as needed.

The key here is to get agreement from the client that implementing a programme of work for them is not an exact science and that the actual costs and time taken will, inevitably, vary a little from the original estimates. After all, you will be negotiating to get the best prices for all bought-ins and sometimes a little extra time (fee!) spent negotiating can deliver cost savings in excess of the extra fee incurred. So under-spends on the cost side can be used to fund over-spends in time and vice versa.

You will agree, absolutely, not to exceed the *total* budget but sometimes it may be appropriate to split the budget a little differently than originally anticipated.

That way, if you find that *unplanned write-off* is building up, there may be some flexibility to pay for it out of savings in the cost budget.

Taking this concept a little further, imagine this: the client wants to negotiate a mark-up rate lower than your standard 17.65%. Maybe they don't want to be charged a mark-up at all! If you agree to a lower rate or even a zero rate, provided that you have a 'total budget' understanding, then the cost savings that the client has made simply leave more money unspent in the budget and available for fees!

I have used this approach very successfully in the past and it has a number of big benefits:

- You can be seen to give much more in a negotiation because the saving remains available to earn back in fees. So what appears to be a big give costs you much less than it appears.

- Asking for a little more in fees to cover additional input is always easier if you know that the money is in the budget.

- Having a certain amount of switch during a programme is much more realistic than pretending that the original estimates were spot-on and that a fee of exactly £xxxx per month (usually an unfeasibly round number) just happens to be totally accurate.

The second assumption that I have made in putting the scoring system together is that you have two rate cards – a standard rate card and your discounted contract rate card (see Part 1, Chapter 3b).

Given this assumption, I have further assumed that you would treat any rolling contract that has only a one month (or less!) notice period as a project and apply the standard rate card to it.

Finally, I have assumed that the concept of giving *investment time* in place of discounting is one that you have understood and accepted as a substantially more advantageous approach – the client gets the free time at full value but the cost to you is zero because you have budgeted to give away this *non-billable* time anyway.

Finally, before looking at the scoring system, one more point: you must understand that the scoring used here is based on the standard T&Cs that *I* would use and that *they may be different from yours*. To make this work for you, you will need to adapt either your standard T&Cs to match those implied here or adjust the items and/or scores to suit.

The principle here is simple: for every 'give' that you make in response to a client 'request' you lose a number of lives; the total number of lives lost determines the potential profitability of the account in question. Then all you have to do is decide whether or not to proceed. Simple!

The Good, the (not too) Bad and the Ugly Scoring Table

Client 'request'	Lives lost	Explanation
Cut margin on 'bought-ins' by **any** amount	1	Agreement to cut the margin has minimal impact in reality as the money remains in the budget overall and can be earned back in fees
Give investment time instead of discounting rates or account costs or instead of free programme planning	1 per % point of fees that the time represents	I suggest a **maximum** of 7.5% and only for the very biggest and most valuable clients
Invoicing fees monthly in advance rather than quarterly in advance	2	
Extending credit terms beyond 30 days	2 per each additional 15 days	
Discounting account costs	2 per each % point reduction	Discounting account costs from 8% to 7% is identical to offering a 1% discount on your hourly rates
Not charging interest on overdue invoices	2	
Discounting hourly rates	2 per each % point reduction	
Reducing minimum contract period from 18 to 12 months	3	This may be by agreeing 6 months fixed + 6 months' notice or 9 months fixed + 3 months. 11 + 1 would not score here as that would be a 'project' – see later in the list
Reduction in notice period from 6 to 3 months	3	I would use the same score if it was agreed at 4 or 5 months too
Invoicing fees monthly in arrears	4	
Agreeing to a fixed-term contract	5	Zero if standard rates apply
Using blended team rates	5	Unless it can be varied if the team mix changes
Invoicing quarterly in arrears	6	
Notice period reduction to 1 month or less	8	Zero if standard rates apply

From the table it is easy to add up the number of lives lost by many potential scenarios that may be requested by a client. That said, there are many more possibilities that might arise from time to time, which don't appear in the list but it's not too hard to assess them as best you can and add them in.

Once you've added up the lives lost for any scenario then simple reference to the guidelines below should enable you to determine how best to proceed:

Up to ten lives lost – the Good

> You are being offered a very **Good** and profitable deal. Negotiate as much as you can to improve the situation but settle without too much of a fight.

Between 11 and 20 lives lost – the (not too) Bad

> This is where the strong negotiator can make all the difference. At the lower end of the scale the deal is a reasonably good one and likely to be profitable but the nearer to 20 you get, the less attractive the deal becomes. Negotiate hard to get below 15 if you can and you should be fine. Between 15 and 20 the deal is **(not too) Bad** but you're being pushed to give quite a lot. Look for some extra security or additional opportunities to justify settling up here.

More than 20 lives lost – the Ugly

> This is the danger zone. Settling here means that you are sacrificing most, if not all, of your profit and there needs to be a good reason for doing that. Even then you should negotiate hard and be prepared to walk away if the score is much above 25 and there is no strong reason for 'giving' that much. You'll be amazed at how a clear preparedness to walk away can often be the lever that turns an **Ugly** deal into an acceptable one.

Before moving on, let's look at a couple of examples to see if the system really works.

Example 1

> The client will agree to your contract and standard T&Cs provided that you will amend them as follows:
>
> - Initial contract to be for one year fixed term only (no notice period)
> - Invoicing to be monthly in arrears (not quarterly in advance)

- Credit terms to be extended to 45 days (from 30)
- Account costs to be 5% (from 8%)
- Mark-up on 'bought-ins' to be 5% (not 17.65%)
- Hourly rates to be discounted by 10%

So how many lives would be lost if you agreed to all of this?

Have a go yourself by referring to the previous Scoring Table.

Example 2

The client will agree to your contract and standard T&Cs provided that you will amend them as follows:

- Three months' notice rather than six months
- A minimum contract period of 12 months (nine months fixed + three notice)
- Invoicing monthly in advance
- Mark-up on 'bought-ins' at 10%
- Free 'investment time' of 5% (ie 5% extra free)

You'll find the answer to both examples at the foot of the page.[*]

Finally, before moving on to the next section, once you have the answers, think about how you would respond to those possible deals; how would you negotiate and what would you trade?

---

[*] *In Example 1 the number of lives lost is 38 made up of (in the order presented) 5, 4, 2, 6, 1 & 20 = 38*
In Example 2 the number of lives lost is 14 made up of (in the order presented) 3, 3, 2, 1 & 5 = 14

d. Dealing with the common objections

During the course of any negotiation, there are bound to be issues that need to be dealt with on the spot. Sometimes these are simple questions that can be answered easily but other times they can pose quite a challenge.

What I am referring to here are not so much the 'requests' that we dealt with in the previous sections but what sales people would refer to as 'objections'; the barriers thrown up by a client or customer to avoid making a decision to go ahead or to agree to specific contract terms. And the secret to achieving a sale is overcoming the objections.

Sometimes they do overlap with the previous requests, but the point of this section is not to look at how we assess the *cost* of such requests but how we *overcome* them; how we can remove the barrier and move on to agreement.

As on previous occasions throughout this book, I am not going to provide a definitive list of all objections and how to overcome them – that would be extremely long – because, as I stated at the outset, this is about understanding the principles and concepts, not really about providing crib-sheets!

So the list of objections below is just a representative sample of the sorts of things you might face. As you go through them, I hope that you will begin to see a pattern emerging, which will help you to overcome many of the barriers put up by clients on the way to a final agreement.

Sometimes the argument might work, other times it won't. There is no magic formula, simply a logical approach to overcoming the barriers – and sometimes they just can't be overcome. Often objections, which are presented as deal breakers, are no such thing and your apparent willingness to allow the deal to fall over that issue can be enough to make the client back down. Fortunately, that doesn't occur too often because where there is a will, a compromise can most times be found.

I've worded each objection as a client statement with how I would approach overcoming it below:

Client: "My word is my bond, I don't sign contracts."

Agency: "I understand and respect where you're coming from on that and

I think there are a couple of ways we could accommodate you.

"Within XYZ we have a number of 'ad hoc' clients as well as our formally contracted clients. The only difference is that formally contracted clients provide us with greater security, as you appreciate, and so we give them special, discounted, contract rates – which are 15% lower than our standard rates.

"In our budgets for you we have assumed all along that you would be formally contracted so everything has been costed at the special rates. However we could switch to the standard rates and work on an 'ad hoc' basis if you prefer?

[Need to gauge the reaction here before deciding whether or not to move on.]

"Alternatively, there might be a better compromise; God forbid that anything happens to either of us but in the event that the metaphorical bus comes along and takes either of us, why don't I simply write down what we agree as the arrangements between us and we each hold a copy. That way, if the worst did happen there would at least be a record of what we agreed and I could justify holding to the special contract rates for you?"

Client:	**"We have our own contract that we'd like you to sign."**
Agency:	"Okay, I can understand that, but if you want us to base our relationship on *your* terms we'll need to get our lawyer to go through it to make comparisons with *our* standard terms and conditions. Provided you're happy to pay for that we'd be happy to do it. In my experience it is likely to cost about £xxx."
Client:	**"I'm not paying 17.65% for you to buy goods for me."**
Agency:	"That's fine because there's no obligation. If you prefer to buy the goods direct then that's your prerogative. We'd prefer to remain in the loop because that way we can be accountable to you for the quality of the *whole* programme and, in our experience, when things go wrong – as they do occasionally – we don't want to be arguing over whose responsibility it is; that can be very damaging

to the relationship.

[Here is another case where the client is left with a choice, to do it direct or to accept that it is preferable for you to do it. Wait for an answer before moving on.]

"On the other hand if you prefer that we control the process and take the responsibility, then we do need to add a margin to cover our costs, after all we will be handling all the ordering, order processing, payment, re-invoicing and so on. So what margin would you suggest is reasonable?"

[Remember the principle of 'fixed budget'; if you charge less mark-up the saving is left in the budget and could be used later for additional fees.]

Client: **"I expect you to carry the cost of the time spent learning about my business."**

Agency: "I understand and respect where you're coming from on that and over the past x weeks, whilst we were preparing the proposals for you, that's exactly what we have been doing – over £xxx worth of time in fact. So I'm afraid that we really can't give any more, otherwise we will never be able to recover the significant investment that we've already made."

Client: **"I'd prefer you to bill me after you have done the work not before."**

Agency: "Okay, may I just check what you are asking for here? Are you saying that you don't want to pay upfront but would prefer to see the work done before paying for it?

[In every likelihood, the client will say 'yes' to this. It isn't exactly what he asked for originally because it substitutes 'paying' for 'billing'. Assuming you get a yes proceed as below.]

"Okay, that's not unreasonable. So, for the work we do in April, say, you'd be happier to pay at the end of the month after the work has been completed? So if we invoice on the 1st of the month, our normal 30 days credit would mean that nothing would be due until the month was over and the work done. We'd be happy to do that."

Client: **"I'm not paying your account costs – they're part of the cost of running your business."**

Agency: "I think there's been a misunderstanding here because we'd never ask you to contribute towards the costs of running our business; account costs are the costs we incur on *your* behalf and are costs of running *your* business."

Client: **"Your hourly rates are simply too high."**

Agency: "I'm interested to hear you say that; what are you comparing them with?

[Once again this conversation could take a number of routes but often the client will most likely be comparing your rates with those of the other agencies who pitched and lost.]

"We may be more expensive than some of our competitors, although I'm surprised to hear that because we check our rates annually to ensure that we aren't out of line; that said, you knew our rates when you appointed us and rejected cheaper competitors. Without wishing to be at all arrogant, that does suggest that you see us as offering a better overall package and value."

Client: **"To keep it simple I'd prefer to pay a single 'team' rate rather than all these different rates."**

Agency: "That's fine, we can calculate an average rate for you; but to do so we need to agree that if the programme demands that the mix of the team changes, we will need to adjust the rate accordingly – either up or down depending on the amount of senior/junior input. Provided you're happy with that we'll put it in place."

Client: **"If I decide to terminate the relationship I don't want a long**

handover, I'll want you out within a month."

Agency: "That's fine, long handovers really aren't necessary. There are two ways we can do this: either you can pay us in lieu of the remaining notice period or we could move to a simple one month notice arrangement. In the latter case we wouldn't be able to offer you the discounted contract rates that we have based our costings on so far; we would have to revert to our standard rates, which don't include the 15% discount.

"However, if neither of those options appeals and it is the six month period which is causing you concern, then why don't we compromise on an initial three months' notice – which would entitle you to the contract rates – and then build it back up to six months over time as you become more comfortable with us – say by adding a month each year?"

Client: **"I want to pay for results, not for your time."**

Agency: "I understand and respect where you're coming from and we do have that as an option. The way it works is like this: we need to agree exactly what the results are that you are expecting and to ensure that they are reasonable and achievable.

"Then, we need to agree exactly how those results will be measured and who the 'unbiased' final arbiter would be in the unlikely event of there being any difference of opinion between us.

"Finally, the way we would bill is at 85% of our normal rates for the work done; a further 15% – on a sliding scale – for performance up to 'expectation' and then a further 15% – again on a sliding scale – for performance beyond expectations.

[The aim here is to ensure that any performance-related payment is limited to the margin you earn, not the whole fee. It is perfectly reasonable to risk the margin but not, in my opinion, the contribution to overheads.]

"That way *we* take a risk on *all* our profit margin should we perform below par, but have an incentive of an equal amount to deliver extra."

Client: **"Let's just sign up for 12 months initially and see how it goes."**

Agency: "That doesn't seem like an unreasonable request and there are a number of ways that we could achieve that. If we were to move to a simple, 12 month, fixed-term contract, then you wouldn't benefit from the discounted contract rates – which are 15% lower than our standard rates – so that's probably not the best route.

"What we should do is to reduce the initial period before you could give us notice to six months; that way, in a worst case scenario, if things really aren't working out – and six months ought to be plenty long enough to know – then you could give us notice and it would all be done within the year."

As I said earlier, this is by no means a definitive list, nor is it meant to be. It simply provides a few examples of how some of the more common objections might be dealt with. Each of the examples could go in many different ways and you need to be prepared for that. You won't have all the answers but you may be able to deflect or overcome the objection if you are clear, in your own mind, what you are and aren't prepared to do.

Be confident and be firm. There is nothing more dangerous than an apparent lack of knowledge or strength. It will be exploited mercilessly.

And remember, no-one ever gets it all right!

Chapter 5

MEASURING CLIENT SATISFACTION
(Why high profitability doesn't mean low service)

Managing client profitability

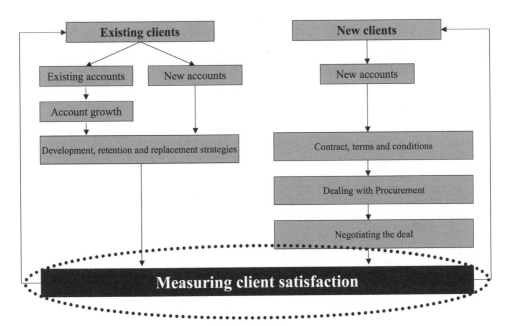

If you have read this far, you may be feeling a little overwhelmed by the pressure to be more commercial in setting up relationships with clients. Maybe you're even a little worried that the level of commerciality implied by all the previous chapters could be damaging to your firm's reputation – maybe it could turn you into a firm overly focused on money rather than client service?

It's an understandable reaction because for decades the marketing and communications environment has been dominated by a 'Client Service' mentality.

Now don't get me wrong here, there is nothing wrong with excellent client service – far from it – it is a prerequisite for good commercial results. What is wrong is the domination of client service over commercial judgement.

And it would be equally wrong the other way round!

As with most things in life, there needs to be balance.

And here, that means a balance between high-quality delivery and proper payment. There is no reason why our marketing and communications industry should be less well remunerated than any other professional service – provided that we deliver valuable results that are worth the cost.

The problem is, and always has been, how to measure the results and value that we deliver.

It is a thorny problem and one that many better brains than mine have wrestled with for many, many years. Fundamentally, *I* believe it comes down to being able to set and agree *measurable objectives* before you start.

Once that has been done it can, sometimes, be quite easy to measure the results – especially when there is a direct and unadulterated relationship between the work we have done and the outcome obtained. But all too often it is impossible to really evaluate the impact of our work on the client's bottom line, for example. Frequently, that is because we can't separate out the results of our activities from those of other communications or 'environmental' effects.

I could write a whole chapter, maybe even a book, on all the different approaches but, to be honest I'm not sure it would make any difference, partly because it's been done many times already but, more importantly, because some things in commerce, as in life generally, simply aren't easily quantified.

Is it worth even trying to quantify how much it matters that we attend our child's first school play? Or remember our wedding anniversary or partner's birthday. We know that failure is damaging and that doing it matters – a lot. Sometimes that's enough, isn't it?

Commerciality isn't all about measuring everything and benchmarking and calculating percentages and converting everything into numbers. Sometimes I think we lose sight of the realities of business and spend far too much time doing stuff that has no purpose other than to show or prove to others how clever we are and how well we're doing. Sometimes using good judgement is just fine.

So I am not going to devote this chapter to measurement and evaluation for all of those reasons.

Here I want to focus on ensuring that improving the commerciality of your firm doesn't impact adversely on your client *relationships*; and that means keeping a regular and vigilant eye on exactly what is happening as well as how it feels.

The recipe for ensuring good commercial/client service balance includes a little discipline, a bit of process, a lot of sensitivity and a healthy dollop of honesty. Together they add up to a mix of activities that will keep you well informed and aware of any potential client issues before they become big problems – and early enough to deal with them!

a. The informal imperatives

Okay, before I start this section let me make a prediction; before you get very far down this page you'll be thinking: 'We do all of this already, everybody does, it's just good account handling'.

And you may well be right – nearly!

Most people do *most* of what I am about to suggest, *most* of the time.

But few do it all, all of the time.

And you should.

So what am I talking about here?

Here's a list:

> *Sensitivity…*
>
> *listening…*
>
> *questioning…*
>
> *clarifying…*
>
> *on every call…*
>
> *at every meeting…*
>
> *not just with those present…*
>
> *openly and honestly…*
>
> *leading to action.*

Let me explain a little more.

Many clients, in my experience, don't raise every single, tiny issue that they have with your firm or team or performance. They know that every relationship has flaws and that things do go wrong from time to time.

If the problem is a big one, then it will get raised; but it is the small, almost insignificant ones that I am focusing on here. And the key word in this paragraph is 'almost'.

These are the issues that *accumulate* to undermine a relationship by stealth. No one thing is the cause; it's the cumulative effect that creates an almost imperceptible undermining of trust or belief – the appearance of typos in reports; the deadlines missed by just a little; the promises to return a call within half an hour, which takes 40 minutes in reality… You know the things.

Sadly, they often go un-noted and only get raised when the relationship has *been* undermined and when it is too late to do anything about it.

The solution is to be aware that even the best relationships have these problems and to be on the lookout for them.

That's where the above list comes in.

You need to be proactive; to probe for the issues and to deal with them; to watch for the body language; to hear the voice intonation; to recognise that when a client says "everything's fine", it could mean just that – or it could mean quite the opposite!

It's the skill of the account handler – the critical skill – that turns a good one into a great one.

But it doesn't stop there because you need to go beyond your day-to-day client and make sure you get feedback from a wider group too: from their colleagues, their boss, the CEO…

Ask your client what others think of the programme/results/whatever. Ask those 'others' directly, too.

And do it frequently; keep your antenna on full alert all the time; on every call and at every meeting.

Only then will you be able to say, for sure, that everything really is okay.

It may sound obvious and rather pedantic – and I'm probably over-playing it a bit – but there is a natural human trait at play here; the trait to look and listen for what we *want* to see and hear. We all do it much of the time – we look for the compliments and positive feedback, we don't go looking for the problems.

In this business it pays to look for the problems; and if you do, the positives will follow.

One final point – don't be tempted to get defensive. It is an easy thing to do when you have probed for the issues and found one! Take it on the chin, accept it and deal with it.

If it really is unreasonable, find the right opportunity to talk to the client about it – it probably comes down to unrealistic expectations and, almost always, that is the agency's fault for not getting the expectations aligned upfront.

These are hard things to do and we all get better and more confident with experience. We all get them wrong sometimes, so don't beat yourself up too much if it doesn't work out every time. Just try to get it right more than you get it wrong and the balance will swing in your favour.

b. The more formal approach

Having looked at the informal imperatives in the previous section, you may wonder if anything more formal is necessary. Often, if the informal processes are working well, the answer will be no, not really.

But no processes work well all the time and when you factor in our natural preference for good news rather than bad, there will always be a need to 'check' whether or not the informal processes are doing the job.

It may sound a bit spy in the sky, but it doesn't need to be.

There are two ways to approach the more formal side to monitoring client/agency relationships – through the regular review meetings that many of us hold and through a purpose-designed, annual review. Let's take a look at each in turn.

1.   Regular review meetings

Most firms seem to hold a regular, diarised, monthly or quarterly meeting with their main clients aimed at reviewing progress to date and firming up future activity. Sometimes these are just working meetings and sometimes a little more formal – it depends to a large degree on the firm's style or values.

Either way, it makes sense to ensure that the subject of 'working relationship' gets on to the agenda and is discussed. Some firms prefer to do this senior-to-senior without the rest of the team present, whilst others are happy in an open forum. I have to say that I've used both and tend to prefer the open forum but with an understanding that any personal or sensitive issues would be held back and discussed senior-to-senior.

That way, the whole team gets used to the idea that an open and honest approach to dealing with relationship/performance issues is perfectly normal and acceptable.

Ideally, it would make sense to ensure that, on a few occasions during the year, the most senior 'interested' client joins the meeting together with your firm's MD/CEO. From the client side this may be the MD/CEO or whoever is ultimately responsible for the area you are working in.

This achieves two things: it helps to cement the relationship between the two firms by exposing the realities of the programme to those who wouldn't ordinarily see them and it helps build the senior level relationships that are crucial to account/client growth (see Part 2, Chapter 1b).

If your firm doesn't hold 'diarised' review meetings, then all I can say is that you should. They don't have to be long or tedious nor do they have to be particularly frequent. Once a quarter may be fine – the choice is yours – but you're missing a critical opportunity to monitor and maintain the health of the relationship if you don't do it.

2.   **The annual review**

This is quite different to the above and is aimed, exclusively and unashamedly, at checking the state of the relationship and performance.

As the name suggests, this is a once a year overview of how everything has gone and should be conducted between the most senior client and (ideally) a third party on behalf of the agency. By 'third party', I mean someone who is qualified to conduct such a meeting but is not involved day to day with either the account, the client or the agency. Ideally they should be a consultant or third-party research firm.

Using someone who is not involved is critical. It ensures that the meeting can be impersonal and objective – and that is the whole point.

If it isn't possible or appropriate to involve a third party (and it can be very expensive), then a non-involved director would make a good substitute. It should *never* be the director in charge of the account.

The meeting is set up in advance by the director in charge of the account and the purpose explained to the senior client: 'to review our working together over the past year, to see if there are areas where improvements could be made and how they could be achieved'.

Being a formal meeting, a certain amount of preparation is needed on both sides to ensure that the meeting is productive.

The best way to do this is by developing a simple form, which both 'sides' complete ahead of the meeting and which is used as the basis for the discussion.

The form works well if it asks open questions as well as asking for a score. That way, if both parties agree on a score (assuming it isn't poor) the discussion can be quite quick. If, on the other hand, there is a clear difference in the scores, then that is where a healthy discussion might reveal the hidden issues and lessons that need to be learned.

This is a two-way review – client of agency and vice versa – although it is fair to say that it will, inevitably, tend towards a client review of the agency. So both parties need to be well briefed before the meeting and the forms need to be completed with input from the whole team on both sides.

After the meeting, both parties need to debrief their respective teams and revisit the agreed actions after, say, three months to ensure that they have been/are being done.

So what would the meeting discuss?

The answer, in short, is anything that is relevant to improving the relationship.

In my experience that falls into a number of headings that are generally common across disciplines and others that are specific to the services provided by your firm.

You will need to decide what areas you want to cover in your annual reviews, but here are a few suggestions to start you off:

1.	Agency team and individuals
	– *Director
	– *Account director
	– *Account manager
	– *Account executive(s)
	– *Planner(s)
	– *The team overall
	– Etc.

2.	Account handling
	– ★Pro-activity
	– ★Knowledge of client/market
	– ★Response to deadlines
	– ★Consultancy capabilities/delivery
	– ★Frequency/quality of meetings
	– ★Budget control and financial processes

3.	Strategic planning
	– ★Research and analysis
	– ★Strategy development
	– ★Integration into wider business strategy

4.	Creativity
	– ★In programme development
	– ★In day-to-day problem solving
	– ★In writing
	– ★Other

5.	Quality of delivery
	– ★Proposals
	– ★Written work
	– ★Production work
	– ★Events management
	– ★Outcomes

6.	Overall performance
	– Criteria used to judge overall performance
	– ★Our performance against these criteria
	– Comparison with other firms
	– Best aspect of working together
	– Worst aspect of working together

7.	The future
	– The big issues coming up for the client
	– Role for the agency in facing the issues
	– Other areas of potential involvement
	– Possible referrals

8.	Action points arising from meeting

★ *These are the items where a score would be appropriate.*

The scoring system can be whatever you choose, but in my firm we used a simple 1–5 system where:

1 = poor
2 = acceptable
3 = good
4 = very good
5 = excellent

As you can see the scoring approach was a little 'un-centred' as 3, the mid-point, meant 'good'.

We targeted the directors to achieve an average overall score of 4 and reckoned that a client who gave less than that was potentially less than satisfied and worthy of some extra investment to ensure that things improved.

What did become clear was that not all clients score in the same way. Some were overly generous whilst others rarely gave more than a 2.

That's why section 6, 'Overall Performance', is so important. It provides a baseline from which to judge the harshness or generosity of the client's approach. If a client generally scores low but, when asked to compare XYZ with other firms, said that XYZ was significantly better, then you could mentally adjust the scores up a notch or so. And the same is true in reverse.

The beauty of the annual review process is this: provided you keep the system consistent, year on year, you can track your firm's performance on an account and the relationship with the client, in each area individually as well as overall. You can see if the client's perception of your creativity is improving or declining; you can judge whether or not any team changes have had an impact; you can tell immediately whether or not your increased commerciality is causing the client to change their perceptions of your firm.

But one benefit overrides all others: simply by **doing** these reviews you will enhance the client's perception of your firm overall, because very few firms do them!

I can't recall the number of occasions when the opening comment by a client at the annual review was to tell us how pleasantly surprised they were that we were bothering to invest so much senior time into ensuring that things were working out well.

Worth the time, wouldn't you say?

c. Why measuring satisfaction generates more business

Just a few words ago, at the end of the previous section, I wrote:

*But one benefit over-rides all others: simply by **doing** these reviews you will enhance the client's perception of your firm overall, because very few firms do them.*

But I lied.

There is another, even more compelling reason.

Because it generates additional business.

A third party (or a senior non-involved director) is in a unique position when doing an annual client review; they have uninterrupted access to the senior client, one-to-one, for a reasonable period of time, focused exclusively on the relationship between the two firms.

That leads, more often than not, to discussions at quite a high level about where the client's business is going and the issues they face.

Someone experienced and senior will always be able to spot possible opportunities and turn the discussion to how XYZ could help.

The issue underlying so much account development is the one discussed much earlier of pigeonholing (see Part 2, Chapter 1b). All too often the client only sees the day-to-day team as being the people who do a, b and c. They aren't seen as being the people who could do e, f or g.

The third party or non-involved director can point out the wider capabilities of the firm without it seeming like they are selling. They can offer a discussion with another 'specialist' to help on an issue; they can arrange to introduce another office or country; they can open up dialogue on additional services.

It will seem like help and support rather than selling; and because it is done at the most senior level, there is no political or personal agenda in play; the decision can be taken there and then.

I would say that on average, about one in every three annual reviews flags up the potential for extra business and that around half of those eventually convert into increased income or new accounts.

I stated earlier most account directors ought to spot these opportunities in their day-to-day contact but the truth is that most don't; if they do, they either don't feel it would be appropriate to 'sell' so overtly or get blocked. Few make it all the way through the process.

Non-involvement has some big advantages; and that's exactly what section 7 of the annual review form is really all about.

Even if you feel that you don't need to do annual reviews because your other formal and informal processes are excellent, would you do them to generate extra business?

Now there's a question.

d. Tracking the overall performance of the firm

In the previous sections of this chapter, we have looked at how we monitor and measure how we are performing in our relationships with our clients.

The approach, so far, has been *client by client* and whilst tracking individual aspects of performance enables us to monitor our year-on-year performance across a variety of areas, it only relates to the *specific accounts* in question.

Here, we are going to look at how we can monitor and track our performance *as an overall firm*. Are we getting better or worse? Are we building on our traditional strengths? Are we overcoming our weaknesses? Have we developed new strengths?

Initially, when I thought about this, I felt sure that the *annual review* results could be pooled to provide all the information we need to do this. After all, if we averaged the scores for each of the question areas across all the annual reviews we would have a picture of the overall firm's scores; and that's what we want here.

But there were problems.

First, the annual review process is, essentially, a qualitative one. The purpose is to get clients to reveal any issues or concerns (as well as praise) they have for the work done. The scoring system was subsidiary to the qualitative element and really only to help get into the issues.

Secondly, the annual reviews are spread across the year and so, to average a full year's worth of scores would mean that some reviews were already a year old (looking back a further year), whilst others were current (looking back over the past 12 months). Not ideal.

Third, whilst some of the questions and answers were general enough to provide good data for a 'whole firm' survey, many generated scores that were influenced by a specific event or individual; in other words, not quite generic enough.

Finally, the scoring system was too narrow – ideal for the face-to-face discussion but too limiting for a broader survey. After all a difference of 1 in an annual review score represents a 20% change. For the whole firm approach that could be too volatile. It could have been changed, of course, but then that would have changed the tenor of the annual reviews – and that wasn't appropriate.

So the only way forward was to devise a specific annual satisfaction survey, which could be completed by all clients simply and quickly, on-line, using a 0–100 scoring system.

The technology exists and is simple, inexpensive and easy to set up.

So all that remains is to establish the questions.

And that, of course, is up to you.

All I would say is don't get carried away – it's easy to devise more and more questions which end up producing fewer and fewer responses. Most clients would answer five questions, but how many would answer 1,000?

So keep it very focused on what you really want to know; keep the questions short and clear; word them carefully so that they can be answered on a 0–100 scale and have no more than 25 questions in total!

Then give your clients advance notice of the event and ask them (maybe even incentivise them) to complete the on-line questionnaire by a given date. Remind them at appropriate intervals as the deadline looms.

That way you stand a good chance of getting a healthy response.

How you analyse and present the scores is up to you but remember, this is not a one-off event; it is intended to be the first, annual survey and what is important is how your scores change year on year, for the 'whole firm'.

Analysing individual client responses is very tempting but resist. The annual review does that job much better. Just in case the temptation is too great, why not make the survey anonymous?

So what would I ask?

Well I said a moment ago that it was up to you but since you've asked again…I think I'd stick to these (or similar) – all ranked on a 0–100 scale like that below:

| 1 | 10 | 20 | 30 | 40 | 50 | 60 | 70 | 80 | 90 | 100 |

1.	Thinking about the team that work/have worked on your business, how would you rate their:
	– Stability (personnel changes)? – Skills? – Experience? – Leadership? – Overall 'brightness' and ability?
2.	Thinking about the team's performance, how would you rate their:
	– Availability? – Responsiveness? – Pro-activity? – Level of understanding of the brief? – Chemistry (between agency/client)?
3.	Thinking about the handling of your account, how would you rate the:
	– Communication? – Fit with your 'ways'? – Keeping to deadlines? – Management of budget? – Attention to detail? – Reaction to changes? – Overall efficiency?
4.	Thinking about the professional skills deployed on your account, how would you rate the:
	– Strategic thinking and advice? – Understanding of your market/environment? – Independence of thought? – Use of logic rather than instinct? – Creativity of ideas? – Execution of ideas? – Overall professionalism?
5.	What would be your overall assessment of the agency's performance?

Obviously the specific questions, how you word them and how many you ask is entirely your business.

Use some or all of the above if you wish or make them appropriate to you. Use simple, unambiguous words and a large enough scale to register small movements.

Then, when you have the first set of results share them with the whole of your firm. Explain what they are saying and how you are going to use that information to guide improvements in the business.

Share out the tasks, monitor them carefully and make sure that actions are taken.

Oh, and it wouldn't be a bad idea to share the overall picture with your clients too together with the actions you are going to take. They'd find that reassuring.

Then next year, compare the results and look at what's changed – if you've done a good job you could be in for a very pleasant surprise.

Chapter 6

CONCLUSION AND 'HEALTH WARNING!'

When I set out on the path of writing this text I had only one aim in mind – to help marketing and communications firms to improve their profitability through the application of some (relatively) basic commercial skills. I stated that I felt most firms could probably double their profitability within a year – and I stick to that. Many, I feel, could do even more than that over time.

But the proof of the pudding is in the eating and at this point I should point out that I have worked with a number of firms and trained many senior staff from others. They tell me it works and often give me updates on where particular elements of my approach have helped them achieve results that they had never achieved before – clients agreeing to substantial budget increases; staff working more billable hours during a shorter working week; contracts in place with six months' notice; invoices being paid promptly as a result of 'interest' charges being implemented....

The end result is greater profitability. More money for investment, better training and marketing budgets, higher dividends, reduced liabilities, stronger balance sheets…

Will it work for you? Well time will tell I guess.

However, before closing I felt it would be worthwhile taking a few moments to collect together all the main points from both sections of the book to see what effect they might have on the 'average' firm – both individually and collectively – and to see what you might reasonably be able to achieve for your firm.

I can't offer any guarantees of success but, with a little patience, a well-structured programme and a strong hand on the tiller, there are many benefits to be gained.

So here goes…

Part 1 - Managing the Firm and its People

Chapter 1   **Planning the future of your business**
(Where are you heading?)

This chapter isn't about improving profitability per se so the impact on your bottom line is nil. However, this is where it all starts and it is the most critical element in planning your journey to improved profitability. Without a clear strategic plan and a realistic financial plan, you aren't controlling the development of your business, merely reacting to circumstances as they happen.

And that's a bad way to manage.

If you want to get somewhere, define where it is and then plan the route and resources you will need. Then get started and monitor your progress regularly, taking whatever action is needed to keep moving forward and on the right track.

Chapter 2   **Capacity management and utilisation**
(How to make money along the way)

Here is where the first of the real profit improvements comes into play.

The first key to achieving improved profitability is in understanding that you are selling *time* and that the more time you sell the better off you will be. Most firms don't achieve the profitability they deserve because they give away too much of their 'stock' through over-servicing or write-off.

Simply getting control over your billable time can be worth as much as an **extra 1 or 2%** on your bottom line and minimising unplanned write-off could be worth five times that – or more – say, **another 7.5%**.

Chapter 3   **Different payment systems**
(What's profitable and what's not)

Selling time and lots of it is great – provided that you have set your hourly rates properly! There are lots of ways to come at it and getting it right (together with selling the right amount of time per person employed) enables you to make the profitability you desire. Up to 30 or even 35% is possible but probably unsustainable; a sustained 20–25% is more realistic. The right rates allow you to set billable norms that are achievable consistently without working your staff too hard and relying on their 'free' overtime.

Get this right and it could be worth **another 5–10%** on your profitability.

Chapter 4   **The key ratios**
                (What they are, what they tell you and how to measure them)

The key ratios don't make you money but enable you to ensure that your approach is working and on track. That said, getting the debtor ratios right and collecting the cash promptly could save you an **extra 1%** on its own.

Chapter 5   **The FD/CFO/accountant**
                (Friend or foe?)

The principle behind using a good FD or accountant is simple: they will often save you from expensive mistakes and keep you from giving in to your professional side too often. They're worth their weight in gold!

So they may not add to the bottom line but 'sure as eggs is eggs' they will prevent some 'loss' or other. I reckon that an average of **1–2% saved** each year would be a reasonable estimate.

Part 2 – Managing client profitability

Chapter 1   **Building profitability through growth**
                (New business – the life-blood?)

Adding clients and accounts is essential for any agency or consultancy. We all know that. But the cost of winning new clients can be substantial. If we all put a little more effort into keeping and growing our *existing* clients – through planned investment time – we would, undoubtedly, grow faster and at a lower cost. Add to that the planned replacement of small, lower profit 'legacy' accounts and the impact on our profitability could be significant. Together, the approaches suggested could easily add **another 1–2%** profitability.

Chapter 2   **Contracts, terms and conditions**
(The legal bits for non-lawyers)

How long is a piece of string? That's pretty much the answer to how much strong contracts, terms and conditions can add to your margin. Of course it takes time to filter through because you can really only introduce all the principles here to *new* clients as they come on board; and that's likely to be restricted to around 15% of your revenues each year. Even so, a deal that gives 5% greater profitability across 15% of your revenues **adds almost 1%** to the bottom line in year 1; and that will grow as you get better at negotiating and as new clients come on board.

Chapter 3   **Procurement – the new enemy?**
(The client's new face)

I can't put my hand on my heart and tell you that knowing 'procurement' will earn you extra profit – it won't. But it will help you to minimise the hit to your bottom line. So I'm going to be hard on myself here and deduct a couple of percent for the impact that procurement will have. So we'll **take 2% off** the tally so far, just to be fair.

Chapter 4   **Negotiating the deal**
(Why what you and your client value are different)

Using the traditional approach to contract negotiation is hard and biased towards the client. 'The Good, the (not so) Bad and the Ugly' reduces the difficulty of 'balancing the trades' and ought to result in a better deal for you than you would have got before. Being pessimistic, it ought to add 3–5% to your profitability – but again, to be fair, I don't want to double count so I'm going to deduct the 1% margin improvements from having a stronger contract (chapter 2) in the 3–5% from here and call it just **a 2–4% improvement.**

Chapter 5   **Measuring client satisfaction**
(Why high profitability doesn't mean low service)

This is probably the hardest one to quantify as there are no direct profitability improvements to be had. However, if just one account is saved from loss or one additional account is won, the effect could be well worth having.
I think a modest +1% would be fair wouldn't you?

So, what does that lot add up to?

	Low %	High %
Capacity management and utilisation	1	2
Reducing write-off	7.5	7.5
Rates and rate cards	5	10
Key ratios – debtors	1	1
FD/accountant	1	2
Targeted growth	1	2
Contracts, terms & conditions	1	1
Procurement	(2)	(2)
Negotiation	2	4
Client satisfaction	1	1
TOTAL additional profitability	**+18.5**	**+28.5**

And that sort of fits with what we now know – that the 'average' firm is making about 10% margin; with work that could be improved by, say, 23.5% points (the mid point above). That equates to a 33.5% margin.

Earlier I said that 35% was possible but probably unsustainable. That would seem to be borne out here as, to achieve it, you would need to implement almost *everything* in the book and manage the business consistently and very tightly indeed. Realistically, achieving half the possible benefits would be a good outcome – an additional 11–12 % points giving 21–22% overall. And that should be relatively easy to maintain, consistently and yet with further improvement still possible.

And, in truth, that's about as far as I got.

Interestingly, I have come across several firms recently who have hit the 35% level (usually during the 'earn out' following a sale of the business), but not one that has sustained it for more than a year or two.

So to round up – unless you're making a margin of around 20% (or more) already, doubling your profitability ought to be quite possible within a year, provided that you focus on the key issues and work in a controlled way – shouldn't it?

Finally, *please* read the health warning overleaf and good luck and good fortune!

Health Warning!

This book contains a huge amount of information and is designed to provide a complete picture of how a 'perfect' firm might operate.

I have never come across or run any business that does it all and I am confident that no such firm exists.

I am far from certain that it's even possible.

So please, be cautious.

Read and digest the book as many times as you wish, as quickly or slowly as you like and dip in and out at will but...

...choose what to implement selectively and carefully.

Make changes slowly and with proper involvement and consideration.

Take it step by step.

The objective is to improve the profitability of your firm *progressively* over a number of years – not all in one go.

Doing too much at once could be too much of a shock to the system.

~ the end ~